D1008346

THE
NEW
SOVIET
ELITE

The New Soviet Elite

How They Think & What They Want

Jeffry Klugman

PRAEGER

New York
Westport, Connecticut
London

Library of Congress Cataloging-in-Publication Data

Klugman, Jeffry.
    The new Soviet elite: how they think and what they want/
Jeffry Klugman.
        p.   cm.
    Bibliography: p.
    Includes index.
    ISBN 0-275-93152-8 (alk. paper)
    1. Elite (Social sciences)—Soviet Union.   2. Executives—Soviet
Union.   3. Social networks—Soviet Union.   I. Title.
HN530.Z9E44   1989
305.5'2'0947—dc19   88-27510

Library of Congress Catalog Card Number: 88-27510
ISBN: 0-275-93152-8

First published in 1989

Praeger Publishers, One Madison Avenue, New York, NY 10010
A division of Greenwood Press, Inc.

Printed in the United States of America

The paper used in this book complies with the
Permanent Paper Standard issued by the National
Information Standards Organization (Z39.48-1984).

10   9   8   7   6   5   4   3   2   1

To Leah, Zoë, and Seth

CONTENTS

ACKNOWLEDGMENTS

There are many people I would like to thank for their diverse contributions—both direct and indirect—to this book. First, there are the people who were the subjects of the interviews, as well as those who helped me track them down. They provided a unique resource that both inspired and intrigued me, and that became the mainspring of what is before you. Then, there are my research assistants, Herminia Ibarra and William Wohlforth, who greatly deepened my effort in the areas of organizational behavior and the Soviet management psychology literature, respectively.

I would like to thank those who read various versions of the manuscript: Jack Snyder, Chick Perrow, Leon Lipson, and Phil Pomper. They have made this book much more readable. I shall retain responsibility for what murkiness still remains.

In a less direct way, I have received much help and encouragement from the members of the Yale faculty seminar on arms control and international security, especially Bruce Russett, Bill Foltz, and (formerly) Dick Nelson. By taking my ideas seriously, they helped me to take myself seriously enough to pursue so large a project. In a similar way, I would like to thank Bob Jervis and the members of his seminar on the political psychology of international relations.

Finally, I would like to thank my wife Karen and my children, who put up with my travels and absences (whether on the road or in the office) and always provided a comforting and supportive place to which I could return and recharge my energies. My children also provided the indirect inspiration for this book, for it was my concern for them that led me (in a tortuous fashion, and with my wife's help) to the study of this subject.

1. *APPARAT AND APPARATCHIK*

How can we understand the psychology of Soviet leaders? Juicy bio-graphical tidbits are in short supply. We can learn something fairly general from Russian culture and Soviet childrearing practices (as dis-cussed in Appendix A, "Bringing Up Ivan"). But how can we learn what makes the Soviet elite, in particular, tick? One way is by studying the process of becoming a Soviet leader.

SOVIET LEADERS THROUGH THE LENS OF CAREER BUILDING

The Soviet Union is one tremendous (albeit clumsy) organization. It is like an Appalachian coal-mining company town writ large: People shop at the company store, live in company housing, and—if they want to get ahead—get a company promotion. In such a situation the company shapes the lives of all the townspeople, and controls most completely the lives of those who want to get ahead. Anyone with ambition has to become, in essence, a "company man." Similarly, in the Soviet Union, the leaders are the most highly socialized (shaped and controlled) people in a highly socialized society.

The new generation of Soviet leaders—the post-Brezhnev elite who are still in the process of taking charge—have had orderly careers, rising through the ranks to achieve their positions of power. Their success in

Throughout this book "Russian" refers to the dominant ethnic group in the U.S.S.R., while "Soviet" refers to the whole U.S.S.R. Almost all of the top Soviet leaders are Russian.

building those careers—their repeated advancement within the giant Soviet organization—has been both a selection process and a socialization process.

Who, then, were the most likely to survive the selection process? What skills and personality traits have been conducive to success? These questions are inevitable when we look at the elite as the survivors of a selection process.

What have been their common experiences in the course of attaining their success? How have those experiences affected their way of looking at the world? These questions are raised when we study success in terms of socialization.

In order to learn about getting ahead in Soviet organizations, I interviewed 20 former Soviet citizens who had participated in—or observed—the career-building process. They were managers, journalists, a diplomat, and party and trade union officials. Our conversations averaged a little under three hours and were free form, but were always directed toward understanding the art of advancement and the organizational context in which that art was plied. In order to have some perspective on these interviews, I found a broader context by researching what has been written about getting ahead in Western organizations—from case studies of particular corporations, to interview studies of (literally) thousands of businessmen and managers, to "How to Succeed in Corporate Skullduggery"–type books—as well as more general studies of Western management, the Sovietological literature on management and politics in the Soviet Union, and the Soviet literature on both selecting and training managers and the psychology of management. My aim was to study how one rises to the Soviet elite as a means of understanding elite psychology.

At first I found the interviews frustrating. I was told that getting ahead was straightforward for people with well-placed relatives and for those with technical talents and an interest in nonadministrative, technical careers. But for those without connections who wanted an executive career, there was no answer to the question, "How does one get ahead in Soviet organizations?" "It's very personal," said one subject. "Everything depends upon your particular surroundings," said another. Or, as still another said, "Nothing is in general, especially in Russia." Following these disclaimers of a general theory of Soviet success, each interviewee would tell me stories—rich in detail and incident—about the lives of various individuals trying to get ahead in their particular circumstances within the Soviet system.

The importance of the idiosyncratic, situational requirements of success seemed a barrier to understanding until I realized that it was the key to understanding: If nothing is in general and people on the rise must adjust to a variety of superiors and situations, then the prime requirement for success is the ability to adapt—a chameleon-like flexibility.

First, one must know what is wanted—understanding, for example, even the unexpressed needs of one's patron or superior. When asked what it took to get ahead, one interviewee replied that it was a visceral sensing of others' needs and feelings—the ability to read other people's moods "like an animal."

But "social antennae" are not enough. Subtle perceptions must be put to use. The career builder needs responsiveness and flexibility—a repertoire of behaviors varied enough so that there is something for (nearly) everyone. Doing well with one boss on the basis of a lucky compatibility is not enough to rise again and again—to succeed with a multiplicity of others in a multitude of situations. Time after time, the career builder must prove useful to those who are in a position to help his or her career. Competency and drive—single-minded careerism—contribute to that usefulness; but above all, the career builder must be adaptable.

In the extreme, such adaptability can become a kind of emptiness. Having no views or beliefs whatsoever, the climber is then merely the perfect opportunist. Whether this is the case, however, depends on the psychology both of the individual in question and of the superiors with whom that individual comes in contact.

Soviet executives are not so adaptable that they don't care with whom they work, however. (I shall use the world "executive" to refer to those with administrative power in any Soviet *apparat*, meaning apparatus or organization. "Executive" refers to party leaders at least as much as to industrial managers.) Executives need to "fit" with one another because they need one another to do their jobs.

Thus, juniors and seniors are always seeking useful connections and always trying each other on for size. Some searches look like a kind of rotation dance: Each climber systematically tries out many partners, looking for the right fit.

"How to Succeed as an Apparatchik"—Part I of this book—describes the career building process by presenting the material from my interviews. Chapter 2, "Pathways to Success," describes how one gets on the ladder, the differences between the ladders of various suborganizations (the party, the trade unions, and so forth), and the various routes to higher office—especially, climbing within a single hierarchy versus being transferred to more central or peripheral hierarchies. Chapter 3, "Climbing the Apparat Ladder," details the social skills needed for advancement; it focuses on how one must manage both cooperation and competition with peers, as well as the all-important relations with superiors. Chapter 4 is the story of a former *komsomol* (youth league) official; it illustrates the themes of the section by painting "A Portrait of the Apparatchik as a Young Climber."

HOW SOCIAL IS SOCIALISM?

The study of Soviet bureaucratic climbers raises the question of whether getting ahead Soviet-style is any different from getting ahead at General Motors, AT&T, city hall, or the U.S. Postal Service: Is the Soviet organization man any different than the U.S. counterpart? Can the psychology of U.S. managers give us insight into Soviet power brokers? To each of these questions the answer is yes and no.

Many of the interpersonal as well as technical skills, the energy, and the devotion required for success are indeed the same in any large organization, East or West. There are important differences, however, which stem from both Russian culture and from the peculiar institutional context of Soviet society—specifically, the fact that the Soviet system is, at base, only one big organization. Both the cultural and institutional factors make the Soviet social process all the more intense, and this leads to differences in mind-set between Western executives and Soviet leaders.

Part II, "Putting the Social in Socialism," is a broad, comparative look at the social skills required for success Soviet-style, and at the implications of those skills for both interpersonal and intrapsychic functioning. Chapter 5, "Social Skills and Success, East and West," discusses the role of social skills in management and leadership as revealed in the literatures of Western business and Soviet industrial management as well as in the interviews themselves. Chapter 6, "Social Structure: Teams, Networks, and 'Families,' " discusses the importance of interpersonal relationships, sponsorship, alliances, and systems of alliance among groups of managers. Again this discussion compares Eastern and Western practices. The term 'family' is introduced through a comparison of groups of Soviet managers with the Mafia's organized crime families. Chapter 7, "Socialized Thinking," examines the ways in which the Soviet elite's style of thinking is affected both by Russian culture and by the selection and socialization process involved in the rise to power. (See Appendix A, "Bringing Up Ivan," for more cultural background and its psychological implications. See Appendix B, "What Makes Vanya Run?" for some speculation about the psychodynamics of Soviet leaders.)

Social skills are central to success because the career-building process shows the Soviet system to be essentially a social system, not an economic one. Without an impersonal marketplace, all interactions take on the flavor of personal relations. "Don't have a hundred rubles, have a hundred friends," quoted one interview subject. Social relations are the Soviet Union's semiofficial medium of exchange.

The organizational climber is a social climber, rising by means of the relationships that he establishes.* First and foremost, this means rela-

---

*For reasons that will be discussed later, very few women attain leadership positions. I therefore will usually use "he" instead of "he or she."

tionships with higher-ups: bosses, sponsors, and mentors. The path to leadership is successful subordinacy—making oneself useful, trusted, and crucial to the superior's well-being and success.

The climber must join the "team" that runs the organization in which he works. This team exists because a group of executives who interact around getting their jobs done tend to create a system of informal, interlocking alliances based on bonds of mutual trust, mutual dependency, and mutual vulnerability. Such a group must all fit together in order for such bonds to form and for the team to do both of its jobs: running the organization, and protecting team members. In general, a variety of pressures force Soviet organizations to have a single executive team. Only in complex central organizations—mostly those in Moscow—can two or more teams coexist within one institution.

Teams are bound together most strongly by the vertical ties between patrons and protégés. Vertical ties are stronger because of the competitive tensions in horizontal (peer) relations. To get ahead, the climber must form successful working relationships with his peers, but peers within an organization have trouble becoming true allies. Thus the team looks like a small inverted tree, or the familiar pyramidal organization chart.

But wider social connections—those without any formal and direct organizational links, and therefore outside the team—are also important. Friends, relatives, former schoolmates, former colleagues, and former bosses and subordinates all form the climber's "network"—people who can be called on for various forms of support and aid. These connections matter because the better the climber's connections, the more he can accomplish. And the more he can accomplish, the easier it is to trade favors and make still more connections. A strong network is necessary for success, and has the added advantage of being able to protect (to some degree) an individual who either has trouble with a boss or has a boss in trouble.

The interlocking teams and networks form extended "families"—named by analogy to Mafia crime families. These intertwine business and personal relationships in the furtherance of both business and personal interests. These families differ from Mafia families in that they exist within the context of a formal organization and are based not on true kinship relations, but on somewhat less personal relations of loyalty and mutual utility.

Living in such a socially dominant system, Soviet executives become socially minded. They see groups as, in some sense, more real than individuals; they are collectivist minded. Within their own groups, their personal attachments are all the greater, because these group comembers manage to stand out precisely by establishing personal relations with them. Outsiders are seen not as individuals, but merely as the representatives of other groups. After all, groups control and monitor individuals. Thus it makes (a kind of) sense to punish groups, families, and so on, for the deviations of representative group members. Thus, too, the Soviets administer by quota and group—which accounts for General Secretary Mikhail Gorbachev's (to us, amusing) suggestion that the United States set up autonomous regions for its minorities. To the socially minded, what matters is group clout, not individual rights.

Other consequences of a social outlook include a tendency to view competition as zero sum, and reinforcement of the Russian culture-based tendency toward having relatively few mental categories (see Appendix A). Categories are viewed as almost concrete, delineated by very strong, clear boundaries. This also shows up as a tendency toward black-and-white thinking. Andrei Gromyko's Central Committee speech nominating Gorbachev as general secretary specifically praised Gorbachev for an ability to rise above what Gromyko called "the law of black and white." "There may be intermediate colors, intermediate links, and intermediate decisions," said Gromyko. "And Mikhail Sergeyivich [Gorbachev] is always able to come up with such decisions that correspond with the party line."

Both cultural and institutional factors predispose Soviet leaders to a certain style of thought—specifically, to favor deductive (not inductive) thinking. This means that they have a (nonconscious) bias toward the analytic method of scientific socialism—reasoning from the general to the specific, from the abstract to the concrete, and thus from policy to reality.

The process of Soviet leaders' getting ahead also promotes in them an energetic (but not necessarily anxious) vigilance; they exercise a continuous scanning of the world for opportunities and dangers, not an inward focus on their own tasks. This fits with their social-mindedness and their interpersonal, outward orientation. Any organization splits its energy between the social tasks of maintaining the organization and its productive tasks—doing its job. Soviet organizations devote a great deal of energy to their social systems, and Soviet leaders do the same. The lack of alternatives—since there are no competitors or alternate employers down the street—means that Soviet executives are always surrounded by the system, with no outside to escape to or relax in. This fact in combination with the importance of personal relations—the primacy of the political—leads them to feel enclosed (in both positive and negative senses), on display, and careful to avoid a negative.

The world around Soviet leaders is tightly integrated—full of pitfalls, but with opportunities that must be continuously scanned for. Occasionally they can knock out a potential competitor, but the utmost care must be taken in such dangerous maneuvers. They work with all their skills—both technical and social—to fulfill the demands of the world while at the same time seeking to improve their positions, building and maintaining good working relations, and cataloging competitors' weaknesses that might be exploited at a strategic moment. All this is very personal and specific—not diluted even in part by an impersonal marketplace or by the knowledge that they (or their allies or competitors) can go elsewhere.

AN ORGANIZATIONAL LOOK AT THE SOVIET SYSTEM

Studying Soviet career development sheds light not only on the psychology and social relations of the Soviet elite, but also on the Soviet system itself. Part III of this book is therefore about "Psychology and Organization: Managing the Soviet System."

In general, the most mobile careers pass through the party: Party jobs are stepping-stones to high nonparty office as well as to party office per se. The fast track in any Soviet organization is via the party; and in this, the party is like the headquarters of a large Western corporation. This comparison is the theme of Chapter 8, "Career Paths and the Organizational Role of the Party."

Corporate headquarters personnel get centrifugal promotions: They go from staff jobs in the center to high-level administrative positions in divisions and subdivisions. Similarly, party officials are promoted to jobs in the organizations supervised by the party committee in which they work. This pattern holds at all levels of the Communist party: the central, the regional, the local, and within the party organizations of the workplace.

The industrial and service side of the Soviet system (virtually all of the state, as opposed to party, apparatus) is what Western corporations would call "operations"—the production function, for the most part. And while the state is involved with production and operations, the party has the role of overall coordination and management—a centralizing function, which also includes strategic planning, personnel (a key function in this system), and coordination of (what in a corporation would be called) the human relations function (ideology, and so forth). These are headquarters' functions.

In this light, various Soviet personnel practices that may seem political to the point of being Machiavellian are revealed as standard corporate procedures serving legitimate organizational purposes (albeit political as well). To look at Prime Minister Nikolai Ryshkov as "vice-president for operations and ex officio member of the board," and General Secretary Mikhail Gorbachev as "chairman of the board and chief executive officer" may seem silly or trivial, but it does illuminate some things:

1. Fast-track careers pass through headquarters. An executive with a job in a division of a large corporation gets a headquarters staff position and afterward

is appointed to a much higher position back in a division. This is functional—not just political—for both individual career development and for the organization. For the organization, headquarters needs to know and trust the local managers, and local managers need to be connected to headquarters to do their jobs properly. For the individual, exposure at headquarters allows for an evaluation by the major, central players and also provides a broader perspective to bring back to the division. But the party is headquarters in the Soviet system—a dispersed and huge headquarters because of the size of the organization, but headquarters nonetheless by virtue of its centralizing functions. Thus, fast-track industrial careers should pass through the party.

2. The dual subordination of state officials—to both the party and the state—is not just a way of maintaining political control, it is a standard matrix structure by which a corporate headquarters manages relations with its divisions. For example, in a Western corporation, the head of personnel in a division is subordinate to and reports to both the division chief and the head of corporate personnel at headquarters. In the Soviet system, an enterprise head is subordinate to both the relevant ministry and some level of party organization; the ministry represents the divisional line of authority, while the party represents the corporate line.

3. The *nomenklatura* system (whereby a party organization must approve of appointees to certain jobs) is not merely a mechanism for political control: It reflects the fact that high-level hires in a division have to be approved by headquarters. A friend of mine is a vice-president in a division of a multinational corporation. He could not be hired, nor could he be fired, by his boss—the general manager of the division. He had to be approved by his boss's boss (the group executive) and the headquarters personnel officer, as well as (pro forma) the company's president. Thus, he is in headquarter's nomenklatura. Translate this to a much larger organization with a multilevel matrix structure such as the Soviet Union and (surprise!) standard corporate procedure becomes the nomenklatura system. This does not mean that procedures are carried out in the same way or necessarily with the same intent, but that the structure of nomenklatura may serve a functional purpose that in no way contradicts its political purpose.

On a broader level, tracing career paths reveals that what it takes to get ahead varies over time. Who becomes a manager or leader of an organization depends in part on the organization's needs at that historical moment, and on how the organization was structured and run while the leader-candidates made their way up the ladder. There are different managerial styles appropriate to various stages in an organization's development. Building a new organizational empire requires a different kind of manager than running an already developed, complexly structured organization. This contrast between entrepreneurial empire-building and the professional management of complex organizations resembles the broad differences in managerial and political style between the early years of Soviet history—especially Stalin's time—and more recent years. In organizational terms, Soviet history has been and is still a rather standard story of evolution from entrepreneurial to professional-style management—the subject of Chapter 9, "Managerial Evolution and 'Brezhnevism.' "

The entrepreneur—the founder or builder of corporate empires—is characterized by a lack of delegation of responsibility, skipping organizational levels instead of going through channels, personalistic decision making, and a demand for personal (as opposed to corporate) loyalty. The entrepreneur is paternalistic, intrusive, dictatorial, and often punitive. Henry Ford, for example, maintained a corps of secret police that monitored the personal lives of Ford employees.

The entrepreneurial manager refuses to plan for a successor, and won't share responsibility; so, as the organization grows—increasing in size and complexity—he becomes overloaded, and organizational performance deteriorates. Thus, under the demands of growth and increasing complexity, organizations experience pressure to move toward a different style of management: cooler, less personalized, with better delegation and more respect for organizational channels and procedures—in sum, a more professional style.

In the Soviet Union, the party itself has been an entrepreneurial manager, taking its lead from that apotheosis of entrepreneurial managers—Josef Stalin. Nikita Krushchev marked the beginning of a transition, but he was quite affected by his exposure to and utilization of an entrepreneurial style under Stalin. Under Leonid Brezhnev—while there was increasing professionalization in the lower ranks—the top ranks became stagnant. Yuri Andropov and now (most clearly) Mikhail Gorbachev can be seen as implementing a more professional style of management at the very top of the system. Thus the 70 years of Soviet history can be seen as the evolution and growth of a huge organization, with the last half of those 70 years (since the death of Stalin) including a slow, fits-and-starts evolution toward professional management.

The evolution of the Soviet Union to a professional style of management has been slow for a number of reasons. Being a single organization without domestic competitors has limited the pressure to change. Also, since all leaders must rise within the organization—there is no outside to bring professional managers in from—leaders have been socialized into an entrepreneurial style. Another retarding force has been the longevity of Soviet leaders and the entrepreneurial manager's characteristic unwillingness to let go and retire.

More than anything else, however, the evolutionary process got held up by a demographic quirk: Stalin's purges resulted in the execution or imprisonment of most of the older officials—and thus put the Brezhnev generation into office all at once, and at a relatively young age. This produced an "age lump" (Downs 1967), which occurs when most of the high officeholders in an organization are of approximately the same age. As an age lump advances in years, it is associated (in the West, at least) with conservative and stagnant policies. And for 20 years the Brezhnev-generation age lump clogged the upper levels of the Soviet system.

One of the most conservative policies of the Brezhnev years was the policy of "stability of cadres"—tenure for high officials. This tenure policy was the elite's attempt to increase its own security after the mortal insecurity of the purges and the job insecurity of Krushchev's reorganizations. Thus both the tenure policy and age lump were late effects of Stalin's purges.

Stability of cadres meant giving up the "stick" of being able to fire nonperforming officials. Like tenure for university professors, it had the essentially decentralizing and organizationally disruptive impact of leaving officeholders free to pursue their private—as opposed to public and official—interests. Under Brezhnev, officeholders furthered their interests informally, or even illegally. At the institutional level, this policy meant that each organization was given authority within its own bailiwick, with each "baron" running his own realm.

Meanwhile, the age lump meant that there were few "carrots." High-level jobs opened up so rarely that the possibility of promotion was not a meaningful incentive. Western studies of people who are "stuck"—without prospects for promotion—show that they have low morale, perform poorly, tend to spend their energies on bureaucratic politics, are fiercely territorial in protecting their own prerogatives, and over-supervise their subordinates (indulging in what the Soviets call "petty tutelage"). All of these phenomena were characteristic of Brezhnevism.

In sum, then, the stagnation under Brezhnev can be seen as in part the result of frustrating the normal career development of officeholders. The pathological and corrupt behaviors that grew under Brezhnevism are typical of the stuck—people who, for whatever reasons, have no hope of promotion. Such people have their motivations unhooked from the organization's; they pursue their own—not the organization's interests. Thus, the stagnation of Brezhnevism is no more intrinsic to the Soviet system than were the high economic growth rates of the 1950s (which at that time were indeed considered intrinsic to the system).

REFORM

If Brezhnevism was the result of low opportunity, then changing personnel policy should affect people's attitudes and behavior and, ultimately, the economic performance of the system. This is the subject of Chapter 10, "Personnel Policy and Economic Reform." My conclusion is that currently proposed economic reforms have the capability of overcoming resistance (both organizational and psychological) and greatly improving the system's functioning—all without radical structural change. By this I mean that the essence of the system—its essential unity under the leadership of the party—can remain intact because delegating authority does not reduce the power of top organizational leadership. In fact, delegating authority focuses that power, and thus makes it all the more effective.

Perestroika means restructuring in the same sense that Western corporations use that term: slimming headquarters' staffs and pushing decision-making lower in the hierarchy. Better delegation (not—for the most part—divestiture) will allow for better, somewhat more independent functioning of the system's economic subunits.

Economic reform and a meritocratic permanent purge will remove the incompetent and thus provide opportunity for the capable. This, in turn, can recentralize motivation—getting people to do what's best for the whole system instead of what's best for their little piece of it. But this is a formula for greater organizational efficiency: recentralizing motivation while decentralizing authority.

In fact, many of the required policy changes are either already being put into place or have been hinted. These include more wage differentiation, more turnover of managers, increased lateral job rotation, and—in essence—a meritocratic permanent purge.

Discipline and restructured incentives—including changes in both compensation and promotion policies—can centralize motivation. The party organizations, the KGB, the new workers' councils, and the media under *glasnost'* (openness) can theoretically all play the role of what are called "parallel organizations"—maintaining discipline and, in the case of the party and the councils, actually fostering innovation. Job rotation has been proposed (by Secretary Yegor Ligachev of the Central Committee) as an antilocalism measure, but will have a number of other benefits for the system: reducing personalism, selecting for better social skills, increasing the interchangeability of managers, fostering broader perspectives and less parochialism, encouraging more innovation, and allowing for an improved, multiple-sponsorship system of personnel advancement. This in turn will encourage better delegation of authority and more interest in fully developing junior personnel.

In a less personalistic organization and with more opportunities, executives will be less cynical, less divided within themselves, and more committed to the overall system. Better commitment, in turn, means that they will handle delegated authority more appropriately, and not just twist it to personal or local ends. This will improve systemic performance.

However one judges the probability of such a managerial transformation of the Soviet system—increased efficiency through better management without changing the core concept of an essentially one-organization society—it seems to me that this is what the new leaders have in mind. Although they may disagree with one another about exactly what policies will be required to achieve the goal, this is the goal. And more consensus about the tasks and goals of management allows for more trust and better delegation, without any loss of authority for top management.

But as skilled veterans of organizational life, the new Soviet leaders must be aware of the scale of the task that they have undertaken. The Soviet system is immense. GM's Chairman of the Board Roger Smith has been trying to reform and reorganize General Motors for about six years, and hopes to see results soon. Scale that effort up to what is required for the much larger, more inclusive, and more complex Soviet system—and the scope of the task becomes clear.

Starting at the top, the new leaders must continue to exert unremitting pressure to push managerial reform down through the levels. Compromising when they must and adjusting their pace to the realities of the situation, still they must not back down. It is a delicate political balancing act—and one that will likely not be completed for many, many years.

One guidepost along the way will be evidence that the new broom is still sweeping clean: At some point, new generation appointees will have to be removed for nonperformance. (It is not clear whether Boris Yeltsin's removal as Moscow party chief and candidate Politburo member qualifies here.) Otherwise, recent personnel changes will just mean that a new gang has replaced the old one, without a change in the personnel process—and thus without its potential benefits for performance. More radical still would be the institution of some sort of up-or-out policy for mid- to high-level managers. This is a standard policy in many bureaucracies to prevent rigidities and stagnation. Another major shift would be the implementation of a mandatory retirement policy at the highest levels.

The Soviet system's slow diminution in personalism and its increasingly rational-technical approach to managing complexity has promoted the growth of "nonideological reality": The system is gradually depoliticizing an objective reality. For example, first (after Stalin) the Soviet Union had to learn that genetics are not really subject to dialectical analysis, then (after Khruskchev) that corn won't grow at the North Pole, and most recently (after Brezhnev and Chernenko) that it is not economically sound to make rivers run backward. This process still leaves ideology its own important realm, however—that of social reality, the socially constructed system of meanings and values that underpin motivation, behavior, and policy choice.

But professional managers—less tied to parochial interests and more willing to see an economic reality beyond ideology—will be more likely than their predecessors to change perverse incentives. Thus, the same phenomena that promote better delegation within organizations may also promote a better division of labor between organizations, with enormous potential benefits for the Soviet economy. In part because impersonal relations have been so unreliable (and thus, for example, a factory might not really come through with what the plan says it will deliver), there have been great pressures on every organization to become as autarkic as possible. Thousands of tons of nails are shipped in and out of Leningrad every year because the nail factories are subordinate to different ministries, and no ministry wants to trust another to deliver essential supplies. Every enterprise maintains "dwarf workshops" because the workers must make—since they can't assume that they can buy—spare parts for their equipment. If professional management will allow for more impersonal trust and more rational relations between organizations, great improvements in efficiency will then become possible—again, without radical systemic changes.

The social and political orientation of the system will still limit its economic potential. But it should be judged on its own social standards.

THE EMERGING ELITE

As they become more professional in style and better adapted to the complexity of the system, the population of Soviet executives is being shaped by a selection process. Somewhat more autonomy will be required to function efficiently in a more loosely connected system, while increased discipline will require a more internalized form of self-control. Meanwhile, as job rotation better unites the system horizontally and discipline better connects it vertically, the need for everyone to fit together creates pressure for still more impersonality and interchangeability. The system along with its leaders is being homogenized even as it is being decentralized.

Who then are the new—and the coming—Soviet leaders? Managerial evolution and the personnel policy that will accelerate it exerts a selection pressure on Soviet managers, tending to mold them into what I call "real new Soviet men." (This is analogous to calling the Soviet system "real socialism." See Part IV, Chapter 11.) The emerging managerial elite are characterized by greater systemic trust, more internalized discipline, greater ability to function independently, greater homogeneity, greater adaptability, better motivation because of greater identification with the system as a whole, more breadth, and more skills. Not necessarily as idealistic as the mythic, ideologically proper new Soviet men, the real new Soviet men are becoming just as socially motivated and attuned. They "fit" the system. And perhaps they are—or are becoming—altruistic, at that, since it will be easier to be altruistic in a system that is improving its performance and that offers them significant opportunities for advancement.

For now, we can only say that the current leaders were successes themselves. Gorbachev—for example—rose very quickly, and the high mobility of his own career history (as opposed to, say, Ligachev's 20 years in one job as an *oblast*—region—first secretary) helped promote his eager belief in the possibilities of improvement and change.

THE PSYCHOLOGY OF FOREIGN AFFAIRS

State policies affect individuals' motivations, which in turn affect the system's economic performance: Thus the functioning of the Soviet system is intertwined with individual psychology. This is one example of the general theme of Part IV: the relationship between "Individual Psychology and Institutional Behavior."

But state policy may be intertwined with individual psychology in another way: The social orientation of the Soviet elite can be seen as subconsciously influencing Soviet international relations. In Chapter 12, "Psychological Models of International Relations," I hypothesize that the relations between people and the relations between organizations experienced by the new Soviet leaders as they made their way within the Soviet system provided them with a model of how to think about relations between nations.

The personal experience of rising within the Soviet system in some ways reinforces an ideologically proper view of foreign affairs (in much the same fashion that cultural and institutional factors reinforce the official deductive thought style of scientific socialism): Soviets view the world as an integrated whole, not as a collection of discrete entities. Everything is seen as connected to and affecting everything else.

More specifically, Soviet leaders tend to view international relations as a social system, a system of ongoing relationships, a true (nonidealized) community of nations—a social system in which states maneuver for prestige and influence and power in ways not so different from those that they themselves used in making their way up the Soviet hierarchy. This is in contrast to the U.S. tendency to see the world as a collection of autonomous entities. For example, this difference shows up in conflicting meanings for "peace." While to us the word *peace* has connotations of isolated tranquillity and a live-and-let-live philosophy, the Russian word *mir* connotes harmonious, coordinated togetherness.

In the eyes of Soviet leaders, there can be no arm's-length relations within the international system; instead, there is a mutual involvement in which one maneuvers for position—much the same as the bureaucratic social system in which they spend all their lives. Like a social system, the international system is seen as dynamic—ever changing both in its external realities (the "objective conditions") and in its social jockeying for position. Thus too, for example, the "correlation of forces" is far more dynamic as well as more broadly inclusive and interactive than the Western notion of "balance of power." Similarly, to the Soviets, the idea of "businesslike" might connote long-term mutual engagement (like Japanese business relationships). (But they are most likely aware that, in the West, the word "businesslike" implies a cool, rational exchange; and they may play on these meanings.) Linkage between various aspects of a relationship seems quite natural and understandable in the social-system context. Symbols and procedures are emphasized as the embodiments of relationship.

The "words" and the "music" are both essential aspects of interpersonal communications, and can simultaneously send entirely different messages. (The words are the concrete content of communications, while the music is its tone or emotional coloring.) By analogy, the rhetoric of Soviet international communications is of great significance (which is not necessarily to say, of great sincerity), and U.S. rhetoric is closely examined in the Soviet Union for its hints about the nature of the U.S.–Soviet relationship. In fact, the training of Soviet officials as unofficial Kremlinologists—always looking for hints about official and unofficial wishes and intentions—might lead them to find clues to Western intentions and feelings even when none are there, let alone intended.

All of these differences in approach between East and West may be softened by the emerging Soviet professional-manager style. The cooler, more professional, and goal-directed style will no doubt apply to foreign affairs as much as to domestic ones. The cultural factors and institutional experiences of having made their way within one big organization, however, means that Soviet leaders will maneuver internationally ever more skillfully in their bureaucratic-social way.

These aspects of Soviet behavior pose a complex problem for Western governments, which need declaratory policies acceptable to public opinion. The intensely competitive nature of U.S.–Soviet relations leads us to evaluate events by asking, "Who's winning?" But in a long-term relationship, there may be other questions to ask. It is quite difficult— but nonetheless necessary—for us to see U.S.–Soviet relations as a long-term relationship to be managed, not as a problem to be solved.

However, these reflections come at the end of a long train of inferences. Let us now turn to one of the engines of that train—some data that are both more mundane and much richer in human detail: the actual stories of people making their way up the ladders of various Soviet organizations. These stories give us a real feel for the successful Soviet bureaucrat—a sense of who the Soviet leaders really are.

PART I. HOW TO SUCCEED AS AN APPARATCHIK

The following three chapters summarize and illustrate the 20 interviews that I conducted with former Soviet citizens on the subject of getting ahead in the Soviet system. The chapter "Pathways to Success" describes how one gets on the ladder; some differences between the ladders of the party, the trade unions, and the KGB; and the various paths to higher office—climbing within a single hierarchy, being transferred to more central or peripheral hierarchies, and so on. The next chapter, "Climbing the Apparat Ladder," examines the social skills required for success, looking closely at how one must manage relations with both superiors and peers. Finally, "A Portrait of the Apparatchik as a Young Climber" illustrates most of the themes of the preceding chapters by tracing the history of a particular young man on the rise.

2. *PATHWAYS TO SUCCESS*

This chapter focuses on the externals of success. Some of these externals are personal attributes: nationality, marital status, and appropriate family and friends. Others are behavioral: selecting an organization to fit into, taking part in the appropriate activities, and attaining the proper positions. Most broadly, the organizational context of success—the organizational structure (which bureau is in charge of what factory)—determines which positions are available as stepping-stones, as well as determining precisely where those stepping-stones might lead. Thus (with success as with greatness), the future *apparatchik* (bureaucrat) is best born with the right personal attributes, must achieve the right behaviors, and has his organizational opportunities thrust upon him.

PRELIMINARIES

In order to be successful, the future apparatchik must have a spotless *anketa* (literally, a form; but here short for *anketnie dannie*, meaning biographical particulars or personal history). This, in fact, means not only a spotless personal record—no troubles with authority ever—but also a clean record for family members, friends, and so forth. The higher the position, the more distant the relatives who must have clean records. The chief of the organization department in a Baltic city's komsomol (Young Communist League), for example, had an uncle who had been in the resistance, and therefore the young man's career prospects were limited: He couldn't rise much higher than the position that he already held. Given the difficulty of assuring clean records for relatives, one official reassured a job candidate by remarking, "You have a good an-keta; your father's dead."[1]

Factors that might disqualify candidates for political jobs include hav-ing relatives abroad, being of the wrong nationality, or being divorced. One of my interview subjects had paid his wife to keep their separation quiet so that he could keep his party job. This went on for about a year prior to his departure from the Soviet Union. Thus he protected both his job and his chances to travel abroad. Homosexuality is another dis-qualifier; one komsomol official whose homosexuality was discovered was sent to run the party organization of a *kolkhoz* (collective farm) in a remote Siberian *raion* (district).

THE FIRST RUNG: VOLUNTARY ACTIVISM AND NETWORKING

The process of getting into the political world starts with voluntary activism. This can be in the komsomol for high school, institute, and university students; in the *druzhina* (the voluntary auxiliary police); or in the party or trade union organizations of the workplace. Such activism requires much more than mere passive acquiescence to the political system, or even ritualistic, formal participation. It is instead (at least the appearance of) energetic and enthusiastic public spiritedness, expressed through officially sanctioned channels. The usefulness of voluntary ac-tivism for career building is that it provides future apparatchiks with the opportunity to make connections and to prove their trustworthiness and usefulness.

Youth Activism

According to Subject #1, the "young but early" (*molodoi no rano*—the Soviet version of "fast-trackers") are activists who are characterized by their "social work": giving lectures, helping write wall newspapers, organizi g meetings, and so on. They start these activities very early, even as children. They carry the flags or the pictures of Politburo mem-bers in organized demonstrations; they are the front-liners; they lead the student brigades.

But even prior to such volunteer work, future apparatchiks have al-ready started building their networks of acquaintances and connections. The young-but-early always choose the right friends; they create groups. They and their friends are always "positive"—never "negative." They choose the right wives, and the right style of life. While Americans seem to need a Jerry Rubin who can organize "networking" parties for them at Studio 54, the Soviet Union's future executives start networking in kindergarten.

Subject #4 agreed. Contrasting the "self-built career" with both the nonpolitical technical career and the career based on well-placed relatives, he said that such a career often has its beginnings by age 14 or 15 in the youngster's participation in komsomol or other voluntary activities. One must start serious activism no later than age 18, he said. The future KGB officer might express his activism not so much in the komsomol as in the druzhina. "Older people are not afraid of competition from these youngsters, so they are willing to help them and teach them."

Well-meaning adults encourage a youth's activism. One subject had been prevailed upon by his history teacher and his parents to accept a position as leader of the ideology section of his secondary school komsomol. "It might be helpful to your career," he recalled being told—and, in fact, it was.[2]

To attend an elite school such as the Moscow State Institute for International Relations (MGIMO)—where Soviet diplomats are trained—activism must have started by age 14, according to Subject #9. This is because of the various recommendations that must be obtained merely to take the entrance examination for the school. These recommendations—from the secondary school komsomol, the class komsomol (for example, the class of '88 has its own komsomol organization), and the school-faculty party committee—are by no means automatic. For one thing, at least two-years' tenure in the komsomol is required, meaning that the youth must have joined at the earliest possible age (some youngsters put off komsomol membership for a year or two). Also required is a roster of "useful deeds" or assignments, such as being a komsomol section leader or a member of the class komsomol bureau (leadership committee). Early disciplinary problems disqualify a student for these useful deeds, and thus have a lasting impact on his career.

For the future diplomat who is building a résumé, being appointed to the komsomol positions mentioned above requires the support or approval of the class leader (the teacher assigned as what we would call "class advisor"), the principal, the komsomol leader (the faculty member chosen by the school party committee as the advisor to the komsomol), the (student) chairman of the school komsomol committee, and the general meeting of the komsomol. Another subject emphasized the need to be popular with fellow students in order to succeed in the komsomol, since the first step—becoming a komsomol section leader—involves true election from below. So many people to please!

In general, the successful apparatchik must have a high degree of self-control and acceptance of authority from an early age. This contrasts with the possibility of attaining success (including political success) in the U.S. system without any early activism, and in spite of an errant youth. Note also that the future apparatchik's early activism may be goal-directed (careeristic) or it may be an authentic expression of social or political interests—even, idealism. Who, then, becomes the "new Soviet man"? The new Soviet boy!

For those who have not begun their political careers in secondary school, there is ample opportunity to become serious activists as university or institute students. Activism during higher education can help establish lifelong contacts among fellow activists, make connections with local political figures, and even lead directly to career opportunities.

As a university or institute komsomol member, the student activist has opportunities to meet various officials with whom he can establish useful relations. For example, a komsomol member may organize an "oral journal"—a series of guest lectures. The guests will usually be party officials at the level of instructors at the *raikom* ("county"- or district-level party committee), who are themselves about 30 years old and therefore not in direct competition with the komsomol student. The guests will be offered a stipend, and the student organizer gets a chance to establish a relationship with each guest. The student organizer also becomes the gatekeeper to the lectures—giving tickets to peers whom he wishes to ingratiate, allowing certain people to stay late or have lunch with the guest, and so on. The oral journal provides an official reason to approach a more senior person in a personal, somewhat informal way, thus breaking the ice.[3]

In one instance, an institute student running an oral journal established a relationship with the ideology secretary of the raikom. When central authorities called for a youth anticrime campaign, the student volunteered to plan a program for his institute. He drew up a plan for ten guest lectures, ancillary student meetings, and so on. He actually arranged for one or two lectures, to which all the raikom and institute bigwigs were invited. The other meetings never occurred, but were glowingly described in the report that he wrote for the ideology secretary. Furthermore, he then volunteered to write an even more brightly glowing report about the anticrime campaign in the whole district, which the ideology secretary proceeded to submit under his own name. This report was praised by *Pravda*, and the program cited as a model for the nation. The ideology secretary, the student, and the relationship between the two all benefited.

Komsomol activism at the university or institute level can lead directly to a political career. Subject #16 described a fellow student at his technical institute who had become secretary of the student section, then a secretary of the class's komsomol organization, and finally a member of the bureau of the institute komsomol. He was then made a party member and, after graduating, got a position working in the city komsomol. At the age of 29, this climber became an instructor in the regional party organization (*obkom*).

Activism in the Military

An alternate route into politics is via the military. Going into the army—either directly from secondary school (before university) or from the university—can help one's career in a number of ways. Army service looks good on one's anketa. Furthermore, many of the elite educational institutions such as the school of international relations, the school of international journalism, and Moscow State University have a quota for people who have served in the military, thus easing their strict academic entrance requirements. Most important, however, is that one can join the party in a relatively easy manner while in the military, much more easily than in places where there is a high level of competition for the party slots available: at a university or institute, or in any white-collar job.

One subject worked for a time in a republic komsomol's central committee. There he learned just how difficult it was for university students to attain party membership. With 8,000 students at the university in the republic's capital, there was a quota of just 5 students per year allowed to join the party. Since komsomol secretaries at the university had to be party members, the republic komsomol's central committee found it necessary to recommend that the university komsomol look for potential officials among those who had been made party members while in the military.

Activism in the Workplace and Local Party Organizations

For those who have become working adults without having begun their political careers, there do remain some political opportunities for the ambitious to seek out. Those interested in industrial management and not politics per se also know that they will advance more quickly by taking the party road.

According to Subject #15, the great number of engineers competing for relatively few high positions produces a very strong pyramid effect. "An engineer needs special tools to move ahead—he must be a party member, and he must have connections among the nomenklatura. There is a Russian proverb, 'Don't have a hundred rubles; have a hundred friends.' "[4] Also, he said, a party leader from among the workers will surround himself with more workers—"his brothers"—and thus block positions for which an educated man might otherwise be suited. Thus, rising as an engineer is a difficult proposition.

Subject #5 compared party activism to a highway that allows one to bypass the heavily congested traffic in the industrial hierarchy. He described how an engineer who wishes to rise in management should first become involved in the plant's primary party organization. (Each enterprise with at least three party members has its own party organization.) The engineer should then approach the raikom to volunteer his services as an auxiliary raikom instructor. These instructors act as troubleshooters, coordinators, and auditors who monitor local industry for the district party organization. (See Hough 1969, for the role of raikom instructors and voluntary instructors. Hough emphasizes the managerial role and not the recruitment aspect of the voluntary instructorships.) Working as a voluntary instructor, the engineer becomes known at the raikom and has the opportunity to prove his usefulness, trustworthiness, and general reliability. If a sufficiently good impression has been created (more on how, later), the engineer will be asked to fill the next opening for a full-time instructor. By holding this kind of party job for a few years, an engineer may then be appointed to a much higher industrial management job than could have been obtained by staying in the industrial track.[5]

Even at low levels, party activism helps in pay and promotions. Subject #7 told of a junior engineer who was mediocre in his work, but who always spoke up and "said the right things" at meetings, went to voluntary workdays (*subbotniki*), and so on. When the subject did not put this man's name on a promotion list because of his mediocre work, a higher-up said, "Where is this person? He went to [some specific] meeting, he always goes to the subbotniki, he's good when we visit the kolkhoz," and like that. And so his name was added to the list.

Subject #7 also told of "a good engineer" who decided he could advance better by being an activist in the plant party committee. Within a few years, this fellow rose to become deputy director of the enterprise. His path was that of engineer, senior engineer, member of the party committee (voluntary, part time), chairman of the party committee (full time), and then deputy director of the plant. The key transition in this list was his getting on the party "bypass"—from part-time voluntary activity to a full-time political-administrative job.

DIFFERENT LADDERS FOR DIFFERENT CLIMBERS

In each social organization—the komsomol, the *profsoyuz* (trade union), and the party—young people learn the organization's "proper behavior" through their exposure to higher-ups. They learn what behavior is expected of them in general, and they also learn to sense what various individuals expect of them. Each organization provides its younger members with opportunities to meet higher officials, both within their local enterprises or institutes and in the social organization's own hierarchy.

In the komsomol, said Subject #4, people learn to say "the proper words . . . *yes* to all requests." They need not necessarily actually do what they have promised to do—that depends—but they can never argue, question, or make excuses. The answer must always be yes. They learn to deliver the proper paper (report) on time, with it looking right. In the trade union, on the other hand, it is permissible to question or even resist. "You can ask for compensation," said Subject #4. In the party and komsomol, compensation may not be prenegotiated. It is expected, but unstated—subject to a kind of trust that can be violated. One can actually lose by never being rewarded. Given these differences between the cultures of the profsoyuz (the trade union) and the komsomol/party, it is obvious that different personalities will be better adapted to one or the other.

While the profsoyuz tends to get ex-army personnel, "sportsmen" (ex-athletes), and in general a more rough-and-ready group, the party road requires more self-control and greater faith—at least in the sense that one cannot negotiate a quid pro quo in the party. One must commit oneself with faith in an eventual reward. In turn, when the reward comes it may bear no direct or obvious relationship to the contributions that one has made.[6] The profsoyuz, which requires the lesser commitment, deals in the smaller blessings of life: bonuses, vacations, housing, and so on. The party concerns itself with high policy and systemic power.

According to Subject #9, at MGIMO, students with problems were both the object of the KGB's scrutiny and also one source of its recruits. (This is my own synthesis of the subject's observations, not his direct statement.) Students would be called to the chief of class's (KGB) office if they had some problems with their studies, were caught arriving late, and so on. Once, Subject #9—while riding the subway—complained to his student monitor (the keeper of attendance records, and so on) about having his *propusk* (pass) confiscated when he was late, which was going to require a visit to the chief of class. "Just go to G [the chief of class] and have a little talk," said his companion, "and you won't have such troubles again." The monitor was apparently a KGB informer and was suggesting that, by cooperating with "G," the subject would get more leeway about the rules.

Subject #9 thought that cooperating with the KGB would not be sufficient to compensate for long-standing poor academic performance (as party activism perhaps would be), and he thought that someone who cooperated would eventually have to remedy his or her problems (of whatever nature)—having bought some time by acting as an informer. The subject was not able to conceive of a way, however, that one could—once started—stop acting as an informer and sever one's relationship with the KGB. Thus, mild disciplinary lapses become KGB recruiting devices, and the mildly deviant characters who become the policemen have the privilege of continuing their mild deviations, to some degree.

STRATEGIC CHOICES

While personality "fit" may determine the best hierarchy or social organization in which an individual will be able to build a career, the choice of technical specialization will be determined by the individual's intellectual capacities and understanding of future opportunities. Subject #9 chose a particular country and language to study as his area of specialization because "relations could develop between the Soviet Union and [that country], there were few specialists in the area, and so there would be more chance for advancement." Subject #6—when asked about how to succeed—talked about the importance of predicting and riding on trends, of foreseeing what skills and areas of knowledge were going to be the most useful in future years so as to position oneself to take advantage of the resultant opportunities. This process, Subject #6 thought, was identical in the East and West. It is worth noting that, when he was applying for emigration, this subject arranged to become consultant to a ministry department that was studying how the corresponding industry was run by Western corporations—thus preparing himself for future employment.

Previously, I mentioned Subject #15's description of the strong pyramid effect in the case of engineers. Being an engineer himself—and daunted by what he observed—this subject decided to change careers. In general, this is not an easy thing to do, but he found a way to be called an engineer while in fact changing areas: He went into NOT (the scientific organization of labor, operating according to what is essentially Taylorism). Because NOT had been in and out of political fashion, it was a very backward area with few specialists. Thus, Subject #15 decided, it was an area of great opportunity; and indeed, he managed to build a very successful career, rising to become a *candidat* (Ph.D.) and professor at a prestigious institute.

Similarly, Subject #16—in describing the career of the komsomol activist who became an obkom instructor—mentioned that, although both he and the activist had been students at a technical institute, the activist "saw that being an engineer was a dead end." So he made "a strictly logical, intellectual decision" to pursue a political career.

One can sometimes misread the tea leaves, however. Subject #10 told a story about the time when Dzherman Gvishiani, who was a deputy to Politburo member Andrei Kirilenko as well as being (Prime Minister) Aleksei Kosygin's son-in-law, founded his (then) new institute of systems analysis. Kirilenko's other deputy was S. P. Trapeznikov, the director of the Institute of Control Problems (of the Academy of Sciences and the Committee of Automation, Instrument Building, and Control Systems). One of Trapeznikov's deputies, Emilianov, left to become Gvishiani's deputy. Emilianov was a corresponding member of the Academy of Sciences; and he apparently thought (according to the subject) that Gvishiani was both well connected and too busy to run his new institute, and so would make him (Emilianov) the de facto director as well as helping him to become a full academician. Emilianov turned out to be wrong: Kosygin died; Gvishiani ran his own institute and hired two other deputies to boot; and it was unknown to the subject whether Emilianov ever made it to full academician.[7]

THE SECOND RUNG AND BEYOND

In all the political success stories related above, voluntary activism eventually led to a full-time political job. This transition from part-time involvement to a full-time release from one's ordinary occupation is a key step in any political career—the making of which requires both delicacy and energy.

Amusingly enough, at times some of the energy required can come from an unexpected direction: from nonpolitical people who want to rid themselves of activists. For example, the mediocre engineer whom Subject #7 was forced to include on the promotion lists greatly irritated the subject. This engineer's work was mediocre, which was bad enough—but worse, he made speeches in the lab. For example, if a few other engineers arrived at work early and were discussing information from Voice of America radio broadcasts, Subject #7 would—as manager—pretend that he did not overhear. (Other managers asked their workers not to talk about such things.) The activist, however, would make speeches about the capitalist encirclement. (Actually, there was a KGB informer in the lab, as usual; and periodically Subject #7 would be called to the first department—the KGB—to be told about the poor attitude of certain of his workers. Subject #7 would then dutifully tell the miscreants to be quiet—and exclude them from promotion lists.)

Subject #7 knew that he could not complain to his own superior about the activist's poor work. His superior was a party member and himself an activist. So instead, Subject #7 went to his superior and said, "[The activist]'s great; let's push him up." Thus he proposed to keep promoting the activist until he could promote him to someone else's section. One day, Subject #7 ran into the head of the trade union committee, who—he knew—was looking for a new man. "I have a great guy for you," he said. "I hate to lose him, but I know it would be better for you to have him." Thus, the activist got a full-time appointment to trade union work.

Similarly, Subject #4 told of one engineer who was both disliked and not especially competent, and so was continually sent away to special courses. Thus, the most disliked and incompetent engineer became—at least on paper—the best trained engineer in the plant. It later emerged that this fellow had a high-level contact, and a deal was made with the managing engineer—who was in line to become chief engineer—to stand aside so that this man could be promoted to chief engineer. The understanding was that he would not be in that position very long; and, indeed, two years later he was promoted to the ministry. Subject #4 said that he saw similar things happening in the U.S. corporation for which he now works. One difference, he said, is that in the U.S. company only a close friend or relative would help a stupid person, while in the Soviet Union everyone will help any sort of person who is an activist—out of self-defense!

In the Soviet Union, which elevates office politics to the level of national politics, impersonal activism (not dependent on personal relationships) may suffice to get one started on the road to a political career.[8] It may even be sufficient for obtaining a low-level job in the *mestkomi* (political organs of the workplace) or perhaps a low-level managerial position. (This creates a stratum of activists who may be mediocre, but who have a modicum of authority and set the tone for all dealings within the enterprise.) Impersonal activism is not sufficient, however, for advancement within the mestkomi or to higher organs. Activists' social and technical skills determine their prospects for further advancement.

VARIETIES OF PROMOTION

Coattail Riding

Getting promoted by establishing one's usefulness to someone who is a rising star has been called, in the West, the "crucial subordinate strategy"; and it works as well in the Soviet Union as anywhere else (see Chapter 5). Subject #17 was brought along when a deputy minister for whom he had done much work was made chairman of a committee of the Kazakstan *sovnarkhoz*.[9] Subject #10 described how his good relations with the director of his institute led to his own appointment as head of the trade union committee; and Subject #11 described how a minister's aide had followed along with the minister on the last three steps of the minister's career path. The minister himself was being moved along his own career path via connection with a Central Committee secretary.

Subject #2 noted that the director of a regional construction authority had formerly run one of its subunits, and that when the director was promoted he brought many of his subordinates to the head office with him. It was as if the whole collective had been promoted. The collective was not impermeable, however; and some new administrators were brought into the regional office from other subunits.

Bringing along one's own team also occurs in the West, when a manager calls on old and trusted colleagues and subordinates in order to have underlings whose capabilities are known, and with whom informal relations have already been worked out. This is all the more important in the Soviet system, given what we shall be discussing in the next chapter: the necessity of mutual cover, and the prominence of informal relations in accomplishing one's tasks.

But there is an alternative to rising with or under a single boss: getting transferred to a higher position under another boss. However, the mechanisms for moving to a higher position in another organization are slightly different, depending on whether the new position is closer or further from the center than one's current position.

Transfers Up and In

A centripetal transfer is a move upward and toward the center. Most often, a person gets such a promotion through the recommendation of his or her current boss. This pattern was illustrated by Subject #12, for example, who got a position on the Georgian sovnarkhoz on the recommendation of his raion (district) party organization's first secretary.

Subject #5 told how a raikom (district party committee) secretary might bring a protégé to the *gorkom* (city party committee) "to show him"—for example, in response to a remark by a gorkom secretary that a new instructor was needed for the city committee staff. Such an occurence implies, first, that—as we would say—the protégé "has good chemistry" with the raikom sponsor and, second, that it is in the interest of the raikom secretary to place the candidate in the gorkom.

In fact, if the raikom secretary is successful in having this candidate accepted and the candidate does a good job, the raikom secretary benefits both indirectly by demonstrating an ability to find and develop talent, and directly by having a useful contact at the gorkom. For example, in a parallel case, Subject #12—having been placed on the sovnarkhoz under the sponsorship of his raion secretary—was later called on by that secretary to help get an ice plant for his district. Thus, ability to place protégés will be a reflection of the sponsor's own power and prestige with peers and superiors. (And mutatis mutandis, the position of the sponsor may be weakened by attacks on his or her protégés and allies. This is familiar to bureaucratic politicians everywhere.)

Centrifugal Promotions

The alternative pattern of advancement is centrifugal, in which one is promoted out from the center. For example, an instructor from the

Central Committee department of propaganda was promoted into the position of editor in chief of *Moscow Pravda*—a position in the nomenklatura of the propaganda department. (A party organization's nomenklatura consists of a list of positions in subordinate party or nonparty organizations, appointment to which requires its approval.) Similarly, the head of the cadre department in each ministry—who has the rank of deputy minister—is usually appointed from the staff of the Central Committee department supervising that ministry. (This process—along with the nomenklatura system in general—emphasizes the party's intense supervision of personnel policy, one of its two main functions along with centralization/coordination. Ultimately, the party exercises its authority via the personnel function.)

Note that centrifugal promotion involves a supervisory organization moving its own personnel into high positions within the organizations that it supervises. This is directly analogous to the practice in Western corporations of promoting corporate headquarters' personnel to high positions within divisional organizations, divisional headquarters' personnel to supervisory positions in subordinate plants, and so on. Such promotions are motivated by the desire of those in the center to place known and trusted actors in the more peripheral organizations that they supervise. The necessity of headquarters' knowing and trusting its divisional managers is, in fact, what is formalized in the nomenklatura system (see Chapter 8).

Patrons Other than One's Boss

If not one's boss, then a friend or acquaintance can sometimes help in getting one promoted. Many subjects reported finding jobs through various friends, schoolmates, former coworkers or bosses, and so forth. One subject stressed that "you can't pick up the paper and read ads" to get a management job. Everything depends on knowing who to talk to and on finding out about opportunities through private channels.

In rare cases, one can make a higher contact on one's own, bypassing the sponsorship of one's boss. Subject #5 said that it might be possible to meet a higher party official at a resort or at official meetings, but he thought that this would be very difficult. Subject #4 noted that too obvious an attempt to make higher contacts could be seen as a threat by one's immediate boss or sponsor, and thus be quite dangerous.

Best of all might be an ex-schoolmate who had attained a high position. Such a person can be quite helpful: Witness the minister who quickly moved through three levels to reach the ministry, propelled by an old friend who happened to be a Central Committee secretary. The stories of highly placed relatives helping careers are too numerous even to mention. The highly placed sponsor who guides and aids a protégé's career is called a *ruka*, meaning a (helping) hand.

CLIMB A RUNG; STEADY YOURSELF; CLIMB ANOTHER RUNG

After each promotion—however obtained—there is first a phase of proving one's technical competence. During this period, one solely responds to requests and pressures from above. Later, there is a more complex political phase in which one becomes something of a player and then has some initiative with which either to succeed or fail.

This alternation of the technical and the political was nicely illustrated by Subject #9's description of the diplomat's career. In secondary school, there is first a phase of proving oneself as a good student, and then a phase of taking a leadership role in the komsomol. At MGIMO, there is first academic performance, and then the increasingly complicated social relationships formed around the students' maneuverings for early party membership (a necessity if they are to progress in a diplomatic career, and an advantage if achieved early) and for advantageous career placement. (These interpersonal maneuverings will be discussed in Chapter 3.) Once placed in a job at the Foreign Ministry or an embassy, life becomes simple again: The graduate works hard at impressing superiors with his competency and also strives to cultivate personal relations with his elders. The latter process involves doing favors both professional and personal: doing a special translation of a radio intercept, for example; on the other hand, voluntarily writing a report for someone, or bringing back gifts or letters from diplomats in the field and sneaking them past customs or censorship (a small but real risk taken by junior diplomats in order to ingratiate themselves). Eventually, the climber tries to socialize with his seniors—ingratiatingly befriending their wives, and perhaps also exploiting their weaknesses: providing spirits for those who drink, obtaining women for the "skirt chasers," and like that. Finally, as higher status is achieved, there are more complicated political maneuverings and alliances; one's own protégés must be placed strategically; and so on. With each promotion, the phase of proving competency diminishes, and the political phase increases.

The tendency for the political aspect to grow in importance as one ascends the ladder is the case even for those careers that are technically oriented—for example, in becoming an industrial or scientific administrator (as is also the case for administrative jobs in the West). But the absolute level of politics versus technical competency varies across different career tracks.

At each step along the purely political career path (the party's "bypass highway"), there is always the option of moving back (at a significantly higher level) to a more technical track. Thus, the komsomol chairman of Subject #9's academic section—having attained party membership after three years—immediately became less active politically. With the "leg up" of a party card, the former komsomol chairman chose to focus more on his studies so as to pursue a straight diplomatic career. One of the teachers at MGIMO, on the other hand, pursued a political-administrative career for a prolonged period before moving back into the diplomatic track. He had been very active politically while still a student, and had become a party member during his third year at the institute. Rumor would have it that the dean had approached one of this man's teachers and asked him not to fail the young activist when the latter had some problems in his language courses. In fact, the fellow did not like the country that he was specializing in, and went on to graduate school at MGIMO instead of seeking a placement in the Foreign Ministry or at the embassy. (In general, graduate school is considered a "plum.") He was active in the party organization, became a teaching assistant, went up in his party position, and became assistant to the dean of foreign students, then himself dean of foreign students, then rector of foreign students, and eventually first secretary to the Soviet embassy in Washington, D.C. (not his area of study). Note that by taking the party route he was able to climb relatively quickly within the educational administrative hierarchy until he could enter the diplomatic service at quite a high level and in a choice location.

It is odd—but interesting—to note that this man who eventually became first secretary at the Washington embassy via the party route was described by Subject #9 as looking 15 years older than his age. The subject remarked on how easily the man dealt with more senior officials, relating to them as a peer—as if his appearance were a truer indicator of his generation than his calendar age. One other interviewee told a similar story of a very successful activist who appeared much older than his years. Apparently, this prematurely aged look distinguished by gray hair and wrinkles carries the stigmata of anticipatory socialization—the truest and deepest signs that one has been attending to those above instead of to peers.

SUMMARY

As children, the future apparatchiks must keep their noses clean. In fact, their entire families must have kept themselves out of trouble, possibly for several preceding generations. Their childhood friends are the proper, positive sort. They may start their political careers as early as kindergarten, although it is sometimes possible to enter politics as an adult.

Young climbers assess their personal skills and the opportunities ahead as well as they can, seeking the path to success. Each individual finds an organization—komsomol, trade union, KGB, or primary party organization—whose "culture" is particularly suitable; and there he or she becomes an activist, a volunteer. As unpaid part-time workers— whether writing wall newspapers for the komsomol or acting as petty informers for the KGB—they establish themselves and seek a route into the apparat.

Once in the apparat, climbers look to rise, either directly up the ladder or by transfer. The opportunities available—whether the next move will be to a more central or a more peripheral organization, for example— are determined by the individual's particular position in the system— by what kind of job he or she does in precisely what organization—and by that individual's particular set of contacts and connections. In each position, though, the climber must first prove his or her technical competency—an ability to get the job done. Then he or she must maneuver socially as a political player, making the right connections to activate the next advancement.

NOTES

1. This remark, the fact that it was considered so amusing, and many other little remarks and stories that I heard in my interviews all pointed to the significance of the father–son relationship. For example, one subject had made a conscious attempt while still a youth to analyze how people got ahead. His father had died when he was a boy, the subject said, and so was not there to give him advice. This subject told me how he had envied the paternal guidance that his friends received. The father–son relationship will be explored somewhat further in Appendix B.

2. If carried too far, this encouragement from adults can be experienced as pressure, and can foster resentment—either conscious or unconscious. This may have been the case with this particular subject, who chose to leave the system on the death of his father. Again, we find the theme of fathers and sons.

3. According to Subject #4—who described this process—in the United States it is easy to make a first informal contact, and progressively harder to make a second and third. In the Soviet Union, it is hardest to make the first personal contact, and then progressively easier. This fits the pattern of Russians having relatively few mental categories, characterized by very rigid boundaries—compared to Americans' myriad of intermediate, hazily defined categories. See Appendix A.

4. Here, *nomenklatura* is used generically to refer to the Soviet elite. The specifics of nomenklatura will be discussed later in the chapter.

5. In organizational terms, the party road is a bypass to high positions because industrial work in the Soviet system is purely (what in the West would be called) operations, while broader management functions are performed in the party. High-level operations managers are expected to have a broad background, and so must usually pass through a party position. Another way to see this rela-

tionship is to realize that industrial work is divisional, while the party has headquarters' centralizing functions. Working relations with headquarters staff and experience at headquarters is essential to proper divisional functioning. See Chapter 8.

6. This is reminiscent of the art of gift giving in Japan. The gifts of the highest practitioners bear no obvious comparability to those that they have received, but are nonetheless just right.

7. Years later, Emilianov was one of those purged as part of the fallout of the Chernobyl accident.

8. In the West, by contrast, even the lowest level of office politics will be personal.

9. *Sovnarkhozi* were regional economic administrations that existed for a time under Khrushchev.

3. CLIMBING THE APPARAT LADDER

The primary requisite for success is social skill, especially of the variety that helps in maintaining good relations with higher-ups. This chapter begins by describing the various social factors that go into pleasing the boss. The boss also wants good job performance, however; and for this, the assistance of peers is essential. But these peers—whose help and friendship are so useful—are the very same people with whom one is competing for promotions and the boss's favor. Thus, a tension is created. Managing this tension requires a nice balance between one's public dealings and one's private thoughts and behavior.

PLEASING THE BOSS

Attending to those above, who can help one in getting ahead—being useful and trustworthy in their eyes—is one key to success. But exactly whom does one impress? And exactly how?

1. *Have the right background.* Being educated, for example, is an asset. Subject #13 described an acquaintance, a "smart guy" who had relatives in the Central Committee Secretariat—another asset. This fellow went straight from the university, where he had been a party member, to a job as an instructor in the propaganda department of the Moscow gorkom (city committee). While working there, he continued his studies and achieved his candidat in the philosophical faculty. On achieving this degree, he was given a job in the international department of the Central Committee.

Note that this job bore no relation to the area of his studies; it was the subject's observation that, after 1965, education per se became an important criterion for promotion. A bright, educated person could get a position based on ability and connections; educational specialization was not required, but education itself helped.[1] Note too that Mikhail Gorbachev thought it worthwhile to pick up an agronomy degree while he was first secretary of the Stavropol *kraikom* (regional party committee—comparable to an obkom).

2. *Be available*. If you're not there to do what is necessary to please your boss, someone else will be. Women are not so active in the party in part because, although an activist has to say yes to all requests, "a woman may want to say 'yes' but has to go home to take care of a child."

3. *Be attractive to those in power*. One subject knew a student who tried to make it as a political activist, but who failed because his father was Jewish. Although the student had a Russian name and Russian nationality on his passport, "he had a Jewish face," and—said the subject—there is a saying: "When people beat you, they don't beat your passport; they beat your face."

When—as described in the previous chapter—a raikom secretary brings a protégé to the gorkom "to show him [off]," the protégé has "to have his ears cleaned." He is dressed up and put on his best behavior. Any behavioral gaffes or even his appearance ("He is too short") can make all the difference in this process of personal chemistry. If the protégé has been well socialized in the skills of "good listening" and learning to read what individuals want of him, then he has a better chance of succeeding in this interview. But there is no way to help being too short.

Subject #11 told of meeting a minister's *referent* (assistant or staff aide). He expected little, he said, when he saw "a handsome man, with a communist face." He looked "like a piece of furniture," or like a poster—"they never smile; like a machine, they say only what is official." Someone else described this type of apparatchik as like "stone"—never relaxed, never discussing "any normal thing." (In fact, the referent with the communist face surprised my subject with his directness when he offered the subject a job implementing the illegal procurement of supplies.)

Being attractive is an asset, East or West; but it is clear that, in the Soviet Union, "a communist face" settled in the correct expression—manifesting the proper control—is an even more useful thing to have. The poster image is the ideal, and official portraits are airbrushed to bring them closer to that ideal.

4. *Be useful*. Subordinates help superiors by doing jobs for them, finding them opportunities for exposure, writing reports for them, tutoring their children, and so on. In return, superiors may provide their subordinates with career opportunities.

5. *Fit with the boss*. Promoting trust and making communication easier makes one more useful to higher-ups. One who "fits" will understand his instructions more easily, require less supervision, and thus—in the eyes of the boss—deliver better, more appropriate performance.

The process of making oneself useful is illustrated by both the story of the student who ran the anticrime campaign, and that of the voluntary raikom instructor who proved his worth to the raikom secretary (see Chapter

2). But why did the raikom secretary promote this eager voluntary instructor over all the other eager voluntary instructors? Perhaps this instructor was more competent—and so, more useful. But perhaps there was some personal "chemistry" or fit between him and the secretary. Similarly, why did the student running the oral journal attach himself to the ideology secretary, and not to some other official? His activity allowed him to meet many officials; he courted those with whom he hit it off, to whom he could provide useful services, and who could in return help his career.

Other voluntary activities might provide similar exposure. There occurs a kind of rotation dance in which people keep changing partners, looking for useful contacts with others with whom they fit. This fit is in part a matter of having the proper talents: A voluntary instructor working for a party secretary for industry needs different skills from someone doing a job for the ideology secretary. But fit is also in part a matter of very personal likes and dislikes: Does the boss smoke or not? Do you have the right outside interests? (But see Chapter 4 for examples of someone *making* himself fit.)

When Subject #13 was chief of his department at the newspaper of a large city's party organization, he secured a full-time job for one of his part-time reporters. Why this man, and not one of the other part-timers? This fellow had worked as a part-timer for a few years; he was a good worker and a "nice guy"—but not so good at writing. Subject #13 felt that he himself could help the younger man with the writing; and most importantly, the subject liked him. The subject's boss had his own candidate for the position; but Subject #13 criticized the other candidate as unqualified, and managed to convince the boss to accept his own candidate. Thus, the personal chemistry between this part-time worker and his supervisor led to a full-time appointment.

6. *Never object or disagree.* Subject #5 described how a volunteer instructor must be "a good listener" at the raikom. The instructor must be willing to provide personal favors and services, to go buy beer for a meeting (this has perhaps changed since the antialcohol campaign), to carry groceries for the department head's wife, to remember the birthdays of the department head and the department head's family. The instructor must be ingratiating and become the department head's "man." ("Whose man is he?" is a question that people ask.) Therefore, the instructor must both be good at the assigned official tasks and establish loyalty and trustworthiness before expecting a promotion to full-time political work at the raikom level.

But one does not have to be a complete "yes man" in every case. Careful criticisms can be made if they are basically positive and useful. In a broader context than the superior–subordinate relationship, Subject #7 said that in the early 1960s he had noticed a change in activists' conduct at public meetings. Instead of being unremittingly positive, smarter activists began to make small criticisms—being careful to describe their targets as local problems that were not any particular person's fault, and ending with a statement that to correct such problems, "We need to work harder," or something to that effect.[2] Subject #7 was quite specific in dating the beginnings of this phenomenom to the years before Brezhnev—and, in fact, thought it had something to do with Khrushchev's secret speech denouncing Stalin in 1956. The subject recalled his own shocked reaction to hearing about the speech and its revelations; he considered that speech (and probably Khrushchev's own criticisms of the party's and state's performance and organization) to have set the tone that allowed for criticism of the means to attaining communism (but not the goal).

Thus, certain criticisms are accepted if they are ultimately useful to those in authority. That is, at least some superiors appreciate respectful and useful criticism. One must be careful to know which kind of superior one is dealing with.

7. *Being useful can involve both official and personal activities.* Subject #10 told of the support that the head of the software department at a Moscow institute got from his director, based on the fact that the software man was doing a Ph.D. thesis for the director. Furthermore, Subject #10 told how the software man managed to use his friendship with the editor of a party journal to get an appointment with Kirilenko, who was then a Politburo member and chairman of the committee for science and technology. Why did Kirilenko see him? "Men in that position are always looking for good ideas." And so they are.

8. *Get the job done*—either on paper, as in the report on the youth anticrime campaign, or for real. Subject #12 told how he earned the support and respect of a local party leader during World War II by getting his small textile factory to turn out—in three months and at the direct command of Lavrenti Beria—3,000 winter underwear sets for the troops. This led to the subject's promotion to chief engineer for local industry in his raion, and years later to a position on the staff of the regional economic council (sovnarkhoz).

Thus, part of being useful is being technically competent. Subject #10 described how the director of his institute chose as deputy not the candidate with whom the director was personally close, but the more useful candidate—the better scientist, manipulator, and administrator. Subject #6 told of evaluating his own subordinates in strictly utilitarian terms; in fact, his manner implied the derogation of personal relationships. Subject #5, who had spoken of the importance of carrying groceries for the boss's wife, made no bones about the necessity of also getting the job done—and better than one's peers.

Subject #7 described how the director of the plant in which he worked derived his power and prestige from technical competency. This director came into contact with high-level politicians through his scientific work, and even had friends on the Politburo. (The plant was in the Ukraine, and I asked if he meant the Ukrainian Politburo; but he said no, the one in Moscow.) "His power was in his technical ability to solve problems on a large scale." In order to perform the technical tasks on which his strength was based, the director surrounded himself with excellent engineers—choosing the heads of sections, labs, and so forth, solely on technical grounds. In fact, this director gave short shrift to politics; when he addressed meetings, he would say things like, "As soon as we can get this Lenin's birthday business out of the way, then we can get down to work." Moral: If you are useful enough, you can build a career outside politics even in the Soviet Union.

But politics always help. This director was eventually replaced by a political manager who knew nothing about the technical work of the enterprise but who made sure that slogans were put up in each workshop, that more workers turned out for demonstrations, and so on. This manager, in turn, chose more politically oriented submanagers.

9. *Be aware of the boss's needs.* The boss may not tell you about the groceries that need to be carried, the children who need to be tutored, and the errands that need to be run. You have to deliberately search out such opportunities to prove your worth—your usefulness and loyalty.

Subject #6, who was a relatively new emigrant from the U.S.S.R., apparently came to believe I was in a position to help him get a grant to write about the Soviet Union. At first, he reacted strongly to my questions by telling me that there were no differences in how careers are built East and West (in this, he is to a large degree correct), and that Gorbachev had built his career by the ancient principles of Machiavelli. He implied that I was wasting his time. Then he visibly seemed to catch himself, whereupon he carefully began to cultivate me. All hint of criticism disappeared; he told me how important my concerns were, and that he could help me become "a top expert" on the analysis of careers in totalitarian systems—if only I would arrange for him to get a large grant. He had adjusted to me in the hope that I might be his new patron.

One of my subjects was instructed by a minister's referent (aide) to procure illegally an expensive Grundig tape recording/playing apparatus—"It must have weighed 150 kilos"—for the minister's *dacha* (summer home). "It was to be a surprise for the minister, to come in and see the whole wall of tape equipment, all installed and ready to play." The minister was known for his interest in music; and the referent took it upon himself not merely to respond to the minister's requests, but to sense what might please his sponsor and to supply it proactively.

Subject #7 told me about a friend of his who had been stationed abroad and was allowed to bring along his family, and who had then defected to the West. From the fact that he had been given such a posting and allowed to bring his family, it was clear that my subject's friend had enjoyed support at high levels and was completely trusted. In fact, this man says that he did not defect because he was disaffected politically, but because office politics was making his position more and more uncomfortable. His support higher up had been weakened because of an ally's departure from the home office and also—it is clear in retrospect—because he had failed to bring his superiors gifts when he visited Moscow. "I felt uncomfortable about bringing gifts to superiors," the defector was quoted as saying, "but then I could tell that they were waiting for gifts." Someone with stronger support had decided that he wanted the Western posting. Agreements with companies in the host country—agreements that had already been negotiated and approved by the incumbent's higher-ups—were then renounced or criticized as poorly handled. His son—a fine student—was denounced for supposed misbehavior in the local school maintained by the Soviet government. When the pressure became too great, the man "chose" to defect. Subject #7 commented that "The higher the level, the less they care." The same general pressure tactics may be used at every level; but the higher one goes, the more ruthless the application.

10. Thus, *bring the boss gifts*. One institute director took up an involuntary collection at his institute—forcing employees to kick back part of their salaries—in order to buy gifts for his superiors in Moscow. The most extreme case of "gift giving" (to stretch the definition a bit) that I heard was the story of a man who had an early career in komsomol, and then became an instructor in the propaganda department of the Central Committee Secretariat. The propaganda department had in its nomenklatura the position of editor in chief of Moscow *Pravda*, and this instructor was given the appointment.[3] Later, he was appointed deputy editor in chief of *Isvestia*. The subject said that this fellow was a nice enough guy—and of average competence—but attributed the man's success to his attractive wife. She was active at high levels in the Committee of Soviet Women, and "she was very flexible." When pressed for an explanation, the subject said that she was reputed to be having affairs with some high-level politicians. Her husband, the subject thought, must have found out something about this because at one point the couple separated for a number of months, but then were reconciled.

Spouses can perform useful services in less dramatic ways, too. Subject #15 told me of a teacher who wished to get into the party. Her husband had a private driving school, and among his students were various party officials who helped the teacher to get a party card. The only other party members at her school were the director and his deputy, so the teacher immediately became the secretary of the thus newly formed—since there were now three party members—school party committee. In this position, she helped the director to make the teachers' schedules—she assigned classes, and so on—putting her in a powerful position vis-à-vis the other teachers.

Subject #16 described a veterinarian who joined the party and became "close friends with the elite," managing to be appointed editor of a veterinary journal and then of a children's nature magazine—a position allowing for frequent foreign travel. This man met his influential friends through his activity in komsomol and the party, but their friendships were based not on his official work, but on the fact that he—a country boy—was a hunter. For city residents in the Soviet Union, hunting is a high prestige activity, especially because of the necessity for gun permits. As someone who could play guide on hunting trips, he ingratiated himself to people on the level of deputy ministers of agriculture and apparatchiki at the Moscow gorkom.

11. *Get credit for successes, and avoid the blame for failures.* Subject #5 told of an incident in which a bridge—the construction of which he had organized—was visited by the first secretary of the republic. On hearing that this bridge was the first of its kind in the Soviet Union, the secretary intimated that medals might be handed out. Because it was indeed the first of its kind—and thus fraught with risk—officials had distanced themselves from the

project as much as possible. Now, however, as completion neared and medals were a prospect, the subject's nominal supervisor in the city government began to elbow him aside, finding reasons to raise questions and criticisms. Although all the questions were satisfactorily answered, the superior wound up getting the medal at the bridge opening ceremonies, while the subject was left standing in the crowd watching. It was at this moment that he decided to emigrate.

His story reminded me of the tale of the little red hen, in which all the other animals avoid the work of growing grain and baking bread, only to make claims on the hen's bread when it comes out of the oven. For all their avoidance of this potentially risky project early on (and the details of this will be discussed shortly), members of the city government advanced many claims on the credit. In the fairy tale, however, such claims do not succeed.

12. *Be loyal to your boss.* Having made a "strictly logical, intellectual decision" to pursue a political career, a friend of Subject #16 discovered that, in a political career, you must treat people on a political basis. You must remember where your loyalties—that is to say, your own interests—lie. In 1976, while this political fellow was an obkom instructor, the subject and several associates presented their technical work at the (permanent) exhibition of Soviet economic achievements, in Moscow. The group received some medals. These medals were not individually assigned, but the group was told to award among themselves the one gold, one silver, and three bronze medals.[4] The group did decide who should receive what, but this then required the approval of the local political authorities. The authorities told the group that they did not have enough party members (there were none), and that furthermore they did not have enough members of the "root nationality"—(that is, there were too many Jews and not enough Russians (of which there were one or two). Not surprisingly, the group was angry that they could not be rewarded for their award-winning work, and so the subject called his friend—the obkom instructor. The instructor said that he would help, but then discovered that the decision was obkom policy—apparently set by the obkom first secretary himself. At that point, Subject #16's friend switched sides and declared that he would support obkom policy. Loyalty to his master(s) was overriding.

Loyalty means supporting one's own boss in particular—not being distracted by other powerful people with whom one might come in contact. The mediocre engineer who was transferred to full-time trade union work (on the recommendation of Subject #7) found that the senior committee members were competing with one another—and to some degree, with the trade union chairman himself. The competitors gathered damaging information about each other (more on this, later) and also argued over how to execute policy. They all agreed on any major subject, since they all followed centrally prescribed policies. But they could and did disagree over minor matters and policy execution—for example: How should the workers line up to march in next week's demonstration? Twenty rows of ten workers, or ten rows of twenty? A monitor at each end, or just one monitor per row?

("If Ivan Ivanovich is too drunk and wanders out of line, there'll be hell to pay.") The banner in the front or the back? Who can be trusted not to leave the banner on the bus, or to just ditch it somewhere and go off drinking? ("Who has a friend reliable enough to keep an eye on the banner?") On such matters, each senior committee member could attempt to demonstrate his or her superior judgment. Since competitors don't ask one another for help (according to Subject #7), they prefer help from someone lower. Thus, our technically mediocre activist became a supporter of the chairman, speaking out bravely in support of the senior man's ideas.

Be loyal even under fire, and protect the boss. Show the boss that you can be trusted not only to get the job done, but to protect the boss's own interests. Subject #4 told of one raikom secretary who had a policy of harassing new workers for a year to see if they would remain loyal, not complain, not go over his head, and so forth. Once they had passed this trial by fire, they could be trusted. Subject #10 told of the time his boss was out of town when he heard that the party control commission would be paying a visit on the Monday that the boss was returning. Subject #10 called his boss at home to warn him. Subject #11 described how the minister's referent protected and took care of his boss the minister. Subject #15 lost his job at a research institute because, in essence, he would not participate in the maneuverings of the institute director.

Illustrating lack of loyalty (and its desserts), Subject #20 told of a colleague—the deputy head of a department in an institute—who managed to alienate both his immediate boss and the institute director. Instead of going to his boss with any complaints, the deputy would complain at meetings and to other organizations, such as the party control commission. This unwise fellow was kicked upstairs to a dead-end position—and then that position was reorganized out of existence.

Competing loyalties can lead to social failure, and even to punishment. This was illustrated in a story told by Subject #16. In the early 1960s, a Russian engineer friend of his had become interested in English and Hindi, both of which he studied on his own. Soviet–Indian relations were close during that period; and, about once a year, Nehru and his daughter Indira Gandhi visited the city where the subject and his friend lived—presumably on business related to the area's industry. Hearing that there was to be a reception for the visiting Indian delegation one year, Subject 16's friend decided to go meet some real Indians. Being a man of dark complexion who—according to the subject—looked a bit like an Indian himself, the friend wrapped himself in a sheet and—in a stately manner—walked right past the guards into the reception.

There he started conversing with a young woman who—as it emerged— was a niece of Indira Gandhi. She was amused by his story; and, after he left in the same manner in which he had arrived, the two corresponded. A few years later the correspondence ceased.

When Subject #16 was leaving the Soviet Union to emigrate, his engineer friend finally told him the rest of the story. The friend had been approached by the KGB and asked to become an informant. He was told that it would be very useful to have someone close to the Gandhi family. He should share his correspondence with them, and perhaps they would arrange for him to travel to India. He refused. And so he received no more letters, although he continued to write for a while. Years later he was still being punished, hounded out of job after job for no other apparent reason. He had passed up an opportunity that might have led to travel and a rather exotic life, because he did not wish to betray his relationship with the young woman.

13. *Know your place.* Initiative is dangerous for the aspiring apparatchik, unless exercised within the structure of directions from above. As a child, Subject #4 was one of a group of children who went to the raikom to complain about the brutal ways of their school's physical education instructor. The children were severely reprimanded. A friend's father—a successful bureaucrat—gave his son some advice: "Never be at the head of anything. Any initiative is punishable. Initiative must come from above."

Subject #17 got into trouble for not having the proper respect for party organs. Twenty-four branch offices reported to him; and in a certain branch, there were two Jews (out of 22–25 employees). The director of that office was called on by the raikom to replace these two workers, and he called his boss—my subject—who tried to persuade the raikom that they were incorrect in making their request. The raikom then dismissed the office director, who was in their nomenklatura, and expelled him from the party to boot. Subject #17 then went to the gorkom to say that the raikom had no right to do this. (Apparently, although the raikom has the right of approval on appointments to positions in its nomenklatura, it is questionable whether it has the right of removal.) The gorkom reinstated the field office director in the party, but affirmed his removal from the job. The subject felt obliged to offer the office director a job in another city; but the gorkom secretary opposed this, too. It is not clear to me whether the subject was dealing with the gorkom first secretary or the organizational secretary, but the man had a direct line to a Politburo member from his republic. He picked up this special phone and conversed in his national tongue, which the subject did not understand. Whatever was said then led to an investigation of the subject and his dismissal, as well as a personal reprimand from the Politburo member. Subject #17 had not had a proper appreciation of the party's perquisites in the realm of personnel policy.

Part of knowing your place is being very careful about any contacts that you have over the boss's head. For example, the second deputy editor in chief of *Evening Moscow* had come from a job at the Novosti news service, via the recommendations of people that he knew at the Central Committee Secretariat. He had no strong support in the gorkom, however, and his position was officially subordinate to the gorkom. Unfortunately, although he maintained the relationship with his Central Committee contacts, he neglected the city committee. Also, people at the gorkom were put off by his having such high connections. They wondered if he could be carrying tales to the Central Committee, and they were also perhaps a little jealous of the Central Committee itself. He was "a strange guy"; the editor in chief wanted to get rid of him, and the third deputy editor in chief wanted to move up into his job. Thus, he was given a hard time at editorial committee meetings; he had become a scapegoat of sorts, or at least a known and inviting target. The editor in chief then went to the propaganda department of the gorkom and said, "The editorial committee is criticizing him. Not myself—I like him—but it's not good for people not to have respect." The editor in chief himself would not criticize the man because he did not want to dirty his hands, especially as the target must have had at least the formal support of the gorkom to get the position in the first place—not to mention having Central Committee contacts whom the editor in chief did not want to antagonize. The editor in chief knew his place.

Along these same lines, Subject #15 told me that one never reveals one's connections: "It makes you look dangerous, arouses envy," and possibly annoys the connections themselves.

To summarize, the bonds that are formed between a Soviet patron and protégé are more intense, personal, and encompassing than similar relationships in the West. (For U.S. mentoring relationships, see Kram 1980 and Levinson et. al. 1978.) The obedience demanded is absolute. Subject #5 likened the atmosphere to one of a criminal gang: There is no outside authority to which to appeal, and no way to leave and go to another organization; so the gang is one's whole social world. This intensity of involvement is the result of both a lack of other institutions to limit party authority and the necessity for mutual covering relationships seen in any organization (see Downs 1967)—but here in the context of authoritarian power.

PEER RELATIONS AND MUTUAL INTERDEPENDENCE

In order to accomplish one's tasks, it is important to be able to rely on others; one must be able to trade favors, and ask for help. Again: "Don't have a hundred rubles; have a hundred friends." (See Berliner 1957 on mutual aid and *krugovaya poruka*.)

Subject #20 was an economist who relied on her own direct factory surveys for data, not trusting official reports. Her ability to obtain worthwhile information depended on her establishing trust with people in each factory, reassuring them that the data would be kept confidential. She cultivated all the people with whom she had professional dealings: "How are you? How's your wife? The children? I have something for you"—a book, two tickets to the theater, or whatever. Connections are 80 percent of achievement, she said.

Subject #2 was the representative of a city government in the construction of a bridge. He described the complex relationships that he established with people in other organizations with which he had to work. As the representative of the city, his job was to approve and coordinate the planning, the contracting, and the actual construction processes. His main counterparts—those with whom he had to work in an ongoing and closely interactive basis—were the heads of *moststroy* #3 (the bridge-building trust), *mostotryad* #1 (the particular construction division—subordinate to moststroy #3—charged with the actual construction), and the planning–design office. His other significant interactions were with the *gorispolkom* (city government executive committee) and *gorplan* (city economic planning) offices, the Ministry of Transport, and the factory that eventually produced the steel used in the construction. The head of moststroy #3 was especially significant: He was a hero of Soviet labor and had many contacts in the city government, the gorkom, and so on, as well as being a strong leader and administrator intensely admired by the subject.

Subject #2 was in fact the most junior of the administrators who had the greatest responsibility for the project. He got his position because a number of other candidates had refused it. Other candidates apparently felt that the job was too difficult, and the risk of failure too great: Planning was behind schedule (there were no designs done), and the bridge was to be of a new type. My subject agreed to take the position because he had previously worked in mostotryad #1 and in the design institute, and so had preexisting relations with the major players. This gave him some confidence in his ability to do the necessary coordination. When, at first, "K"—the head of the moststroy and thus Subject #2's former superior two levels up—did not seem to pay enough attention to him, Subject #2 went to K and offered to resign. After K told him to stay on, they worked together smoothly for the duration of the project.

There had been a steel factory initially chosen by *gosplan* (the national government economic planning agency) to supply the project; but, in fact, it had refused the job two years earlier (at the inception of the project). No new supplier had been found. Subject #2 was only able to get another steel factory to agree to produce the required new types of steel by: (1) agreeing to pay premium prices, and (2) taking responsibility for the steel actually functioning as intended. In other words, he was personally taking on the risks inherent in moving to a new technology. Further risks were taken when the subject later decided not to spend resources on protecting a construction-phase approach road from possible washout by floods.

In another city, a similar bridge project, which had the special backing of then Prime Minister Kosygin, was unable to get its steel produced because its managers were unwilling to pay premium prices. Without the premium, the steel factory would not take on the work of changing its technology—Kosygin or no Kosygin. (That bridge was eventually completed two years late.)

Paying such high prices for the steel left Subject #2 open to possible criticism if the bridge later went over budget (its budget was approximately 60 million rubles). In order to partially spread this risk, the subject insisted that the following players approve the steel contract: the head of mostotroy #3, the head of mostotryad #1, the design office, himself as director of the bridge project, the gorispolkom, the Ministry of Transport, and the steel factory. This process of self-protection is referred to as "collective nobody-is-responsible"—the antithesis of collective responsibility. (This is similar to *krugovaya poruka*—meaning circular security—except that the latter involves covering for infractions of rules and other legal violations. This instance differs in that it merely spreads the risk of future failure, not legal culpability.)

Note in this instance—and in all the others detailed here—the importance of getting everybody on board. In part, this was aimed at the avoidance of conflict. Subject #2 had a preexisting grievance with the head of mostotryad #1: the subject had married the latter's girl friend and the mostotryad chief had then done certain things to make the subject's life difficult. This had led to Subject #2's earlier decision to transfer to the design institute. Now that he was in a more powerful position, he made no attempt to revenge himself. "If I squeeze them once, they'll squeeze me ten times," he said. If open conflict were to erupt, no one would be able to do the job and all would fail. Note the importance of cooperative, socially oriented behavior.

Relations of mutual trust evolved in which the participants had to rely on one another to cover for them. For example, the subject needed good relations with the woman working at gorplan (the city economic-planning office) who was in charge of his budget. Subject #2 sat in her waiting room for two months before he got in to see her. Finally she said, "What are *you* doing out here? Come in." Each year, she would significantly cut his budget so that her total planned expenditures would remain within her own budget. During the first year he needed 500,000 rubles for design work, but was allotted only 175,000 in her plan. However, she assured him that, by year's end, enough other projects would not have fulfilled their work and expenditure plans so that she could come up with the extra money. Accepting her assurances, Subject #2 then contracted to spend the whole 500,000, thus putting himself at risk if she did not live up to her promises. In a similar fashion, the subject asked an electrical contractor to supply his own cable (presumably from other projects) on the assurance that he would be repaid when the bridge's electrical cable was finally delivered.

This system of *mutual relations built on trust and the sharing of risks*—in which people were expected to cover for one another—was essential to the timely completion of the project. The ability to maintain such relations, then, is essential for the manager who hopes to succeed (at least in part) on the basis of his accomplishments.

Incentives and premiums play a significant role, and can reinforce personal relations. Already noted was the premium price paid to the steel factory. Another ploy was the division of the bridge project into four subprojects: the north section of the bridge, the south section, the central span, and the approach roads. This allowed construction to be done in phases, with achievable intermediate goals; and it also allowed for three months' salary to be paid as a completion bonus on four separate occasions, instead of once for one big job. This provided additional incentives for all concerned to concentrate their energies on the project. Thus, inventiveness in exploiting the normal rules for payment is a valuable managerial asset.

In running his own office as director of the project, Subject #2 created a home for wayward engineers. His chief engineer, for example, had gotten into trouble at the Transport Ministry. While still a candidate for party membership, he had been promoted to work in the *glavk* (main directorate, a subdivision within the ministry). He had created such animosity through his outspoken style however, that he was rejected for full party membership—thus becoming ineligible to work in the glavk. He was transferred to a lower position, and then hounded from that. The engineer then found refuge in the subject's office—which was not subordinate to the ministry, but to the city.

Note that the expulsion of this engineer from the glavk can be seen as more than a mere petty personality clash. If systems of personal relations based on mutual trust and covering for one another are essential for one's functioning in the system, then a prickly personality who cannot fit in endangers both the work of a unit and all the individuals in the unit. It is appropriate and necessary for such an individual to be expelled.

Similarly, in the central committee of a republic komsomol, an instructor was promoted to deputy department head, arousing the jealousy of another—more senior—instructor. Upset, the senior instructor stopped working: He would just go home instead of visiting the districts that he was supposed to be overseeing. According to my informant, this fellow had not gotten the promotion because he was "rough"—and the one who was promoted was "smooth." The rough fellow—whose heavy-handed protest presumably illustrates his personal style—then wanted to be given a position as party secretary at a local college. Instead he was sent to the staff of the republic's party control commission—not a very good job.

The most highly cultivated and extensive personal networks are maintained by politicians and *tolkachi* (literally, pushers, supply and procurement workers who often engage in unofficial and sometimes illegal trading in order to obtain needed supplies). Subjects #3, #8, and #11 worked as high-level tolkachi. Their success was predicated on maintaining relations with large numbers of other supply managers—with whom they traded—as well as with those in charge of distribution at their factories' suppliers. Within their own factories, they also often acted to coordinate the trading of supplies among departments and shops. Thus, shop heads were dependent on the tolkach(i), and were careful to build relations with them. In particular, the shop heads would not complain if the tolkach had genuine difficulty in obtaining their supplies since, if they did, the tolkach would not help them out the next time they wasted or damaged supplies, or diverted them to private use. In both their internal and external roles, then, these tolkachi were dependent on horizontal mutual-covering relations.

Subject #8 supervised about 100 supply workers and kept up relations with "thousands" of other supply agents at other enterprises, trading a variety of goods including—for example—a half ton of gold (for which he had to arrange transportation, armed guards, and so forth), tens of tons of copper, and so on. The gold was "lent" to him in exchange for supplies of gold that his own plant was supposed to receive in three months. This kind of transaction was based on trust and mutual necessity. No official basis existed for such a trade; no contract could be signed; and so, the trade had no official existence or legal standing. The subject emphasized that his good word was his stock in trade: "I lie one time, and I am finished."

Subject #11 got in trouble when he could not supply his boss with some piece of equipment and the boss concluded that he was holding out, or had perhaps gone ahead and sold the equipment. Subject #11 was fired and threatened with legal action until he pointed out that every head of laboratory in the boss's institute would—having cooperated with him—go to jail with him. A friend of the subject's said that someone he knew—a minister's aide—wanted to offer the subject a job. "I talked to him about you," said the friend. "He's interested." "Why?" asked Subject #11. "You connect with many people. You got what you needed," came the answer.

Subject #15 said that the director of his institute was a politician who had been appointed to that position as a demotion. In his new position, the director's only stock in trade would have to be academic degrees; so he quickly gave himself a candidat degree (equivalent to a Ph.D.), and began arranging that they be given to various connections, sons of connections, and so on. It was a case of *"ty mne; ya tebye* (you [give] to me; I [give] to you)," said the subject.

Mutual covering must occur vertically as well as horizontally. Subject #2 described how subordinates' acceptance of unrealistic plans is dependent on their superiors' later accepting the subordinates' excuses. Since the system runs on pressure from above, unrealistically ambitious plans are set routinely. In meetings with the representative of the gorispolkom (the city government executive committee), Subject #2 (who, you recall, was in charge of building a bridge) had to agree to impossible plans and then later find excuses for their nonfulfillment—only to agree to a new set of impossible plans, and so on. Refusal to agree would have resulted in dismissal since, otherwise, such a refusal had to be endorsed and transmitted up a level and so on. Thus the maintenance of working relations requires that the senior official accept the excuses (and/or lies) offered, which happens readily enough if he or she recognizes the impossibility of the initial requests. This constitutes another form of mutual covering, in response to potential criticisms for not meeting the plan.

The superior does always have the option of not accepting the excuses, which might happen if he or she wishes to get rid of a subordinate. Subject #10 described how the director of his institute lost the support of his governing council and so—as part of their campaign to dismiss him—was called to account for his fabrications, instead of being supported in them. In general, though—in the Soviet Union as in the West— assistants cover for their bosses, and vice versa. (See Downs 1967 on the unavoidability of infractions and the necessity for loyalty.)

Relations of personal trust can only develop over time; they can be maintained with only a limited number of others. These limitations contribute to every Soviet entity's drive toward autarky, since without personal relations one cannot depend on the satisfaction of one's needs. Given an economy of shortage, *impersonal relations are unreliable.* Even when ordered by Gosplan, factory X will not necessarily deliver some product to customer Y; thus, what is needed is a captive supplier. This is what lies behind—for example—the Transport Ministry having its own steel factories, and Soviet factories having dwarf workshops that produce needed supplies and spare parts in small quantities (and at enormous expense, compared to the cost of mass-produced parts). *The limits of personal trust mean limited cooperation, and thus insecurity and duplicated efforts.*

CRITICISM

In general, criticism toward individuals (as opposed to criticism of general conditions, which all must pledge themselves to improve) must be negotiated in advance or directed at helpless scapegoats. (It goes without saying that criticism of the system is extremely damaging. Subject #10 was prevented from becoming a candidat because a party member in his office reported some unguarded critical remarks that he had made.) Subject #3 once received a *vygovor* (reprimand) because, having been unable to obtain certain supplies, he was blamed by a shop for their lack of production. The subject had not called on any higher authority for help in obtaining the supplies, because he knew that they just were not available. (Indeed, he knew his suppliers' warehouses better than his own.) Subject #3 would have avoided the reprimand had he called for help, but this could have made trouble for him with his supplier—so he preferred to absorb the criticism.

In order to maintain good relations with party and trade union officials, Subject #7 made personal appeals to his subordinates to get them to attend meetings or demonstrations. He implicitly offered in return such favors as overlooking lateness, excusing absences used to run errands, and so on. The subject wanted the subordinates to attend so that, when the various labs and shops were evaluated in terms of their political activism, "I just should not be put on the end of the list." This was a concern because the person on the end of the list becomes the scapegoat onto whom all political pressures are deflected.

This theme of avoiding the negative and, more specifically, avoiding the position of last—that is, being the scapegoat—is one that appeared in other interviews. But, after all, there is always a last place on any list. Thus, in the Soviet system, *the boundary of acceptability is not an objective or arbitrary standard that all can exceed, but is instead a socially defined, ongoing process of identifying and scolding deviants.*

Sometimes, said Subject #7, a superior would instruct him to "Feel free to criticize So-and-so" at a meeting. The subject interpreted this as an order to criticize So-and-so—and as meaning that So-and-so's career was already over, albeit as yet unannounced. No other direct criticisms were ever made unless permission had been granted by the object of the criticism. For example, before complaining that a project was behind schedule because he could not obtain a certain power supply, Subject #7 would go to the head of supply and ask, "Would you mind if I mention . . . ?" The head of supply might say yes or no, depending on his own needs and position. He might agree to be criticized if he could successfully pass the criticism on to a safe target: either a scapegoat with a dead career, or a target so distant that it would never hear of the criticism (some other ministry, or whatever). Alternatively, there were times when one might agree to absorb a minor criticism in order to build up credits with someone else who needed a scapegoat.

Subject #7's main point here was that "these meetings were *theater*— all arranged in advance." But it is worth noting that the roles in these plays were *negotiated* among the players, and that the process of negotiation was important to the informal structure of the organization.

Thus, criticisms must be made very carefully. When Subject #7 described the advent of careful critics in the early 1960s, he emphasized the importance of their "not saying anything against, not mentioning anyone's name." This is because criticism—or "being last on the list"— is so potentially damaging that one may create dangerous enemies through careless criticism.

Officially required self-criticism also had to be made with care. At plant meetings, the shop and lab heads would have to report on their work and say something good and something bad ("80 percent good, 20 percent bad"). The something bad was usually chosen as being immediately susceptible to correction: For example, a "self-criticism" might be made that a project still had not been completed—in the knowledge that it would be done within two weeks. Each report at these meetings went as follows: first(!), political achievements—"My lab had the best turnout when we celebrated X," "We had so many *politinformatzia* sessions," and so on; second, technical achievements; third, shortcomings.

Official criticism may often be avoided by scrupulously following official procedures. There were two subjects who told of hostile bosses who had been unable to remove them because of the necessity of following proper bureaucratic procedure. Subject #15—who had described how the demoted politician appointed to run his institute began to retail degrees—earned his boss's enmity by giving the director's degree candidates a hard time during their thesis defenses. The subject said that, because he did everything by the book, the director could not get rid of him. Subject #7 was allied with his director in a bureaucratic struggle at their institute. While the director was away, the deputy director— who was on the other side of the struggle—tried to fire the subject. Since the subject was head of the institute's trade union organization, however, his removal had to be approved by the city trade-union organization; and so his job was saved. Similarly, another subject told me about someone who had outspokenly criticized the Soviet intervention in Czechoslovakia in 1968, but who remained in his academic job for three years because his five-year appointment had that much longer to run. Such procedural protections are analogous to civil service protections, and presumably exist to provide some check on the whims of bosses.

Young people soon have to learn how to deal with criticism. Their evolving sophistication in making and defending against criticisms was illustrated by Subject #9, who described the scene at MGIMO every year when each academic section of approximately 12–20 students would meet with its class leader (faculty advisor) for a sociopolitical *attestatsia* (certification or examination). At this meeting, students were permitted to criticize one another; they would mention infractions like telling anti-Soviet jokes, being drunk at a lecture, "skirt chasing," "passivity in komsomol," "passivity in social work," or not being able to maintain good working relations. Among other things, this was a chance for the less successful student to denounce a smarter counterpart and so improve his or her own career possibilities.

One particularly telling and subtle charge was to accuse someone of *tshcheslavia*—meaning haughtiness, vanity, or looking down on people (literally, vanity—a word with heavy religious overtones in the Russian language). This was very difficult to defend against because of its vagueness. One's only hope was in having enough friends or allies pledged to mutual support. These allies would then testify to one's being a regular guy. The accuser might be in an especially good position, however, if— say—he were in the same language group as the accused, while the defenders were not. "How can you know him as well as I? I am with him every day." In the case of Subject #9, there were only four students specializing in his chosen language, and they would obviously be both competing and cooperating with one another throughout their careers.

Before this attestatsia meeting, a tentative evaluation of each student would be prepared by the student komsomol chairman and the student party chairman (if there were at least three party members) of the section, in consultation with the class leader. Votes were taken on both the various statements in this tentative summary and those offered from the floor of the meeting. During the discussion, the class leader would offer an opinion on statements from the floor, and usually—but not always—the group would follow the class leader's opinion. Once a personal evaluation was adopted, it went into one's permanent file—maintained by the KGB.

For the first two years of their studies at MGIMO, students criticized each other frequently in these meetings. Everyone came in for some criticism, and "the discussion was chaotic."

Officially endorsed criticisms made in the first two years (of a five- or—for Oriental languages—six-year course) could be worked off, unless they were quite serious. Passivity in social work during the first year or two could be improved on and then noted as improved in later evaluations, for example. Subject #9 himself was accused of passivity in social work because he was one of only three students in his section who were not listed on the brigadier's honor roll when the school went to a kolkhoz (collective farm) to harvest beets. The following year, the subject worked extra hard doing construction in Central Asia (he says that he was sick for weeks afterward) in order to make the honor roll and thus demonstrate his rehabilitation. If one needed to overcome an accusation of tshcheslavia, on the other hand, it would take years of careful attention to one's social relations. The safest course was to have nothing negative in one's file—ever—and always to have a politically sound justification for one's behavior.

In the later years of a diplomat's schooling, the social process of the attestatsia was much more complicated. Students were now aware of their vulnerabilities; they would prepare their defenses and line up allies before the meeting. While the students were becoming increasingly conscious that they were in competition for the more attractive postgraduation assignments, they also now knew the dangers of acquiring enemies or looking negativistic by making criticisms that wouldn't stick. Thus they became more careful and strategic in the criticisms that they did make. (Apparently, criticisms made in these meetings would not prevent people from developing working relations in later years, according to the subject.) Someone could be knocked out as a competitor only if the case against him could be built up over the years, or if that someone did something that made the whole group angry. This resulted in one or two vulnerable students emerging as scapegoats; they were the safe ones to attack.

The most significant outcome of the sociopolitical reports (the attestatsia) occurred when the institute came to make its decision about which students were eligible to go abroad. In the subject's academic section of 13 students (16 had begun the course, but 3 dropped out because of difficulties with the languages), one student was declared ineligible to go abroad; this fraction was described as about average. The ineligible student had been caught intoxicated at a lecture in the fourth year, and had also had some academic problems. Other negative factors considered in the determination of eligibility for travel might include early disciplinary problems in secondary school, having had an aunt under German occupation(!), and conducting correspondence with a foreigner (including nationals of fraternal socialist countries!).

The Foreign Ministry apparently did not pay a great deal of attention to the records of the sociopolitical evaluations, provided that the student had been approved for travel. Since such a small percentage were actually declared ineligible, one might think that the process was not very significant for the vast majority who did clear this hurdle. However, the social prominence of the attestatsia process along with the need to avoid being last on the list was apparently quite stressful and a significant motivator. Furthermore, the conscious focus on and importance of social relations going back to at least secondary school must have a lasting effect in establishing a calculating, careful, defensive, and extroverted attention. What chords are struck in the mind of a Soviet diplomat who is listening to some attack, criticism, or demand? For that matter, what chords are struck when the Soviet diplomat hears an offer of mutual aid or reciprocity?

Certainly, the process of choosing key people who will be given the opportunity to work abroad is especially careful and controlled. Its intensity, however, only serves to highlight and exaggerate what are systemwide patterns of handling criticism and competition.

COMPETITION

In general, competition is never direct in the sense of being one-on-one without the involvement of others; instead, it entails winning the greater esteem of higher authorities. The simplest result of winning the boss's favor is increased resources to do your job better, which then helps you to win further favor, and so on. Subject #2 noted that each bridge-building enterprise (mostotryad) had about three or four work teams. Each such team had a chief, below whom were three brigades working in shifts—each with a junior engineer as foreman and a senior worker as brigadier. The foremen, who were less experienced, tended to take the advice of their brigadiers; and this advice often in effect consisted of ways to shift lower paid or more difficult work onto the next shift. Shifts might delay moving the crane, for example, since the time involved lowered their output and pay. (Such phenomena are not unknown in U.S. factories—involving, for instance, the postponement of maintenance work so as to keep up piecework production.) Thus, the brigades competed for better pay and work conditions. Competition among team leaders was not so direct, but was instead a competition for the favor of the mostotryad head; and similarly, competition among mostotryad heads was for the favor of the head of mostotroy. Such favor could result in easier or better paid work, better workers, and so on.

More complicated forms of behavior come from the fact that winning favor for oneself may be achieved by discrediting competitors in the eyes of superiors. Accomplishing this requires a good deal of care, however, because one risks looking like a troublemaker and thus discrediting oneself.

I have already described the sociopolitical attestatsia, in which students at MGIMO had the opportunity to criticize—and perhaps eliminate—future competitors. The critics' being students and thus young and inexperienced, as well as their having no one with lower status to front for them, resulted in the remarkable openness of this process.

Describing a somewhat less open process, Subject #4 said that there were three candidates for the position of chief engineer at his plant. One of these candidates arranged that, at a party meeting, a lower level party member would mention the unseemliness of having a chief engineer who was engaged in an extramarital affair—thus eliminating one of the competition, who was known indeed to be having such an affair. In fact, this had been common knowledge for some time, but had never been mentioned officially until it came to serve this political purpose. The subject did not know which of the other two candidates had arranged for the "revelation," but assumed that this was indeed what had happened.

Subject #8 emphasized that, in political meetings, criticisms could not be made by managers at any level. For example, complaints about poor working conditions, difficulties with supplies, lack of uniforms, and so on, were implicit criticisms of the managers in charge of the relevant areas. Therefore, so as not to alienate their peers, managers had to arrange for criticisms to be made by workers. Workers could safely complain because they could not be threatened: They had little to lose; and it was easy for them to find other work, given the shortage of labor.

Recall that in the story of the second deputy editor in chief of *Evening Moscow*, the editor in chief disguised his own criticisms by attributing them to other, lower workers. *It is dangerous to criticize directly, especially because everyone with a managerial or political appointment got it with some higher-up's approval or support.* One does not dare to offend that higher-up. (In telling me this story, the subject compared the process of indirect criticism to the current glasnost'—openness—campaign, in which people at lower levels, local newspapers, and so on, are being encouraged to criticize managers and politicians, thus helping the highest-ups in their campaign against certain higher-ups.)

In describing the political process of the trade union committee, Subject #7 mentioned that the senior committee members gathered potentially damaging information on one another—in regard to drinking, chasing women, and so forth—and released this information at the most strategically valuable moment, preferably via a worker fronting for the superior. Recall that Subject #7 had also described occasions of being told to "feel free to criticize So-and-so" at plant supervisors' meetings, and had concluded that this was an order and that So-and-so's career was over. It is possible, however, that the career in question was not quite over, but that Subject #7 was being asked to participate in its destruction. That is, he himself was the subordinate fronting for a competitive superior. Given the danger of criticizing anyone who might have some power to retaliate, it is likely that such instructions are given very carefully and only after deliberations have led one to conclude that the risk is minimal. Even the MGIMO students described by Subject #9 came to this conclusion after a few years.

This is not to say that open denunciations never occur. The head of a nuclear physics institute in Kiev made a mistake that led to an accident in a nuclear research reactor. One of the physicists, named Nemetz, wrote to party officials describing the mistake; and in a few months the director was removed, and Comrade Nemetz appointed in his place.

Subject #13 was in a position to observe machinations in both the Moscow city committee and the Central Committee. In the course of asking him about competitive tactics, I told him the story of the engineers who managed to make public the extramarital affair of a competitor. Subject #13 replied that, in the industrial field, "people are very open." In the political hierarchy, they are more sophisticated, more sober, and more afraid: Their punishment for any transgression will be much worse. After all, an engineer who is fired or who even goes to jail can still always get a job as an engineer somewhere. A political worker has no skill to fall back on, once ejected from the political world.

This subject knew of cases in which instructors had tried to undercut competitors, going to the cadre office or the chief of the party organization with tales of someone else's misdeeds. The instructor who had carried the tales was usually fired. ("This happened many times.") I asked if the instructor in this situation was ever not fired. Subject #13 said that, if the superior already had a dislike for the person being attacked, then the superior might choose to make use of the instructor's information.

Thus, there is a hierarchy of openness. Technical types, novices, and low-level players are the most open. People in the industrial hierarchy learn, however, that they must have someone of low status to front for them in making criticisms. In more political contexts, even just a few years of experience—such as the MGIMO students get during their five- or six-year course—teaches one to be very circumspect. The political hierarchy quickly eliminates young instructors who have not learned this lesson.

Skilled operators do not approach higher-ups directly with damaging information. In the industrial hierarchy, they find a worker to front for them and—if possible—totally conceal their own role. In the political hierarchy, they carefully assess the relationships among all the people involved, and only reveal their criticism if they believe that it will be well received.

SUMMARY

Pleasing higher-ups is a matter of one's usefulness to them. In order to be useful, one must first of all be available, and one must find ways both official and unofficial to prove one's worth. Personal chemistry is significant because it implies being better able to understand the boss's needs and desires—whether that means pursuing the right interests, taking the right side in policy issues, or giving the right kind of gifts. Technical competency is also a necessity if one is to be truly useful.

The boss must be made to feel comfortable with one's loyalty. This means that the boss must be assured that his interests will be protected even under fire, and that one knows one's place. This helps to establish an intense, personal, and encompassing bond that will make the boss one's sponsor and oneself the boss's protégé.

Doing one's job requires the cultivation of friends and contacts. One shares risks in order to accomplish things; one establishes mutual trust; and one pays people off with gifts, lucrative contracts, and favors.

One must be careful with criticism. If possible, public criticism should be positive, not negative. Personal criticism of competitors should be well documented, or it will redound on oneself. One must be aware of one's own vulnerabilities and protect oneself by suppressing damaging information—if possible—and by lining up support from others.

Competition is not direct. If one wishes to garner support from above, it is best to exercise one's competitiveness by maneuvering in secret. Being too direct looks heavy handed, overly aggressive, and alienates the other competitors' supporters (both above and below). Thus, one must attack only indirectly, via a front. In fact, one should carefully assess the utility of attacking at all—recognizing the political nature of the process, and looking to see who will approve of such an attack and who will benefit or lose by it. A sophisticated player must be very secretive and very careful.

NOTES

1. This subject also observed that it was fairly common for second- and third-year students at Moscow State University to become party members. Given that the average age of attaining membership is (according to Hough and Fainsod 1979) about 28 or 30, this implies that an educated elite on a fast track achieves early membership, while rank-and-file members are co-opted later in their careers. Compare also the low quota of party memberships at the state university of one constituent republic (as mentioned in Chapter 2): 5 new members a year out of 8,000 students.

2. This sounds so much like what is being encouraged now in the Soviet Union that I must wonder to what degree the current news is stimulating the subject's memory. On the other hand, this sort of criticism could not have appeared all of a sudden on Gorbachev's accession to the post of general secretary. Presumably, Gorbachev himself has been a longtime practitioner of this careful kind of criticism.

3. This was considered a promotion because "he could be his own boss maybe 50 percent"; he would also have patronage to dispense in the form of appointing employees, and so forth.

4. What a characteristic procedure! Official Soviet society discerns merit in the group per se, not seeing past the group boundary to distinguish among the individuals. Also, the social process of the group is then intensified by the process of dividing up the medals.

4. A PORTRAIT OF THE APPARATCHIK AS A YOUNG CLIMBER

My most fascinating subject was a young former party official who had been the head of a city komsomol organization and member of the city party bureau—the city's board of directors. Slated to become the city party committee's organizational secretary—the fourth most powerful job in the city—and with a potentially quite successful career ahead of him, he chose instead to leave the Soviet system, for reasons I will touch on later. The story of his rise illustrates all the themes presented in the previous two chapters. It is a brilliant tale of social skills and manipulation in action.

Although he is of Great Russian ethnicity, Subject #19 grew up in one of the Soviet Union's non-Russian republics, and was officially of that republic's nationality. His father was a political-military officer; and, after finishing university, the subject served for a few years in the army as a political officer—secretary for a regimental komsomol.

When he left the military, Subject #19 got a position as an inspector in the organizational department of the republic's komsomol central committee. From this position he received appointments first as head of the organization department of the *gorkom komsomola* (city komsomol committee) of a resort city, and then as the first secretary of that city's komsomol. Both positions were in the nomenklatura of the central committee department in which he had worked, and thus these were centrifugal promotions.

As first secretary of the city komsomol, he also served on the city party bureau and on the city party control commission—a disciplinary body. He was part of what he called the "city Mafia," defined by him as that group of high officials who get together to drink after an official function. This Mafia consisted of the first, second, and third city party secretaries, the chairman of the city *soviet* (the administrative body running the city government under supervision of the city party organization), and the first secretary of the city komsomol. My subject held this last position.

At the time that he defected, Subject #19 was slated to become head of the organization department of the party gorkom—a position that reported directly to the city first secretary and also rated a seat on the city party bureau (it was functionally "fourth secretary"). This position would not have been part of the city Mafia, but was in fact more powerful than the komsomol leader's job. I mention these facts merely to illustrate that the subject was indeed a man on the way up.

To be in the first secretary's career line—according to the subject—one had to be by the age of 30 either the first secretary of a raion or city komsomol, or a department chief at a komsomol obkom (regional committee) or central committee. If one had not attained such a position, then it was almost impossible to go very far. Subject #19 was on track.

The first-secretary career line leads to the most powerful chief administrative positions in the Soviet Union. If differs, for example, from a second (ideology) secretary's career line. The subject and I did not discuss a second secretary's career line in any detail, but it presumably involves more cultural/ideological work and less purely administrative positions. The differences between these lines are not absolutely rigid, but they are quite real.

Being on track implied that the subject was quite widely known among people who could help his career. As first secretary of the city komsomol organization, for example, Subject #19 was in three nomenklaturas: the oblast (region) komsomol's, the oblast party's, and the city party's. Thus he was known in at least these three organizations.

The first requirement for getting ahead, the subject emphasized, is to know what your boss wants even if he doesn't—or can't—tell you. He may want something that is officially against regulations.[1] You have to "help your boss look good, help do the job."

Since the city in which Subject #19 worked was primarily a resort, the main task of the city's first secretary was to host visitors, and the subject's job was to be deputy host. Frequently there would be more than one delegation to be entertained at one time: The party first secretary would be, for example, with people from some all-Union ministry, while the subject was hosting a komsomol delegation or a group of party officials from some other obkom. His job required a great deal of drinking. He said that any party official must drink a great deal (though this may have changed) and not show the effects too much—but that, in his position as host to junketing officials, he had to drink even more. Once, my subject counted 53 straight days of getting drunk. He described one strange scene in which his father—the military officer—happened to visit and was treated to fulsome praise of his obviously drunken son by the also obviously drunken city party secretary.

But pleasing the boss is by no means all there is to building a career: One must continuously look for friends and patrons. This is because the boss may be promoted or moved elsewhere—or, worse yet, fall into disfavor. It is simpler and more straightforward to get ahead in the military, according to Subject #19. There, you just have to be a sycophant with the immediate boss. In the party, you need a whole network of support to get a position; your boss can't just appoint you to a position, even if he wants to. For example, as I mentioned, the subject's position was included in three nomenklaturas. Thus, although his boss's desire to "hire" him was valuable, he required support from three different committees to get his job as head of the city komsomol. (Implicitly, we were talking only about line—not staff—positions.) In the military it is simple because "you don't have to be elected."

The subject's position in a resort city was an especially good one for network building, since his job consisted primarily of being a host to the various officials visiting the area (and secondarily of writing reports and administering the local komsomol activities). Therefore, Subject #19 met a wide variety of officials and established a network of contacts including both officials of the Moscow komsomol organization and people in the international department of the CPSU Central Committee (because of contacts with foreign visitors to the resort). The subject compared his position to that of Gorbachev when the latter was first kraikom secretary in Stavropol—another resort—during which time Gorbachev cultivated the acquaintance, most notably, of the vacationing Yuri Andropov.

Given both the political possibilities of this job and the fact that the city was described as such a pleasant place to live (with its beaches, clubs for entertaining tourists, summer concerts by top Soviet performers, and so on), I asked Subject #19 how he had been given this plum position. His answer was as follows:

As an instructor in the organization department of the republic's komsomol central committee, he had been in charge of overseeing three cities or districts, including this particular resort. In this capacity, he had evaluated the performance of the city komsomol's first secretary, despite the fact that the subject had the junior position. The first secretary was a woman who was somewhat straightlaced, older than the subject, and a bit rigid. He conducted a subtle campaign of undermining her position. The subject never criticized her directly, but would say things at the central committee about how a woman wasn't so good at that job because

of the importance of playing host to visitors, drinking with them, and
so on. He would say, for example, that you couldn't tell a good Russian
joke in front of her because she was a woman. In reality, she was not
very good for the position, and was also not liked by the city party
secretary. As a result, through his campaign of subtle criticism, Subject
#19 managed both to undermine her position and establish his own
understanding of the job.

The city party's first secretary, said the subject, was easy to figure
out: He was a Gorbachev type—interested in high tech and efficiency—
while this woman komsomol secretary was old fashioned. Subject #19
never directly suggested anything to the party secretary; but when he
visited from the komsomol central committee on his inspection trips, he
would present himself as the kind of man that the party secretary liked.
The party secretary did not like smoking, so the subject never smoked
in the secretary's presence; the subject made it a point to talk about the
computer revolution and other interests dear to the secretary's heart;
and he even started dressing like the secretary—in good suits and a tie.
Thus he adapted, reading the signals and responding like a chameleon.

The city party first secretary's brother was a high-ranking KGB officer
who liked the military. Subject #19 made it a point to establish contacts
with the local KGB and let the brother know that his father was a high-
ranking military officer. He kept up these KGB contacts by staying in
touch with the local KGB-komsomol officials (the KGB had its own komsomol and party organizations, just like any other Soviet institution).
Although the local KGB-komsomol organization did fall within his jurisdiction, it was two levels down; and actually, Subject #19 did not
have to spend time with its officials. However, the subject's father, who
was head of the political department in an army division, was friendly
with the KGB officer of the division; and the subject was friendly with
one of the KGB officer's sons. This friend's cousin happened to be secretary of the komsomol organization of the city KGB—which provided
an easy way for the subject to cultivate the local KGB, and so too the
city party first secretary's brother.

Thus, the woman who was the city komsomol's first secretary was
sent to a party school in Leningrad, and the subject was given her job—
having first passed briefly through the position of chief of the organization department of the city komsomol. In fact, this short-lived position
helped to qualify him for what could have been his next advancement
(had he not defected)—head of the organization department of the city
party committee.

While it is fairly clear that Subject #19's efforts did help him to become
the city-komsomol first secretary's replacement, it is a mystery as to
whether—or to what extent—his campaign of hidden criticism contrib-

uted to her being removed from that position. And he doesn't know to what position she was sent after completing the party school.

I asked about the subject's own prospects for rising even higher. These, he said, depended on "how strong I felt, as it was very exhausting."

What was exhausting was the necessity of constantly managing his social relations. Who, for example, chooses a party career? One can "get burned in a party career," the subject said. Because of this insecurity, children of the intelligentsia and of the political elite do not generally choose party careers; they become diplomats or journalists or intellectuals. It is the children of the Soviet "lower middle class"—most often, the children of engineers (that is, white-collar industrial workers)—who go into political work in order to have upward mobility. These were the people with whom Subject #19 worked, and to whom he had to adjust. He had to hide his knowledge of foreign languages, for example, for fear of being considered an intellectual. Similarly, he hid his fondness for jazz. "I said all the right things. There was a show of modern art: I said it was good we had democracy to allow these things, but I like the good old Russian art, good old Russian soul." In addition, there was the constant monitoring of his relations with a multitude of differing officials, always being on display, and always being careful to say and do the right thing.

As an ethnic Russian but officially of local nationality, the subject was in an especially good position, since the party likes to point to "locals" in its hierarchy but prefers people who speak Russian like natives—and Russian party officials relate best to Russian ethnics. However, he was separated from his wife; divorce—which seemed probable—might have hurt him severely. In discreet conversations with friends at the central committee, however, he was told that it would be left up to whoever was his boss whether to overlook this defect.

Had Subject #19 not defected but instead returned to become head of the organization department in the city party organization, he would have been in a good position to then become a gorkom second or third secretary, and then go to the republic's party central committee. Another career possibility was with the international department of the all-Union Central Committee. Because of its location, the city in which he worked had many foreign visitors, resulting in connections with the international department. The third secretary (in this case, the secretary for industry) of the gorkom had in fact been offered a job in the international department. He had refused it because it was off the first-secretary career track: An international department job is essentially a staff—not a line—position.

Had the subject chosen an army career, he would have become at least a general, he told me; aside from his father's position, his father-in-law was also a general. The assurance of success was true, I later realized, precisely because he could have plugged into his father's and his father-in-law's ready-made networks, as well as cultivating his own— a tremendous advantage. He could have built a better network with less effort. And the network is everything.

The subject described some bureaucratic conflicts in which he engaged. The manager of a restaurant chain would not cooperate with the subject in hiring people that he recommended to her, and even in letting someone from the city komsomol committee into a nightclub when it was supposedly sold out. The subject went to the city party secretary to complain about this, and then arranged for the restaurant manager to be reprimanded—not for these unofficial offenses, but for "bad komsomol work." The previous komsomol secretary had also complained about this woman's komsomol work, but seriously—not as a mere pretext for punishing the restaurant manager's disrespect toward komsomol perquisites. The restaurant manager was a friend of the gorkom secretary; and since the previous komsomol leader (the woman whom we met earlier) did not have especially good relations with the party secretary, the complaints at that time were ignored. Subject #19's complaints, however, led to a dressing down of the restaurant manager. I asked if the party secretary had been put into an uncomfortable position. But the subject replied that—on the contrary—the party secretary had been amused, and his respect increased for this komsomol secretary who could put the manager in her place. The manager then came to the subject privately and asked why he had not approached her directly with his complaints. Subject #19 replied that he had, and that she had not listened. "I am on the bureau of the gorkom," he said. "I should not have to complain twice."

In this instance, the subject's good relations with the party first secretary prompted the latter to endow him with a bit more authority. This in turn put the subject in a better position to help his own "dependents" (or the dependents of other officials who might want a favor) with both jobs and perquisites, thus putting others in his debt.

The subject was also a member of the people's control committee— an organization that is supposed to deal with mismanagement, fraud, and so forth, and that has the power to dismiss or fine officials. Although at first Subject #19 viewed this committee as just another bureaucratic burden, he soon realized that it provided more levers for him to get things he wanted. For example, the manager of the city transportation committee wouldn't give him spare parts to repair his car, and wouldn't supply buses for komsomol outings when requested. ("You get ten buses and fill them with kids, bring along some vodka and go somewhere. You say you're celebrating some holiday or visiting the site of a battle from the war. Everyone has a good time and you write a nice report and show how active you are.") The subject then not only complained at the control committee about the transport manager's poor cooperation with the komsomol; he also said that people were drunk while working at the transport service and that when someone hadn't shown up for work and the komsomol committee of the transport service had recommended dismissal, the manager refused to follow this advice. The committee issued an official reprimand to the transport manager, and the subject henceforth got his spare parts and buses.

The subject's positional authority, as well as his strong connections with members of the control committee (again: the network is everything), had allowed him to assert authority over the director of transport. The spare parts made his own life easier, while the buses made his job easier: His reported level of komsomol outings could go up. Thus he could do his job better in the eyes of the people evaluating him at the center of the system.

The importance of personal relations was also illustrated when the subject apparently became the object of a colleague's jealousy at the komsomol central committee. When he arrived at the komsomol, Subject #19 was a candidate party member. He had been made a candidate while in the army, but had not served with any one unit for 12 months; and so he could not become a full party member there. After working at the central committee for the requisite period, he needed references to become a full party member; he approached a colleague whom he thought of as a friend. This fellow was older and somewhat embittered because he wasn't going anywhere in the organization: He looked Jewish, although supposedly he wasn't; and he was too old for the position he was in. This "friend" wrote a critical reference, saying that the subject had not really "met his party obligations." The secretary of the party organization of the komsomol central committee was himself a friend of the subject's; the party secretary intercepted the reference and showed it to the subject. They then both confronted the critic and got him to change his reference letter. I asked the subject how he had made such a mistake, asking this particular fellow for a reference. "I was too young," he replied—too young to really know how to read the man. "If that hadn't been caught, it would have really hurt me." In any event, he was saved by good networking. (Moral: If you can't read people well enough to pick who will give you a good reference, then you won't go very far.)

When I asked the subject about his motivations—for example, in seeking the position of first komsomol secretary in the resort city—he did not talk about career ambitions, but about wanting to have a good time while he plotted how to get to the West. His fascination with the West began when he was quite young, he said; and even if the Soviet Union were really a democracy, he would have gone West. His father was very much the army officer: dominating, a "true believer," a Stalinist. His relationship with his father was not close. However, he was close to his mother, who taught literature. I asked if his mother had been ambitious for him.[2] He said no, she just wanted him to be happy.

Another defector whom I interviewed had an army officer father who was a true believer, but one with a much warmer style. In that case, the subject was close to his father, but not to his mother; he defected immediately after his father's death. In both cases, however, there was the sense of the close parent being fairly indulgent, encouraging a kind of narcissism and self-centered approach in the boy—psychologically allowing for the defection.

Neither of these defectors showed much remorse or concern for those they left behind, even when I deliberately probed. Subject #19 did express one small regret, however, for a friend whom he had helped get a job in the international department; he assumed that the friend had lost that job when the subject defected.

The story of Subject #19's friend illustrates the process of how people get jobs for their own nominees. This is presumably similar to the process whereby officials place their allies and protégés in useful positions. The friend had been komsomol secretary of the republic gosplan (economic planning organization), and was sent abroad for computer training. When he came back home, the komsomol central committee co-opted him (to the annoyance of gosplan) to work on their computer system. Thus he became an information-department sector chief at the republic's komsomol central committee. When the subject was also working at the komsomol central committee, the two became friends. The subject set him up with a friend of his sister's; the girl friend was the daughter of a high-ranking general in Moscow. When the couple then became heavily involved, the subject knew that his friend wanted to go to Moscow to be near her. Thus, Subject #19 recommended his friend to some people in the international department whom he had met in his capacity as komsomol leader of a resort visited by foreigners. The subject mentioned his friend's fluency in foreign languages, his computer skills, and so forth. The friend was put in charge of a sector at the international department. Had the subject not defected and had he wished to pursue a career in the international department, his friend would have been one more good contact to have. (By the way, the general opposed his daughter's relationship; and so the subject had recommended to the couple that they quickly have a child. Perhaps the general was able to protect his son-in-law.)

When the subject wished to go abroad on an officially sponsored komsomol trip (in order to defect), twelve people had to give their approval. The subject was on good terms with every one of them. Among the twelve were these five:

1. the secretary of the party organization of the city party apparatus. Like every institution, the gorkom has *its* primary party organization.

2. the second secretary (ideology) of the gorkom, in the role of chairman of the "travel-abroad commission." This man was an intellectual and a candidat, and did not care for the first gorkom secretary, but the subject (chameleon that he was) managed to be on good terms with both.

3. the head of the komsomol tourist agency (*sputnik*) for the republic. This bureaucrat gives quotas to each gorkom: how many can go abroad, how many to each country, and so forth.

4. the third secretary of the central committee of the komsomol. In charge of ideology, this secretary oversees travel abroad. The subject reported to the second secretary when he worked at the komsomol central committee, but also did favors for the third secretary such as writing articles and speeches for him. He did this as part of his general pattern of currying favor and widening his network.

5. the deputy head of the travel-to-capitalist-countries section of the Moscow Sputnik. A few months before, someone from the republic's komsomol central committee had defected in Spain. A committee headed by this Sputnik deputy (a woman) came from Moscow to investigate the republic's sputnik organization. Since the members of a visiting committee must be entertained, they were taken to the resort city in which my subject worked. There, in spite of the deputy's somewhat forbidding demeanor, Subject #19 went out of his way to be nice to her—seemingly with no ulterior motive, but knowing that sooner or later he would try to travel West. This helped both with the Moscow Sputnik deputy and indirectly with the republic's sputnik people: They were being investigated, and appreciated anything that would help their inquisitors relax a bit.

I asked Subject #19 how he differed from other young bureaucrats, that he would defect? He just wanted a good time, he said, while those others "have an agenda." This means that they wanted to accomplish something—to change things or perhaps get power, but certainly something more than enjoy themselves. Not being pure and simple manipulators and also presumably fitting in more naturally might also mean that the task of maintaining their networks is not so exhausting as it was for the subject.

On reflection, this may be just another way of saying that those who are still struggling and managing and maneuvering are connected to the system, are part of the system, or perhaps most simply *are* the system. They cannot detach themselves so easily. They have less definition as individuals, and are less narcissistic in terms of primary narcissism (pure self-love)—although they may be quite narcissistic in terms of secondary narcissism (seeking the admiration of others). Presumably, the survivors of the Soviet system's exhausting selection process are more balanced than this subject between their ability to step back and be distanced enough to perceive what is really required of them, and their genuine desire to please, to be admired, to accomplish, and to dominate—a desire that makes them true citizens of the social system, instead of merely its manipulators.

NOTES

1. This universal bureaucratic imperative was recently illustrated by White House National Security Advisor John Poindexter when he took responsibility for the diverting of funds raised by the sale of arms to Iran over to the benefit of the Nicaraguan contras. Poindexter said that he did this on his own because, although he was sure President Ronald Reagan would like it, the president could never officially approve the action.

2. Some studies of Western business executives say that the ambition of the mother is an important motivator for "self-made men." See Appendix B.

PART II. PUTTING THE SOCIAL IN SOCIALISM

The following three chapters examine the social skills required for success Soviet-style, and their implications for the social structure and style of thought of Soviet leaders. Chapter 5, "Social Skills and Success, East and West," puts the interview material of Part I into a broader theoretical context, looking at how the literatures of Western business, Soviet industrial management, and Western Sovietology analyze the importance of social skills. Chapter 6 shows how the social activity of the Soviet elite inevitably produces a "Social Structure: Teams, Networks, and 'Families'." Chapter 7, "Socialized Thinking," examines how the intensely social orientation of the Soviet system promotes a certain way of seeing the world—one in sharp contrast with the individualism-oriented Western way of seeing things.

5. SOCIAL SKILLS AND SUCCESS, EAST AND WEST

The ability to make and use relationships is one key to success in any organization. This ability, in turn, depends on social perceptiveness and responsiveness to others' needs, both spoken and unspoken. Because the Soviet system is all-encompassing—providing no extraorganizational routes to success and no alternative systems of value—social skills are all the more emphasized, and social relations are a more important medium of exchange than mere money. Thus, the Soviet system is a social system more than an economic one.

Social relations must not stand in the way of ambition, however. The apparat climber must additionally cultivate single-mindedness in the pursuit of success. He or she must be prepared to sacrifice other interests, friendships, and even family members when they conflict with the interests of the organization.

In order to properly perceive those organizational interests, the climber must have a breadth of outlook that allows for an understanding of his or her place in the system and how the climber can contribute to or even manipulate that system. In turn, this requires an understanding of the boss, the boss's boss, and so on.

The first link in this chain of interests is the climber's relationship with his or her boss, or other sponsor or mentor. From this ambition perspective, understanding one's superiors and establishing one's loyalty and usefulness to them is the highest and most important use of social skills.

SOCIAL SKILLS

The former tolkach asked me if he could smoke. After the smallest hesitation, I said yes; but then it was his turn to hesitate. Finally he lit a cigarette, but made a fuss about how he wouldn't smoke much and how it would relax him for the interview. Later, when he took out a second cigarette, he noticed that I glanced at it; and again he made reference to the issue. In all, he made a great deal more of my reaction than any American ever has in a similar situation. His heightened social sensitivity was probably an important contributor to his ability to establish the kinds of relationships that he had needed for his work in the Soviet Union.

This incident reminded me of a story in a book on American managers, in which a high-level executive received a phone call during the course of an interview with the book's researcher/author. The author automatically stepped outside while the manager took his call. The manager's secretary then remarked to the author that the kind of sensitivity he had just displayed—knowing to leave the room or at least ask if he should leave the room—was a key factor in the success of junior executives. The ones who hang around or—worse—try to listen in never get promoted.

According to a Soviet writer, Soviet analysts of management "have singled out the following traits of capable organisers: psychological selectivity, that is, effective perception of the psychological traits and states of other persons; ability to put oneself in the psychological situation of another person; . . . psychological tact"; and so on (Stolyarenko 1983). These "traits" are a function of good social antennae (see also Popov 1976).

Soviet books describe at length the importance of antennae aimed down at subordinates, emphasizing the need for leaders to have "a precise knowledge of psychological and psycho-physiological peculiarities of workers, [in order to arrange] placement of cadres according to personal and interpersonal peculiarities." They call this process "the emotional-dynamic tuning" of the collective (Golubkov and Fatkin 1984). (Western management writing appears slightly more impersonal than Soviet writing on these issues, showing some tendency to view workers as interchangeable.) Although the Soviet literature does not discuss the application of the same sensitivity upward, it is clear from my interviews that antennae pointed up are needed at least as much as those pointed down, if one wishes to get ahead.

U.S. managers tend to downplay interpersonal skills, thinking that they advance on the basis of rational-technical competency (Bass 1981). But in fact, the higher they go, the more the people-handling skills become emphasized over technical know-how (ibid.; Kanter 1977; and

Packard 1962). Alertness to the environment and the ability to size up situations is said to differentiate leaders from followers (Bass 1981). "Sensitivity—Has a 'feel' for people; recognizes their problems. Quick to pick up 'the way the wind is blowing.' Is considerate of others" describes the successful executive (Randle 1959). "Maze brightness" (Packard 1962)—a feel for knowing one's way around the organization—is another aspect of the social sensitivity required for success. Careeristic books in the West (see, for example, Hegarty 1976; and Kennedy 1980)—along with academic ones—heavily stress social antennae, with the careeristic ones especially focusing on the need to attune to one's boss or other superiors.

Due to the heightened importance of informal relations in the Soviet system, social skills are all the more important in Soviet organizations. And while top U.S. managers rate themselves highest on task motivation (Bass 1981)—not social awareness—they do in fact use skills that are increasingly social as they ascend the corporate ladder. Their Soviet counterparts are just more explicitly social in orientation.

Previous chapters have illustrated the importance of interpersonal relations in accomplishing what in the West would be straightforward and ordinary business tasks. Note the equation made in the compliment given to one of my subjects: "You connect with many people; you got what you needed." Soviet managers must rely on their personal networks—not impersonal market relations—to get things done. And most importantly, they must establish personal relations with those officials who hold the keys to their resources.[1]

Even at higher levels—managing regional economies—the Soviet standard of value involves the interests and attention of individuals. This is because the party organs have essentially replaced the market in determining priorities for supplies procurement and production scheduling. "If, as the eminent Soviet mathematician L. V. Kantorovich has noted, all orders tend to carry the priority of 'very necessary,' 'absolutely indispensable,' these words quickly become debased. In such conditions of 'priority-inflation' how is the plant director to determine which orders are actually 'absolutely indispensable' and which should be produced first within the planned month or quarter?" (Hough 1969). There are so many demands that it is ultimately only the party leaders who set values—by their investment in telegrams, phone calls, and building relationships with officials who can be helpful to them.[2]

"The all pervasiveness of the personal factor in the determination of resources" (Berliner 1957) makes personal relations—not money—the Soviet Union's semiofficial medium of exchange. Thus, in essence, the Soviet system is a social system more than an economic one.

The fact that there is really only one all-encompassing Soviet organization further reinforces this social emphasis. A manager in the West whose mobility is blocked by a slow-moving superior may advance by leaving one corporation and joining another (Jennings 1967). The Soviet executive cannot exercise this option, but must arrange for a transfer within the single, extended organization that is Soviet officialdom. This puts an even greater premium on social skills, networking, and an ability to get along with whomever fate has placed in one's path.

Thus, the observation that the "promotion [of Soviet executives] seems based primarily upon performance" (Hough 1969) must be understood in light of our knowledge, first, that technical competence drops out of the equation when all candidates are well trained and competent[3] and, second, that getting anything done in the Soviet Union requires above all social—not technical—skills. Leadership qualities recommended by Soviet books include "contactability" (*kontaktnost'*—the capability to set up positive social contacts), an "open character," a striving for information, a high level of aspirations, and an ability to create business ties. The manager, it is said, must have the capability to listen and convince, and also the capability to hear both sides in a conflict situation (Fatkin 1984). In sum, the Soviet manager must be socially skilled.

Perhaps, then, we should see social skill as merely another kind of competency—one related in the Soviet case to "political maturity." However we may view it, though, it is clear that the most important category on the nascent Soviet leader's report card (as it is also for Western business executives) is "gets along well with others."

The Soviet executive must in fact have outstanding "teamability"—the ability to find, join, contribute to, and make use of networks. Even in the less socially oriented West, "industry is run by teams today, not individuals." And "the rugged individualist, unless he has the rare quality of being politic, does not last in companies today" (executive search specialists quoted in Packard 1962). An article on the "Keys to Executive Success" appearing in *The Nation's Business* stated that one who would get ahead "must adjust readily to the needs and demands of the organization and also make its essential characteristics an integral part of his own personality" (quoted in Packard 1962). Or, as a Soviet author has put it, the successful leader must "integrate social functions—adapting his behavior to the role expectations of others." One must "be an informal emotional leader and administrator, reconciling formal/legal instructions with informal norms or organizations" (Fatkin 1984).

The nonteam player not only does a poor job in the Soviet context, but also endangers his or her coworkers. Thus, it seems appropriate that this type be extruded from the organizational setting. This was the case in the story of the candidate party member whose membership was not ratified, thereby in effect expelling him from the glavk where he worked—all because of his prickly personality.

Open conflict within an organization is especially dangerous. So, in general, people in the Soviet Union must get along and suppress politics, except for subtle undermining and a rare eruption of outright criticism—preferably channeled via a lower ranking "front." This need to avoid conflict is as true for institutions as for individuals: Enterprises, for example, must try to "live peacefully" with the ministries and other state organs (Berliner 1957). One has to go along to get along.

In fact, the outwardly directed Soviet manager tends to value good personal relations more than productivity. This explains the emphasis in Soviet management literature on the need for "demandingness" in managers' dealings with one another. This issue never seems to arise in U.S. management literature, presumably because U.S. managers are higher on task motivation and less socially constrained.

Luck helps in getting ahead, of course—taking the form of well-placed relatives and schoolmates, a pleasant appearance, being in the right place at the right time, or coming across patrons with a good "fit" in terms of personal interests and personal psychological structure. In the United States, "who you know" can generally only get you in the door, since business (which competes) cannot afford incompetence (Warner and Abbeglan 1955). In the Soviet Union—in the absence of market discipline (and in conditions of lax party discipline)—social relations can go farther.

But even well-placed contacts, correct appearance, and patron fit are only partly luck. One chooses which schoolmates to cultivate; one can screen a variety of officials for fit; one can scan for opportunities and perhaps even predict where one's possibilities are greatest; and, although one can't choose one's face or stature, one can decide how to dress, whether to smoke (and in front of whom), and so on.

Intelligence helps: It needs to be above average, but not necessarily very high. In the West, the IQ of mobile managers is no higher than that of immobile managers: The whole managerial group is above average, but IQ does not distinguish those who rise higher (Jennings 1967). Managers' IQs in general average 120—good, but not great—but IQ tests do not capture the good judgment and people skills that managers need (Packard 1962). According to one study, lower ranking managers are distinguished by "capacity" (mental ability); middle managers by "acceptance" (gaining the confidence of others), and top managers by "dependability" (meeting schedules and deadlines) (Randle 1959). In fact, IQ is most important (in the West) only at the foreman level (Bass 1981), because factors related to capability lose their importance at the top. They cease to be a distinguishing factor among contenders. This is true not only for intelligence, but also for technical capability among lower managers and managerial capability among middle managers. Instead, factors such as leadership, decision making, personality, and (again) luck come into the selection process (Powell 1963).

The keys to success—East or West—are externality and responsiveness, especially to higher-ups. A certain calculating manipulativeness—that is, an ability to apply one's social knowledge—is required. One must disown failure and claim success, while allowing all significant initiative to come from above. One must not stick out from the group; one hides any unusual interests—foreign languages, jazz, or whatever might make one seem strange and different. These are standard bureaucratic political skills, but not so much needed by those who genuinely have the "correct" interests. One must have a keen attention to context and a chameleonlike flexibility. (Even Gorbachev must conceive of himself as *responding*—in his case, to historical circumstances and the dictates of history.) *Freedom—for the "man on the make" and the good Marxist both—is the recognition of necessity.*

Self-control is a must (see Inkeles 1968). The successful apparatchik needs "a communist face." This is just a bit colder than the Western "bureaucratic face" (Williams, Sjoberg, and Sjoberg 1980), with its generally flat affect, formal cordiality, and "plastic smile." The care with which a bureaucratic face presents itself to its various audiences seems quite similar to the control required of the communist face that a Soviet official uses with anyone outside his circle.

One interview subject described the director of a large factory whom he came to know. The director came from a rural village; he was the son of kulaks and had been about ten years old at the time of Stalin's antikulak campaign. According to the subject, this director hated the system; but—as a "good-looking . . . man with ego"—he decided that, so long as he was in the system, he wanted to be on the top. His hatred well concealed, the factory director worked himself up to a very high position.

The director of the institute at which the same subject worked—a man with whom the subject became close—was "two different persons" inside the house and out. At home he liked good food and clothes; he was warm and likable. Outside, as institute director and as a member of the gorkom and the obkom, he was "like stone"—under perfect control.

The successful Western executive also requires emotional control: He doesn't blow up when provoked, expresses hostility tactfully, and accepts both victories and setbacks without showing feelings of pleasure or pain (Packard 1962). But the Western executive need not have quite what the Soviet executive has: two entirely separate modes of being—one public and one private (see Klugman 1986).

In sum, the bureaucratic climber "functions like radar, picking up opinions, ideas and impressions. The scanning approach, a search for contact with people on the outside, is essential to one who calculates power equations. It results in adroit flexibility, but seldom in conviction. Intellectually and emotionally, it is like living out of a suitcase, allowing the person to avoid investments and, consequently, losses. The minimum man [bureaucratic personality] is a survivor, one who clutches power and holds on despite major shifts in goals and directions" (Zelaznik and Kets de Vries 1975).

Subject #18 described a Soviet defector whom she knew as follows: He had everything as a child, and "still thinks he's special." He has "snob psychology," and puts people down unless they have something that he wants. Subject #18 described this man giving talks to different groups in the United States and telling them diametrically opposed things, depending on what they wanted to hear. She called him a "chameleon."

The necessity of dealing with many people implies that it is advantageous to have a smooth, featureless surface, which allows one to tailor whatever image one perceives to be required. This mechanism was clarified for me by one of my (U.S.) patients—a business executive who came to me complaining of anxiety symptoms accompanying his conscious ever-escalating attempts to vary his behavior to please numerous business associates. This patient told me that he viewed whomever he was dealing with "as a mirror," watching facial expressions and body movements to see how he was coming across. He deliberately went through a whole repertoire of behaviors, seeking whatever might be desired of him. For him, though, this process had gone wild because he was becoming both too self-conscious and increasingly confused about who, indeed, he was. The successful apparatchik also sees others as mirrors, but never loses sight of his own identity and interests. This identity itself, however, tends to be less individual and more socially defined than that of an American.

LEADERSHIP AND SINGLE-MINDEDNESS

Studies of 4–11-year-old U.S. children showed that a child who had acquired power in previous groups was able to gain power when introduced into still another, already formed group. The steps that these children used were:

1. The child learned the group's rules and then ordered people to do exactly what they would have done anyway. (Youth leaders might echo higher authority and thus assume power.)
2. The child then introduced small changes and innovations in group procedures.
3. The child assumed ownership and possession of all important objects in the room (quoted in Winter 1973).[4]

Such studies seem to indicate that something we call "leadership" is present at quite an early age.

One study of 2,000 executives identified six factors for early detection of management potential. The first factor was "matures early (early leadership goes back as far as being one of the volunteers to distribute the milk in kindergarten)."[5] The future corporate leader shows both early independence and success in terms of being nominated and elected by others: He or she is president of the class, captain of a team, and so on (Packard 1962). Although it is not essential, such activity helps to establish social links, and is viewed as a predictor of one's capacity to work in groups and develop leadership ability.

For Soviets—as earlier chapters have shown—explicit political activity can start as early as kindergarten, and often by age 14, but necessarily by one's early twenties. Just as in the West, participation in sports and other organized activities as a youth is a plus. In both East and West, then, such extracurricular activities build social and organizational abilities, increase exposure to people, and give some experience in cooperation and social coordination (Packard 1962). "But to the 'mobicentric' individual, the most important activities in life are preparatory to mobility. School, college, marriage, social life, and even religion and faith are central to mobility. . . . The central idea is to become and stay active" (Jennings 1967)—not as an end, but as a means.

Other interests, hobbies, family time, and friends must all give way to a single-minded pursuit of advancement and approval. Thus, U.S. climbers must be available during regular hours, overtime, Saturday, Sunday, and evenings (Hegarty 1976). Be dedicated, the books and the bosses tell U.S. climbers—Work extra hours (Packard 1962). Thus, too, Soviet women are hampered in their party work if they want to go home to be with their children: This makes them unavailable for the voluntary work required to make a good impression. Dependability is important (Hegarty 1976; Jennings 1967), especially at the top (Randle 1959).

The successful leader needs "the ability to maintain a high level of thrust (drive, energy)" (Packard 1962) in pursuit of his or her single-minded goals. Subject #19 emphasized how exhausting it was to keep up—to maintain his vigilance, assess and play to each of his audiences, do his job, build his network, and so forth. Furthermore, since a leader must tolerate uncertainty and make good decisions anyway (Packard 1962) and since Russians have less tolerance for uncertainty, they will attempt to control as much of their context as possible (see Hofstede 1980a and b). This also takes energy. One Soviet source writes of the importance of "stress-stability" (*stresoustoichivost'*), saying that leadership is tough, tense work—especially when work breaks with routine and requires strong-willed, tough, tense action (Fatkin 1984). This endlessly draining quality of the pursuit of success may be why there were many stories in my interviews of people looking for a "quiet life" (see Berliner 1957).

Certainly, U.S. achievers are single minded (Jennings 1967; Packard 1962)—but not quite to the same degree as Soviet leaders. Young U.S. managers worry about their loss of autonomy in pursuing corporate success (see the case histories in Kram 1980). Senior executives maintain some separate identity outside their corporate roles, as evidenced by the fact that high-level U.S. corporate leaders will voluntarily retire on occasion: They have other interests to pursue. Even so, a report on the American Management Association's survey of the lives of 335 top executives concluded: "To get to the top . . . a man has to put on a pair of blinders to shut out everything except business" (quoted in Packard 1962).

Part of what must be shut out are others' feelings. The U.S. executive must be ruthless, and possess "the surgical touch." This means that—supposedly—the executive can fire someone without a qualm, and therefore cannot be too emotionally involved with subordinates (Packard 1962). Soviet managers aspire to even higher degrees of ruthlessness, perhaps in reaction to their tendency to immerse themselves in relationships to the point of lacking "demandingness."

One of my subjects noted that, in a recent case of a Soviet woman wanting to go to Israel to give her brother a bone marrow transplant, the woman's husband was prevented from leaving because of the objections of his father—a physicist named Florov. Presumably, Florov objected because he thought that to do otherwise would harm his career. Another subject told a similar story of a father's sacrificing his son on the altar of his own career. (One is reminded that, in his meetings with Stalin, V. M. Molotov made it a point not to dwell on the arrest of his wife.) Thus, though policy interests as well as personal ones be at stake, the budding Soviet leader's pursuit of success is so all consuming that he or she must sacrifice hobbies, family time, impolitic friendships, and—occasionally—family members.

There are a number of structural factors in the Soviet system that encourage single-minded careerism. One is that, in general, compensation and privileges are strictly related to official position: The only way to get more is to get promoted. Subject #15 said that since coming to the United States he had been in the same corporate position for a number of years; but, while at the beginning he was paid as a novice, now he was paid twice as much without any change in job title. This, he said, could not happen in the Soviet Union, where the only way to get more money is to be promoted. Similarly, Subject #16 said that he decided to work toward a candidat degree partly because his salary depended solely on his title. This strict civil service–like link between title and compensation promotes both careerism and bureaucratic politicking.

Furthermore, *there are no other institutions—such as private wealth—to*

trade off, whether economically or psychologically, against official privilege.
Socially, there are unofficial institutions—*blat* (personal favor; see note
1), nepotism, and so on—that pit informal networks against official position as an alternative source of both identity and economic advantage.
For the most part, however, these informal networks themselves are
maintained through the exchange of favors made possible by official
position, and thus they reinforce official position as a source of both
identity and advantage. Instead of the Westerner's autonomous sense
of self embedded in multiple overlapping social roles, there are for the
Soviet citizen two sharply divided identities: one, private and personal;
and the other, public and official (Klugman 1986).[6]

Subject #20 emphasized that, among the intelligentsia, there was
great dedication to and identification with work. People's identities were
very wrapped up in their professions. For careerists, however, their
work is in promoting their careers: Their careers are their creations.

Political workers, in particular, are the most embedded in their careers.
They have the most to lose in bureaucratic competition since they have
no career alternatives. An engineer can always get some sort of job
somewhere, but a full-time party official has nowhere to go outside the
party. To be relatively secure in a position, the political worker must
make peace with those who have power, forever seeking their approval
and support. And the best evidence of such support is a string of promotions.

I asked the subject who made these observations about political workers if anyone ever opted out of the political game. Did it ever happen
that someone would be just devoted to the job per se (as opposed to
advancing his or her career), or to other interests? Subject #20 said that
he could recall only one such case: a man who was for many years head
of a department at a city newspaper, and who never thought about
promotions. He simply loved his job. The subject laughed when recalling
this, commenting on how strange the man was. Subject #20 also mentioned that there are people who top out—who realize that they can't
rise any higher, and resign themselves to that fate. This is not voluntary,
however. In the Soviet Union (as compared to the United States), the
subject said, one's career is everything. By this he meant that one cannot
become a consultant, get a part-time job on the side, or do other things
to improve one's standard of living. Even money isn't worth much
without position. One's position is everything.

BREADTH OF OUTLOOK

Single minded is not narrow minded. Like top U.S. managers, Soviet
political operators have to be generalists.[7]

The budding apparatchik "simply has no time to be a good Party member, unless he is ready to neglect his professional job. People in various professional lines are thus forced, as they are in other societies, to make a choice between devotion to their specialty and devotion to a career as an operator, manipulator, and organization man" (Meyer 1965). But U.S. managers develop broad perspectives only late in their careers (Dalton, Thompson, and Price 1977). More so than mid- and low-level U.S. managers, Soviet political types (in particular) have to be generalists from the start. Being a local party secretary for industry requires a much broader outlook than being a factory director (Hough 1969), and even being a voluntary inspector in the raikom industrial department requires a different outlook than that of a pure and simple engineer.

What is required, besides people-handling skills, are political skills— what can be called "maze brightness," organizational sense, or system-aimed antennae. The Soviet executive requires "the ability to sense the ever-changing hierarchy of values, standards, and priorities of the top leadership" (Meyer 1965)—people with whom the Soviet executive has no direct contact.[8] Sensing the political winds differs from the social skills discussed earlier: Instead of reading individuals and their psy-chologies, it involves discerning impersonal and organizational phe-nomena.

A broad outlook is also important in the West. A senior manager described one way he helps a protégé by saying: "I can give him an appreciation for what the pressures are as perceived by the top people in the business. Not because he will then do anything directly because of that knowledge, but in effect that his work life and all the little de-cisions that he makes as he goes along, will be done in the context of having that understanding" (quoted in Kram 1980). Presumably this vague awareness of the thinking of top leadership makes it more likely that the protégé's work will be more productive or at least more noticed.

Having a broad outlook means being aware of a multiplicity of de-mands and values. The successful manager, we are told, must tolerate ambiguity. He or she knows how to compromise, balances vague situ-ations and shifting commitments, and knows which rules to follow and which to break (Dalton 1959). Nonetheless, it appears that these pres-sures are less intense in the West, possibly because of the more auton-omous identities of the players, the greater options for changing organizations, and the generally more impersonal atmosphere.

On a more mundane level, an ability to read trends and make strategic choices can be of direct use in building a career. I heard numerous examples of straightforward careeristic calculations. Decisions about choosing a specialty, for example, were made not on the basis of sen-timent or enjoyment, but on a cold-blooded assessment of opportunities. I have mentioned the case of Subject #6 who, in order to prepare himself for emigration, positioned himself in the ministry department that was studying the relevant Western industry. Subject #9 was originally pressured into accepting a komsomol position by his secondary-school English teacher and his parents, who saw this as a way of improving his opportunities. (It did.) Later, Subject #9 chose his language specialty on the basis of the number of specialists already in the area, and his assessment of the possibilities for the future development of relations between the country in question and the Soviet Union. I have also already described how one subject changed his specialty from engineering to NOT (the scientific organization of labor) based on such a calculation, and how another subject said that engineers needed to think about taking the highway bypass—the party road—around the clogged industrial hierarchy. A few other subjects also spoke of engineers who had made exactly that calculation.

Between mundane strategic calculation and general political awareness lies sensitivity to the particular organizational setting in which one is functioning. In general, the need to be useful to a superior means that it is worthwhile for the junior official to tune into the larger system of the boss's world. If one is to rise, one cannot just do one's job, but must also understand how that job fits into the needs of the superiors; if necessary, one must shift jobs or create new tasks to make oneself even more useful. One cannot please enough by passively accepting the tasks assigned, but must eagerly look for bigger and more useful tasks. (A lot depends on the values and desires of the boss—for example, whether the latter is interested in personal services and gifts or in official duties.) The subordinate on the rise must not only know what the boss wants, but—better yet—understand the boss's world well enough to offer what the boss doesn't even realize, or hasn't even said, or cannot (for legal or political reasons) admit that he wants.

Thus, the junior official must raise his nose from the task at hand—the task assigned—and broaden in outlook. One performs one's task in light of this broader outlook, and this reinforces (or at least fits) the Soviet's training in thinking from the top down—the method of "scientific socialism." One learns to think about the broader perspective before acting. Since the boss, in turn, is interested in demonstrating *his* (or her) worth to *his* boss, the junior official would do well to begin thinking at least two steps up; and in like manner, it would be even better to begin on still higher levels. Thus, most generally, subordinates must diligently maintain an awareness of the party's line. This chain—which connects the most junior official to the highest aims of the party—depends on the system hierarchy being so strongly connected that, indeed, the boss really does want to please the boss's boss, and so on. (This condition cannot fully apply under conditions of lax party discipline and stability of cadres.) A key variable in success, then, is the accuracy of the subordinate's antennae—the ability to see not just broadly, but broadly and accurately, on every level from the local and personal to the organizational and strategic and on to the national and political.

RELATIONS WITH THE BOSS/SPONSOR/MENTOR

The key link in this chain is one's boss or, if available, some other sponsor or mentor. Being a good team member requires good relations with the team captain, and finding a captain with a team to join is the first step toward success.

To get ahead—East or West—one must become known, and bring oneself to the attention of people who are in a position to help. The successful executive is usually "a member of everything, everyone knows him" (Hegarty 1976). The first requisite for getting power is sheer visibility (Winter 1973), especially to those above (Packard 1962; Jennings 1967). Starting an oral journal, for example, gives the higher-ups a chance to see you. Going out of your way to have contact with the city party committee's first secretary and his KGB-head brother is the route to becoming first secretary of the city komsomol.

But mere contact is not enough: One must create the proper impression. In the United States, managers prefer—and rate as more effective—those subordinates whose values are similar to their own (Bass 1981). In turn, highly motivated members of a group tend to identify more strongly with authority figures than members who are low in motivation. And individuals who are low in interpersonal confidence tend to be influenced more readily by peers than by authority figures, whereas the reverse is true for persons who are high in interpersonal confidence (Bass 1981; see Inkeles 1968 for indications that this applies to the Soviet population as well). Thus, rapidly promoted executives tend to identify themselves with their superiors as a primary organizational reference group (Henry 1949).

Fast-trackers fit in more with superiors than with peers—in education, experience, age, sex, personal distinctions, hobbies, prestige, race, nationality, religion, politics, manners, speech, personal appearance, dress, habits, and style of physical movement (Dalton 1959; Packard 1962; Powell 1963; Bowman 1964; Jennings 1967; Stein 1976; Hegarty 1976; Bass 1981). Some of these—hobbies and organizational affiliations—are important not only as ascriptive characteristics, but as mechanisms to meet and socialize with influential people in the organization.[9]

"The path to leadership is successful subordinacy. People who advance in large bureaucracies generally understand this principle" (Zelaznik and Kets de Vries 1975). Attention to superiors can go to the extreme of toadying in both East and West. The closed (monopolistic) nature of the Soviet institutional context apparently makes toadying somewhat more common in the Soviet Union (see, for example, *Current*

Digest of the Soviet Press [CDSP] 37:45:4 report from *Pravda*, November 10, 1985). The U.S. climber is counseled: "Perhaps your boss might like an assistant who could help him teach a Sunday school class or wield a second brush when he is painting his boat next spring" (Hegarty 1976). Presumably, at least some Americans need books to tell them this, most likely because of their conflicts surrounding the issue of autonomy. But the natural climber does not need such advice.

Short of toadying, upwardly oriented executives must be open minded (about the boss's ideas), dedicated, loyal, adaptable, and quietly deferential (Packard 1962). The U.S. climber is counseled not to "overinvest" or be too open about his or her loyalty, for fear of embarrassing the boss or even causing the boss to become suspicious (Packard 1962)— "a smart boss can see through any buttering up" (Hegarty 1976). I did not hear of similar moderation being called for in Soviet cases, but this might change with the more rational-technical style of the new generation of Soviet leaders.

Whatever the style, though, if you wish to get ahead, you must be for your boss: Give the boss 100 percent loyalty; find out what he or she wants; help the boss to be right; work the way he or she wants; talk to the boss's interests; tie your interests to the boss's; learn when to argue (in the sense of useful disagreements in which you rescue the boss from his or her own mistakes; see Packard 1962); fight the boss's battles; live with the boss's weaknesses; keep the boss informed; and protect the boss's status (Hegarty 1976). Of all these, loyalty is probably the highest virtue with a boss (Hegarty 1976; Powell 1963; Packard 1962; Jennings 1967); and it is of immense value to be labeled "my man" by one's boss (Hegarty 1976). Furthermore, "it pays to go along with the policies and decisions set by the aboves even though you don't agree with them. Forget any criticism of the company, its policies, and its product. Speak well of the company, its aboves, and other personnel" (Hegarty 1976). The right answer is yes.

Saying yes is not enough, however: To be mobile, the subordinate must serve to advance the career of the superior (Bass 1981). People move up by making their superior look good; and since, in fact, the boss and subordinate make each other look good, mobility is a transaction in which one thing is exchanged for another (Jennings 1967). But again, high performance is not enough: One must have both high performance and trustworthiness (Jennings 1967).

"The future president leaves behind many hard workers each time he is promoted. The fact of the matter is that high performance as it is variously defined is a necessary but not a sufficient cause of upward mobility. One sufficient cause is trust. . . . Few men arrive at the top who are not trusted by someone already there, nor are few placed in crucial positions at any level who are not trusted by their superiors" (Jennings

1967). Among qualities necessary to establish trust are availability, attentiveness to superiors, predictability in the sense of reliability for good performance, and personal loyalty. "Mobile executives and managers never entrust a crucial responsibility to a subordinate who they suspect will sacrifice them for selfish gain or for abstract 'principles' " (Jennings 1967). "Often [the superior] wants hard-working, aggressive, personally loyal, perhaps even submissive subordinates who will fulfill certain requirements that he views as important to his career. [He may expect] obedience, respect for superior position and experience, and always, of course, spontaneous work for his crucial interests. These expectations must be fulfilled if the subordinate wishes to succeed" (from an article quoted in Packard 1962).

"The route to the top is by becoming a crucial subordinate to a mobile superior, by keeping the superior mobile, and by getting out from under him if his upward mobility becomes permanently arrested" (Jennings 1967). Mobility is largely a relationship between two or more people. In most companies, it is impossible to rise solely on the basis of job proficiency: One must also be recognized and tapped by someone higher in the power hierarchy (Packard 1962; Martin and Sims 1956; Jennings 1967). One must have a sponsor, an advocate, or a good "shirttail." One must become a "key subordinate" to the boss; and that subordinate is key who knows how to heighten the boss's effectiveness and sense of well-being (Packard 1962).

In a survey of 1,250 executives mentioned in the *Wall Street Journal's* "Who's News" column, nearly two-thirds reported having a mentor or sponsor, and one-third had two or more mentors. Nearly half had mentors who were immediate supervisors (Roche 1979).[10] Mentors offer concrete help—early transfer to more challenging jobs, access to new positions opening up, special assignments and autonomy in difficult projects. They apply pressure to obtain promotions for their protégés, and advise protégés on good positions and on company politics (Reich 1985).

If you're not connected to someone higher, you're stuck. "Good apparatchiks," I was told, "hit a ceiling" if they do not have a higher sponsor/protector. Subject #5—working in a department of a city party committee—said that he knew who was and who was not well connected by his boss's instructions to "respond to this quickly," or to "ignore requests/complaints from such people."[11]

But if people ignore your complaints or requests, your job performance suffers. If the Soviet medium of exchange is personal relations and you're not connected, then you're broke. Not having a sponsor/protector limits your ability to be useful to another higher-up in order to cement a new relationship. This produces a vicious circle in which lack of connections and impaired performance are mutually reinforced—just like the virtuous circle in which good connections and high performance reinforce each other.

SUMMARY

The young komsomol secretary described in Chapter 4 was just the kind of socially skilled manipulator who can climb rapidly in the Soviet system. He had the right perceptiveness, responsiveness, willingness to sacrifice (especially the willingness to sacrifice any superficial sense of autonomy and independence), vision to see what was required, maze brightness to manipulate successfully the levers of organizational power, and ability to ingratiate himself to—above all—his boss.

Where he failed—in a sense—was in his autonomy or narcissism. Subject #19 was not truly embedded in the system. This is why his quest was so exhausting for him, and why he wanted to leave.

The truly successful apparatchik will have all that young man's skills, but will be a true citizen of the system. He will have an agenda.

NOTES

1. If working relations persist over time, they become established channels for *blat*. The word *blat* describes a personal basis for a favor or exchange, as opposed to an official and formal basis. Unlike bribery—in which an immediate payment is made—in blat, the reciprocity may be delayed and may take different forms. Note that this parallels the party member's relationship with the party. Friendship is considered to be the basis of blat; it is cultivated by means of little gifts. Mutual confidence is the essence of blat; it is not done with strangers. Blat is viewed as a compensation for lack of strength; the high-priority enterprise has little need for it, but its advantage is reduced by the blat of the less important enterprise (Berliner 1957; see also Jowitt 1983). Thus, there are official and unofficial systems of resource allocation, and the two are in competition. Similarly, someone with a high-level *ruka* (sponsor or mentor) does not need a personal network so much as someone without such highly placed help.

2. According to research in Western organizations, politicking is likely to be especially intensive in organizations when contacts are considered important, when there is an emphasis on extracurricular socializing, when news flows by grapevine, and when there is a lack of candor in superior–subordinate relations (Packard 1962). Sound familiar?

3. People who have low opportunity or are discontented tend to emphasize the political aspects of promotion (Kanter 1977), so it is striking how many of my interviewees—people who chose to leave the Soviet system—emphasized the necessity of competency for success Soviet-style.

4. Note the relation to Soviet corruption and the attitude of "la collective, c'est moi."

5. The other factors were: practical intelligence; self-confident, but not ag-

gressively so; broad interests and knowledge; develops his juniors, who then do well; and, willing to admit problems and mistakes (quoted in Packard 1962).

6. Jowitt (1983) discusses this under the rubric of "official identity."

7. Zinoviev (1984) has compared Soviet politicians to athletes who have to compete in 100 events: They must be mediocre, he concludes. But was Bruce Jenner (the 1984 Olympic decathalon medalist) mediocre because he wasn't number one in any particular event? No, he had to be a terrific all-around, nonspecialized athlete. It must be remembered, however, that Jenner could not win on the basis of having an uncle who was in business with an Olympic official.

8. Soviet managers must scrutinize the press carefully for new "campaigns" in order to decipher the latest changes in priorities. "The determination of relative priority is an art, one for which the successful manager must develop a 'feel.' Russians talk much of 'reading between the lines,' a vital talent for the manager" (Berliner 1957). "In attempting to minimize the risks he faces every time he acts, the successful administrator's most valuable skill may consist in sensing to which of his objectives the Party assigns the highest priority and which standards it is least risky to neglect or violate" (Meyer 1965). The manager must continually pick up clues concerning what can be gotten away with and what cannot (Berliner 1957). "The administrator's greatest danger, apart from general failure, lies in sudden shifts of (political or legal) opinion within the Party, sudden decisions to crack down on some violations that have heretofore been tolerated" (Meyer 1965).

9. U.S. managers also need the right kind of wife (Hegarty 1976; Packard 1962; Powell 1963); but this has not been so true in the Soviet Union except in those cases where the wife herself was well connected, or was a social disgrace. Note that executive ladders are male-dominated, both East and West.

10. Many chief executives report feeling that personnel development and management succession are key responsibilities that they cannot delegate, and in which they must personally participate (Roche 1979).

11. Perhaps there were genuine priority projects, and it was my subject's prejudice that led him to interpret such orders as an indicator of good connections. On the other hand, one must ask how and why certain people are assigned to priority projects, and what this implies about their connections or desirability (to higher-ups) for new connections.

6. SOCIAL STRUCTURE: TEAMS, NETWORKS, AND "FAMILIES"

Using their social skills, climbers cultivate potentially useful informal relationships, sometimes—but not necessarily—with the same people with whom they have formal and official relationships through their work roles. Interlocking unofficial relationships tend to fall into three patterns: teams, networks, and organizational "families." In the order listed, these three kinds of social groupings are of increasing size and increasing vagueness (in terms of defined membership and defined methods of mutual aid). The larger, vaguer groupings are nonetheless real, and are important in determining what actually happens in the Soviet system in questions of turf, personnel, and policy.

TEAMS

Since protégés move up with their sponsors, top management echelons (in Western corporations) are made up of interlocking cliques of powerful sponsors and their "men" (Martin and Strauss 1959). Or— focusing on the relationships instead of the personnel—"the executive system in a firm is composed of complexes of sponsor–protégé relationships. For the protégé, these relationships provide channels for advancement; for the sponsor, they build a loyal group of followers" (Martin and Sims 1956).

So, managers group themselves into teams—groups or cliques allied through ties of mutual support.[1] These are not official work teams— groups joined together by assignment to a specific project or task—

although the relationships among team members often start while they are in an official assignment together. Instead, these informal cliques or teams offer broad support aimed at the general political benefit and protection of the team members. In comparison to task groups, the coordination within these teams is more comprehensive (in that it involves the participants across all their roles and duties), more informal, and more persistent.

There are a number of factors that promote and reinforce the existence of informal teams. Executives everywhere want to work with known quantities; and in the Soviet Union—where informal relations are so important—this desire is especially strong. For just such a reason did the minister described previously bring along his referent (assistant) through his last three promotions, and so did that same minister receive those promotions because of his old-school-tie connection to a Central Committee secretary. I have mentioned that the management collective of one division of a construction trust moved up virtually en masse to manage the whole trust. In corporate or bureaucratic organizations everywhere, crucial subordinates are brought along when a boss is promoted. In the Soviet Union, however, there are many, many crucial subordinates. Thus, collectives of executives tend to rise and fall as a team.

To quote a former Soviet factory director:

Each director of an enterprise, big or small, considers the selection of reliable assistants as his primary task. The attitude is: 'All for one and one for all.' The people know they must sink or swim together. This is why the plant director always supports his subordinates. If they get in trouble, he bails them out. His subordinates in turn give their wholehearted loyalty and support to him. In many instances, when the plant director is transferred to another plant, he takes his loyal assistants with him to ensure a continuation of this secure relationship. (Ryapolov 1966; see also Berliner 1957)

The stability of the management group promotes team formation. One source of this stability has been the fact that job rotation—simply changing jobs at the executive level—has been hindered by the Soviet belief in the importance of reinforcing the collective qua collective (see Stolyarenko 1983). Also, the Brezhnev policy of stability of cadres tended to stabilize executive groups. In general, then, forcing people to work together and succeed or fail together over prolonged periods has strongly reinforced the tendency to form teams and subteams. By contrast, U.S. managers are very mobile (Swinyard and Bond 1980), and so their relations are in general more superficial.

At the local level, the common dependence on plan fulfillment unites Soviet managers (Berliner 1957) and party officials, too. The director of an enterprise, control officials, and the officials of the local *partkoms* (party committees) must cooperate. They could get into feuds or battles; but this situation is unstable, and quickly leads to someone's removal. Conflict is risky. "We were all linked together in life," said one enterprise director of his management group's relationships with the local party officials. "We were the enemy of the district Party secretary. We were suspicious of each other, but practical life made us work together" (quoted in Berliner 1957). Natural selection works against overt fighters and in favor of team players.

Local solidarity is also reinforced by difficulty in dealing with—or even fear of—a higher authority. To some degree, central planning pits local groups of leaders and their immediate subordinates against a distant central authority. Loyalty and support for one's local superiors is exchanged for their protection from the larger outside system (Ryapolov 1966). Similarly, in far-flung U.S. corporations, "the outlying people may see the people at the New York or Cincinnati headquarters as an all-powerful, menacing, controlling, to-be-feared 'they' force" (Packard 1962).[2] Thus, the centralized system of management itself encourages the formation of local self-protective groups.[3]

CONFLICT AND CONFLICT AVOIDANCE

The bonds among regional team members are reinforced by the appropriations process. In dealing with the center, plant and party officials support all projects: They do not have to make choices. Because the appropriations are decided centrally—and most likely by different ministries—supporting housing, for example, does not mean giving up supporting a central appropriation for industrial investment (Hough 1971). This reduces the potential for conflict among local officials, channeling conflict into the competition between regions for the favor of the center. But, at the regional level, officials do have to establish priorities when local officials are all demanding resources from the region (ibid.)

Thus, when looking out from a region (or any Soviet organization), other regions (or organizations) are competitors, and intragroup solidarity is reinforced. In the internal affairs of any organization, however, suborganizations will function as subteams competing with one another. So—more than in the West—*every Soviet organization looks very unified in its external affairs, and factional in its internal ones.*

In general, most organizations have only a single, unified managerial team. An enterprise has a relatively small management cadre and a relatively narrow external clientele with, therefore, a focused set of demands. These factors militate toward the maintenance of one—and only one—team at that level of management.

When there is conflict in or around an enterprise, there can be two teams, but only for a brief time. One interviewee described the appointment of a deputy director of a research institute whose job was to check on and ultimately undermine the director of the institute, because the latter had managed to alienate the institute's governing board. In the struggle, each of the two men created a structure of informal alliances woven through the formal organizational charts of the institute's party and trade union organizations as well as the institute managerial structure. Finally, the director and a number of others were forced to leave. Most left en masse for another institute, preserving their team.

Higher level organizations are more complex, and so can sustain multiple teams for extended periods. And complexity probably has an effect on the nature of accession to office. *As complexity increases, so does factionalism* (Tichy 1973; Tushman 1977).

Thus, in the Soviet Union, only complex central organizations (in Moscow, for the most part) can sustain for a prolonged period the presence of multiple teams embodying a variety of orientations. At these higher levels, teams compete—albeit, for the most part, subtly.

People highly interested in power are adept at using social situations to expand their network of contacts or allies, and are concerned to maintain smooth relationships. They prefer to avoid disruption among those around them. Yet they like to compete with others. Thus, they direct their competitive drives outward from their close inner group of associates (Winter 1973). Since they are interested in smooth relations, however, and since there is no Soviet organization or citizen who can be officially labeled "outside" or the "enemy," Soviet executives must try to keep conflict submerged or hidden.

For Russians, who are in general more highly socialized and less individualistic than Westerners, the channeling outward of competition should be even more the case. This contributes to both team formation and interteam competition, while the desire to avoid disruption mitigates—or at least drives underground—the competitive side of interteam relations. Still, *in complex organizations, tensions are played out between— not within—teams.*

"FIT" AMONG TEAM MEMBERS

A group or team works best when it "fits" together. Fit is the collective manifestation of the team members' shared individual characteristics as well as their flexibility or "teamability." As the Soviets put it, in selecting cadres "the job is not just the selection of particular people, but the creation of a whole *management collective*"(Popov 1976, his emphasis).

This notion of group fit—especially fit with superiors—is obvious, and applies even to children. In choosing school komsomol (student) officials, for example, faculty look for "a person they can work with, can exercise some pressure on," according to one interviewee. In return, the student activist receives recommendations and any other forms of patronage that come along—trips or other rewards. Faculty advisors, administration, and student officials all must fit to make a smoothly running political organization.

There was some evidence in the interviews that, in the Soviet case, people whose authority is built on a certain specialized knowledge or interest choose subordinates who will reinforce that specialty. One subject, for example, described a technically oriented manager whose influence was based on his ability to solve technical problems. He chose technically oriented subordinates who helped him deliver the technical goods. He was eventually replaced by a politically oriented manager, who appointed politically minded subordinates.

This contrasts with the U.S. situation in which complementary relations are most important in success—rounding out the skills of a management team, instead of pursuing a strategy of team specialization. There are two main reasons for U.S. managers preferring complementary subordinates. First, executive assignments involve broader, less specialized authority, and require a complement of skills. Second, an executive team with a complementary set of skills can fulfill more of a corporation's necessary role constellation, and can have wider visibility and exposure (Jennings 1967).

In the Soviet system, on the other hand, geographically or functionally peripheral organizations are more specialized than Western organizations. Whole oblasts often define their success in terms of the output of a single industry or even a single product. This specialization, plus the fact that narrower responsibilities are delegated by superior institutions, means that only a narrow range of technical skills are required by a management team to supplement their social skills. Thus, *the specialization of Soviet organizations at every level—from enterprises to whole regions—reinforces the tendency toward the formation within each organization of a single team with a single specialty.*[4]

Thus, although the Soviet system requires the successful individual to have a broad contextual and strategic outlook (as described in Chapter 5), the team is technically narrow.[5] In contrast, a U.S. management team will have more specialization (or division of labor) by individuals and less specialization of the team as a group. There will be less overlap and more diversity of technical skills within the U.S. management group and, in general, narrower but more autonomous individuals.

There are psychological pressures—not just structural ones—reinforcing the supplementary similar-mindedness of the Soviet team. A complementary team has to incorporate within itself various tensions and trade-offs. The intensity of the Soviets' social orientation and, thus, the closeness of the fit that is desired within a team makes these kinds of conflicts particularly stressful. Again, *conflict is better handled between groups than within them.*[6]

Good fit is important to a team because it improves effectiveness. In the mentor–protégé rotation-selection dance, for example, seniors and juniors are looking for useful connections; they are searching for mutual utility and good fit. Fit is determined by personal values, interests, opinions, and policy preferences, as well as elements of personal style. And the junior's flexibility is also an important variable. *Good fit improves mutual utility,* because it implies that the protégé can better anticipate the needs and desires of the sponsor, that the superior can better predict and rely on the behavior of the subordinate, and that the two can better communicate in general.

Teaming is thus comparable to nepotism and tribalism—the advantages of which are that relatives' "modes of perceiving and interpreting reality are very much like the appointing official's"; that the "intimate knowledge of his relatives enables an official to understand their biases faster and more completely than he would if they were strangers"; and that, since relatives are likely to be removed from office whenever the official is removed, their interests will be closely identified with his own. In addition to which, relatives often have a nonrational loyalty (Downs 1967). Thus, *team members are pseudorelatives.*

Recall that one subject described the methods of career building as being: (1) technical and outside of politics; (2) based on relatives; and (3) based on making connections—that is, personal politics. We see now that the third option represents the creation of pseudorelatives for those who lack the real thing.

In the top echelons—where organizations are complex and multiple teams exist—the fit between teams becomes as important as the fit within teams, because there the teams are interlocking. Some teams will fit the larger system better than others, and some individuals will fit better with more teams.[7] Since at high levels there is more shuffling in line assignments, and more mixing of teams in the workplace—a deputy minister, for example, is often not from the same team as the minister— broader teamability as well as diverse and far-flung contacts become important. This is a topic to which we will return in the discussion of personal networks and political "families."

VERTICAL AND HORIZONTAL RELATIONS

In U.S. management, cliques are described as either "vertical" (uniting managers on different hierarchical levels, such as a superior, a subordinate, and a subordinate's subordinate) or "horizontal" (uniting managers on the same level, such as a group of vice-presidents and general managers). Vertical groups can be symbiotic (mutually useful and improving effectiveness and productivity) or parasitic (protective of team members' personal interests). Horizontal cliques promote their members' interests vis-à-vis higher-ups, and can be aggressive (actively undermining higher authority) or defensive (protecting members from higher authority). Horizontal cliques in U.S. organizations tend to be *temporary*, and function to deal with a crisis. This is because the members of horizontal cliques are natural competitors. Vertical cliques, on the other hand, are long lasting (Dalton 1959).

Similarly, Soviet management teams are held together by strong vertical relations, while horizontal ties are in general weaker. Just as in U.S. organizations, Soviet vertical cliques can be symbiotic or parasitic, while horizontal cliques are aggressive or defensive. Horizontal cliques, however, need not be temporary, because the need for their defensive function may be permanent.

Horizontal work relations in the Soviet Union are reinforced by the necessity of cooperation to get work accomplished, and may involve quite complicated trades and exchanges of both goods and favors (see Berliner 1957; and the previous chapters of this book). Risk-sharing devices abound and include, for example, multiple bureaucratic sign-offs (getting everyone on board; "collective nobody is responsible"). In the extreme, horizontal relations include mutual covering for illegal activities—circular support (*krugovaya poruka*). But while mutual covering relations are based on a real and necessary trust, this trust is in a sense negative: It is maintained only by the potential of joint and mutual incrimination and/or joint failure. (Thus this phenomenon is related to localism, as described above.)

Trust in horizontal cliques is the product of a shared fear of higher authority. Thus, although horizontal cliques can help people do their jobs and get things (legal or illegal) done, they cannot provide the pervasive and persistent kinds of positive support that a vertical clique can provide.

That they are not intrinsically persistent and pervasive is one reason why horizontal cliques are of limited utility for climbing the apparat ladder. Another is that horizontal cliques simply lack authority to make higher level appointments, since only a higher authority can promote a member of a horizontal clique. In fact, I heard of only one example of an aggressive horizontal clique trying to help someone get promoted. When a newspaper editor retired, a group of people at the paper campaigned to get one of their number the job, lobbying the higher authorities. They failed. In contrast with the limited value of peer support in getting promoted, there is no doubt about the importance of the boss's favor at every level—both in achieving superior performance and in benefiting from it.

The real limiting factor on horizontal cliques is that their members are natural competitors. As peers within the same organization, they are ultimately competing for the same jobs. This is as true in U.S. (or any other) organizations as it is in Soviet ones. But Americans do not experience their positions as everything. Position is only one part of identity, and having a multiplicity of roles, institutional affiliations, and organizational alternatives softens their competitive process. Thus, as intense as peer competition may be in U.S. organizations, it is more intense in Soviet ones since even more is at stake.

Certainly, everyone in every organization must offer formal support to peers. But as far as I can tell from my readings and the interviews, U.S. senior executives seem readier to offer at least some informal peer support as well (see Kram 1980 on senior managers' reliance on peers). This is in part a result of the closed nature of the Soviet system, Russians' strong cognitive boundaries (the contrast between bosom buddy and alien—*nash* and *chuzhoi*), and the lack of alternatives to ameliorate bureaucratic politics. Again, the inability to get a job in an entirely different organization soups up the Soviets' social process and its competitive tensions.

But climbers must impress their superiors by doing good work, and that necessitates good teamwork. So climbers need good peer relations to excel; they cannot alienate their peers by appearing haughty. They must somehow outshine the rest of the team without provoking hostility.

Factors softening competition include the fact that, just as local party leaders can support all local projects, a boss can support the work of a number of protégés, and propose them for different advancements. (But still, the boss does make a choice about who is to get the best opportunities. There are the favored and the most favored.) Also, since peers are all working their way up in the same system, a peer may be one's boss someday (see Downs 1967), or at least be in a position to help or hurt—another reason to maintain good peer relations.

The tensions of horizontal relations—the trade-offs between competition and good peer relations—also show up between Soviet organizations, not just between individuals. For example, too much success for an enterprise can bring attention, which in turn brings irregularities to light—for example, plans that are set too low.[8] (Similarly, in the United States, the informal peer group may drive out workers or managers who perform too well and thus undermine the comfort of the group; see Dalton 1959.)

Managers who become widely talked about because of rocketing success submit to certain dangers of rumor-mongering. To be sure, there are some who are not deterred from pursuing a career for these reasons, but for many it is merely courting danger to become too outstanding: "It is also unwise to leap forward suddenly in fame. Other people begin to talk about him and find pretexts for circulating rumors about him. Therefore everybody tries to avoid bad relations with other people on his level." (Berliner 1957)

Peer relations are made easier by the fact that there are no direct contests between peers within an organization. The only prize is the boss's favor, or sometimes the favor of a superior institution: the party control commission, the raikom, whatever. Given the personalism of Soviet politics, though, success usually boils down to relations with some highly placed individual or individuals, anyway. People advance through sponsored—not contest—mobility.[9]

But the boss (and the system) far more frequently rewards cooperation than conflict. Remember, for example, that gorkom instructors who criticized their peers not only did not achieve their purpose of self-advancement, but were themselves fired more often than not. So, conflict is further moderated by the fact that success requires the backing or approval of a superior, who usually discourages overt, destructive competitiveness.

Even more directly, at lower levels of party officialdom, the need to be elected means maintaining good relations with both subordinates and peers, as well as superiors. A few negative votes may be understood and accepted by higher authority, but more than a few will call one's local support—and one's social skills—into question.

Thus, *paying too much attention to overtly competitive activity misrepresents the system*. Group membership and acceptance is important, as are mutual covering relations. Furthermore, associates can have a genuine desire to accomplish something, for which the management collective must in fact function as a collective. Peers usually have good working relations, and often even friendship.

But, *maintaining good relations is not the same as having an alliance*. Climbers' competitiveness to some degree limits their capacity for forming horizontal alliances. For the most part, they look for supporters above and below.

For those climbers willing to undertake the risks of competition, horizontal relations are marked by the need to cooperate instrumentally and maintain a functional facade of amiability while awaiting the proper moment for the bureaucratic kill. The "leaking" of information about a competitior's extramarital affairs, for example, or the dissemination of information about someone else's mistakes must be done very carefully.

Summarizing, then, Soviet peer relations are quite delicate. Managing them requires all of those social skills described in Chapter 5. If the lower level official can't manage these tensions, can't balance between peer arrangements and vertical loyalties, can't trade off teamwork and competition, then he just can't make it.[10]

In contrast to the complications of Soviet peer relations, though, vertical relations are quite simple. One succeeds through allying with a superior. Envy and competition don't enter the picture because each party knows his place.[11]

The Soviet sense of hierarchy is quite strict (as is, historically, the Russian sense of hierarchy). One subject described how, at each Moscow raikom, there were separate *stolovii* (dining rooms) for instructors, deputy department chiefs, and department chiefs. The raikom secretaries, meanwhile, would eat in a small room off one of their offices or, if at all possible, ride in a limousine to the gorkom to eat. There they could politic with the gorkom instructors, sector chiefs, and deputy department chiefs—their approximate peers. Gorkom department chiefs and secretaries were their superiors, and so were not approached as casually.

Contact with superiors is mostly only one or two levels up, not multiple levels. With such narrow contacts, a strict hierarchy, and strong boundaries between institutions, a lower level apparatchik is totally dependent on the immediate supervisor (unless there is a ruka—a sponsor or mentor, often a relative, elsewhere high in the system). In the initial stages of his career, then, the apparatchik must focus on pleasing and allying with the boss. The loyalty thus established is intense and personal; and the obedience demanded, absolute.

Constant attention must be paid to maintaining and strengthening ties to superiors. If the apparatchik is stationed elsewhere and visits the home office, then he must remember to bring gifts! How straightforward compared with the complexity of peer relations!

The need to establish unquestioned loyalty is especially important in creating the possibility that the boss will pass the apparatchik on to a higher boss. At that point, dealings with the sponsor (the former boss) move to a more informal footing. The relationship then is not friendship, but it does encompass mutual trust and reliability. One interview subject described the relationship of sponsor and former protégé by saying that they would be mutually useful because "they know each other." "You mean they have a personal relationship?" I asked. "No," he said. "They know each other. They trust each other to be allies." (Also see Downs 1967 on the value of dealing with known actors.)

Western organizations require loyalty, too, but high job mobility and job rotation within organizations reduces the personalism of the loyalties created. Job rotation mitigates the forces that tie together subordinate and superior (for example, the fact that top managers tend to identify the effectiveness of lower level managers with that of their immediate-level superiors; see Fleishman and Peters 1962). Also, everyone knows that he or she can be fired, except in the most paternalistic organizations. And Americans, at least, have a constant awareness of the opportunity to leave—to go to a competitor, to go into one's own business, to become a consultant, and so forth. This lessens—or cools—the average level of loyalty to one's boss or employer in the United States, while creating a diffuse but real loyalty to the system as a whole.

In the Soviet Union—in contrast—loyalty to the system is narrowly funneled through one's superior(s). Loyalty is more focused and personal.

Thus, the Soviet management team can be pictured like a standard pyramidal table of organization, with strong vertical ties uniting superiors and subordinates. Positions are arranged in strict hierarchy, with a branching coefficient of 1–3. That is, patrons have 1–3 protégés apiece (according to my subjects). Note that (except at the highest levels) each protégé has one and only one patron, not counting relatives; anything else destroys the sense of loyalty required for sponsorship. This contrasts with the pattern of multiple—but more dilute—sponsorship in U.S. organizations, with their higher mobility via job rotation and thus their more dispersed social networks.

Soviet teams have been described as "mountain climbing expeditions"—evoking the image of a chain of men roped together, ascending the heights. This is a useful image, but add to it the notion of branching chains and—given competition between peers—the occasional detachment or addition of a subchain.

Subchains—or subteams—do in fact compete for favor up the line; and here, again, the concept of fit is important. Let's examine once more the case of a raikom secretary taking a protégé to show to a gorkom secretary who has mentioned his need for a new instructor. First, it is clear that the protégé has good chemistry with his raikom-level sponsor, or he would not be "shown" in the first place. Also, the better the chemistry of the raikom secretary with the gorkom official, the better chance the raikom secretary has in choosing a winning candidate to present. Thus, the selection of the new instructor from among the candidates of many raikom secretaries will reinforce a certain subteam at the expense of the others. Alternately, the gorkom secretary may have solicited candidates only from certain favored raikom secretaries, reinforcing connections that have already emerged as dominant. And in the end, the future performance of the new instructor will make a difference for relations among the three: the gorkom secretary, the sponsoring raikom secretary, and the instructor himself.

These relations are complicated by the fact that the nominating raikom secretary and his former protégé who is now a gorkom instructor are no longer in a vertical relationship. And they are no longer on the same subteam. "They know each other." They are allies. Their relationship is approximately horizontal, but across an organizational boundary: One works at the gorkom, the other at a subordinate raikom; and neither has direct authority over the other. These two are in each others' "network."

NETWORKS

Teams, as defined, are work centered. Therefore, they do not encompass the multitude of other relationships that may connect people: blood relations, old school ties, prior work relations, and less intense varieties of mutuality such as acquaintanceship and blat. Such relations—based on personal connections and without a formal and direct organizational basis—constitute a person's network. Thus, the network is horizontal, but its relationships are not competitive.

The first example of a network relationship was explored above: the sponsor and a former protégé. In the West, we know that mentor relationships in the business world develop into lengthy relationships: They are maintained. In one study, almost half of those executives who had had a mentor still kept up relations with *all* of their mentors, and another quarter kept up relations with some (Roche 1979). No less is to be expected in the Soviet Union, given the greater intensity of the loyalty demanded and thus of the bonds formed.

The official Soviet system reinforces local and regional network formation by requiring personal contact among local notables across organizational boundaries.

The recruitment of personnel for all responsible positions within the entire society is a formidable task. . . . From the point of view of the Party leadership it is, of course, a very vital concern, and the Central Committee has made it clear that it expects territorial organizations to make nominations only on the basis of personal acquaintance with the nominees. The Party command, at all levels of the political system, is therefore obliged to cultivate personal acquaintance with the leading personalities in all fields of endeavor; familiarity with their record of achievements apparently is not deemed sufficient ground for recommending them. As a result of this obligation, the fabric of high society in the USSR is very close knit. At any one of the various levels of the political system, there is a managerial set somewhat analogous to the country club set in the United States, where the leading citizens from the various professions mingle and become acquainted with each other. (Meyer 1965)

The mutual exchange of favors both across organizational boundaries and within extended organizations, reinforces network connections. Many students get into MGIMO (the school that trains diplomats and international journalists) through family connections in the Foreign Ministry. Ministry officials help their relatives by using their personal connections with those diplomats who serve as school admission officials. Since there are still too many candidates for admission, this results in a *blatbit* (blat fight)—a competition of "pull," in which those with the strongest network get what they desire.

Within the industrial hierarchy, the movement of personnel up to the ministries establishes ties—which smooths the way for blat and for the expectation of ministry support. The ministry is full of former officials of the plants; or, alternately, these officials may know each other from school days (Berliner 1957). "We may have been co-workers with them before. In this case, they may require a smaller plan from us" [ibid.].

"Officials are motivated by both self-interest and altruism to create informal networks of friends, favor recipients, contacts, and communications links based upon primarily personal, rather than official, relationships with others" (Downs 1967). Such networks help in coordinating work both within the organization and in its work with other institutions. This aids organizational functioning, as is demonstrated by the horizontal mutual-cover relations required to get work done.

But we also see that the personal network acts to some degree against the official system, mitigating its demands and formality. Also, it enables an official to build up a reputation and status independent of the particular position held. This is useful preparation for future jobs elsewhere in the organization. Similarly, the personal network reduces the dependence of an official on his superior(s).

Just as, for survival's sake, every bureaucracy desires autonomy—a distinctive area of competence, a clear clientele, and undisputed jurisdiction over some function (Downs 1967)—every official, for survival's sake, wishes to reduce his or her dependence on superiors. The crucial subordinate does not "identify openly and publicly with the superior" (Jennings 1967)—for fear that should the superior's mobility end, so would the subordinate's.[12] In that situation, the subordinate needs to be able to get out from under.

An executive should preserve maneuverability in career planning. . . . He ought never to get in a situation that does not have plenty of escape hatches. He must be careful, for instance, that his career is not directly dependent on the superior position of a sponsor. He should provide himself with transferable talents, and interfirm [for Soviets, interorganizational] alliances, so that he will be able to move elsewhere if the conditions in his current organization become untenable. (Martin and Sims 1956)

Thus, paradoxically, apparatchiks achieve a degree of independence through social immersion, not by developing autonomy. They reduce their otherwise overwhelming dependency on superiors by cultivating multiple, mostly horizontal alliances in the form of their personal networks.

ORGANIZATIONAL "FAMILIES"

As mentioned above, competition between teams and the tendency for teams to rise and fall together means that fit is important between

teams as well as within them. Just as an individual has to fit into the
team, so does the team have to fit into a larger structure of alliances and
working relationships—a "superteam network," if you will, or a political
"family."

Subsuming both teams and networks, "families" are so named by
analogy to Mafia crime families—a frequently drawn comparison. Let
us compare the Soviet "Mafia family" to the actual Mafia crime family
(Ianni and Ianni 1972).

In Mafia crime families, there is a merging of social and business
functions. The assignment of leadership positions is based on kinship.
Closeness of kinship correlates with position in the hierarchy. There is
a requirement for close consanguineous or affinal relationship to be in
the core leadership. The organized crime family can be considered a
clan, where a clan is defined as an associated group of lineages intricately
bound to one another through a network of marriage ties and ritual kin
associations (in this instance, the godfather–godson relationship).

Soviet "Mafia families" are more purely meritocratic. Since connections are not based primarily on blood relations but on mutual utility
and painstakingly established ties of loyalty and reliability, leaders rise
on the basis of a variety of (mostly social) skills.

In the Mafia family, the family—not the individual—is the unit of
importance. The individual exists only as part of this group; and membership is based on familial relationship, no matter how distant. (Kin
who do well rise fast, and a relation who does not do well is at least
assured of a job.) Thus, there is a sharp distinction between the "family"
relationship and the more instrumental "contacts" with outsiders.
Within the family, alliances are based on kinship, mutual interests, a
common outlook on the future, and reciprocal obligations or favors.

In the Soviet organizational family, on the other hand, there are multiple levels of loyalty: to family, to team, to subteam, to network, and
to self. There can be conflicts among these loyalties without clear rules
for resolution. The individual exists only in relationships and as part of
a variety of groups. Since the relations are artificial—not by kinship—
and based in part on utility and performance, there are no guarantees.
Thus, family membership is conditional.

The Mafia organized-crime family has no morality outside of family
loyalty and family values. Behavior is based on "amoral familialism"—
ignoring the laws of the state or the feelings or desires of outsiders in
order to attend to family business (see Banfield 1958). "Social control in
such systems requires that acts against any member of the system activate all other members to right the wrong or avenge the misdeed before
the system can return to equilibrium. It also requires that members of
the system keep faith with each other and not take outsiders into their
confidence" (Ianni and Ianni 1972).

The rules, rights, and obligations of the Soviet organizational family's members are far less clear than the Mafia family members'. And although Soviets distinguish between degrees of connection, there is no family kinship to be the sine qua non of relationships. Also, in some sense, *all* relationships in the Soviet Mafia family are instrumental. Thus, the boundaries of the Soviet family are looser and more permeable than that of the organized crime family.

Structurally, the Mafia crime family is a social system, not a formal organization. It is built on personal relationships. Organizational roles depend on the individuals who carry them out: That is, duties are tailored to the individuals, not individuals fitted into organizational slots.

In contrast, the members of a Soviet political family are fitted into organizational slots, but on the basis of informal relations. Furthermore, Soviet networks will often tend to duplicate formal structures: For example, people within a glavk have to cultivate their relations within the glavk. The rules of the formal organization must be honored, even if only formally and through lip service. The Soviet organizational family, then, may best be described as a social system living in a formal organization.

While in its internal structure the crime family is tightly integrated, the national coordination of crime families seems to be loose—based on a kind of bubble-up of issues and the drawing of turf lines, not on a top-down ordering of tasks (Ianni and Ianni 1972). In the Soviet system, by contrast, there is an interaction of tight top-down authority within the formal structure and of bubble-up issues (concerning turf, personnel, and policy) from the informal networks.

Although Soviet Mafia families are more loosely defined than Mafia crime families, they are both more potent and more clearly defined than the sponsorship networks that exist in Western formal organizations—corporations, governmental bureaus, and so on. Western sponsorship networks are loosely defined, overlapping, and interlocking—especially because of Western organizations' pattern of multiple sponsorship and rapid job rotation. Absent these organizational policies, Soviet Mafia families probably have less overlapping than Western sponsorship networks.[13]

In sum, Soviet organizational families can be defined as extended super networks encompassing many subgroups linked via intertwined personal and business relations. For example, Gennadi Kolbin—appointed first secretary of Kazakstan in 1986—served originally in Sverdlovsk under Nikolai Ryshkov and Boris Yeltsin. He then became second secretary in Georgia under Eduard Shevardnadze. (See New York *Times*, December 17, 1986.) Presumably there were other candidates for that second secretary position (at least informal candidates), and the selection of Sverdlovsk's candidate connected (further?) the Georgian and Sverdlovsk teams. Both groups presumably supported Kolbin's appointment to his new position in Kazakstan, further cementing their relations and opening up possible connections with—and job opportunities in—the Kazak organization. Shevardnadze's having accepted Kolbin as his second secretary forged a link between the Georgian and Sverdlovsk supernetworks analogous to a marriage between two royal families.

Patronage relations among Soviet Mafia-family members are in some ways analogous to those of U.S.-city political machines, such as Tammany Hall or Richard Daley's Chicago machine. Bonus lists are used for factional patronage (interview #10), and loyalists are rewarded with no-show or equivalent patronage jobs (interview #11). But while this kind of politicking is informal in U.S. politics, it is often explicit and official in the Soviet Union—embodied in sociopolitical attestatsia, the inclusion of political criteria on technical evaluations and checklists for promotion, and so on. Just as the nomenklatura is formalized—you don't need sociometrics to find out who is in the elite, but only have to look up the list—Soviet patronage politics is in many ways formalized and bureaucratized. Political machines are in part integrated into the formal organizational structure.

Soviet organizational families have hierarchic levels, like a baseball-team farm system. Powerful sponsors can move protégés through multiple levels of organization; they bring players up from the minors, so to speak, to the triple A club before going on to the majors—like the minister brought up through three levels by his Central Committee–secretary former schoolmate. Selection and competition will occur between teams, among subteams, and among team players.

We can get a sense of one historical family's structure by looking at the very high level, powerful Zhdanov family, whose shape was revealed when it was purged in the so-called Leningrad affair: when second- or third-ranked Politburo member Andrei Zhdanov (ranking behind only Stalin and perhaps Georgi Malenkov) died in July 1948, those closely associated with him were purged, including N. Voznesensky (a Politburo member), A. A. Voznesensky (his brother, who was minister of education of the R.S.F.S.R.), A. A. Kuznetsov (a Central Committee secretary), M. I. Rodionov (chairman of the R.S.F.S.R. Council of Ministers), Shikin (chief of the main political directorate of the Red Army, and the only member of this group of Zhdanov allies at the center who was not executed), and P. S. Popkov (secretary of the Leningrad party organization). "Most of the victims of the Leningrad Case can be pretty certainly regarded as Zhdanov's men, who were or had been officials of the Leningrad party organization under him" (Conquest 1961).

A protégé of Georgi Malenkov (one of Zhdanov's rivals) was placed at the head of the Leningrad organization itself, which was then purged of the Zhdanov family: At least several hundred—and perhaps as many as 2,000—executives were removed. Those killed included all five obkom secretaries, the top four officials of the executive committee of the town soviet, and leading officials of the oblast trade union. In the Moscow city party organization, there was a smaller purge of "secondary associates" connected with Zhdanov's ally A. S. Shcherbakov (ibid.).

When you succeed in identifying *networks of supporters*, they appear typically to *cut right across formal divisions between chains of command and fields of activity*. For example . . . Zhdanov's patronage predominated in the state and party organizations of Leningrad Region and City, and it was prominent without predominating in the Central Committee apparatus, the government of the RSFSR, the State Planning Committee, certain fields of ideology, and the party apparatus in a broad zone in northwest Russia. Study of the various purges and counter-purges in Georgia between 1951 and 1953 gives a similar picture of the ramifications of patronage networks there (Rigby 1964, emphasis added).[14]

Post-Stalin, there has been somewhat less overlapping and interpenetration of patronage networks, and it has been more the case of the powerful running their own organizations (Rigby 1964). This shift is a product, I believe, of the lessened degree of job mobility in the Brezhnev years, which promoted the emergence of a single team associated with each institution. (Reduced mobility and the lack of job rotation thus also provides the institutional coherence that underlies Hough's model of "institutional pluralism" see Hough 1977.)

SUMMARY

The need within Soviet organizations for mutual covering, support, and trust promotes the formation of teams—informal groups or cliques who have direct work relations based on their official positions, but who are allied through informal ties of mutual support. Although individual climbers in the Soviet system must be broad minded, the teams they form tend to be relatively narrow: That is, team members have heavily overlapping competencies. This is in contrast to U.S. managerial teams, which tend to be more diverse as a group, although the individuals making it up are more narrow than Soviet managers. Except in large, central, complex organizations, there is only one team per Soviet organization.

Teams often take the form of "mountain climbing expeditions": a small group of allies arrayed vertically—one above the other in organizational positions—climbing together. Even when not of this exact form, teams still tend to be vertical in the sense that the most important connections are between higher-ups and those below them, not between peers at roughly the same organizational level. The potential competitiveness between peers within an organization also reinforces the fact that true alliances are more comfortable in vertical form.

Teams within Soviet organizations are held together by personal affiliations. Western organizations are, in general, somewhat less personalistic.

But not all relations of mutual support and benefit are between people with direct work relations based on their official positions. A skilled climber cultivates people in many organizations with whom there may be only intermittent official contacts or no official contact at all, but who may at some time and in some way be useful. This group of useful acquaintances, former colleagues, ex-schoolmates, relatives, and friends form the climber's network. Note that the network is mostly horizontal, in that its members do not have official authority over one another.

The network helps the climber do his work, but it also may help the climber limit or alter the assigned kind of work. It also provides the climber with some autonomy by providing an unofficial counterweight to the official power of superiors.

Organizational families are amalgams of intertwined teams and networks. In some ways, these groups resemble Mafia crime families— thus the name "families." They differ from Mafia families in that they inhabit a formal organization—the official Soviet system—while the Mafia family is more purely social. The Soviet groups are more complex, thus leading more easily to the possibility of conflicting loyalties within the family. Soviet families are also more meritocratic, and thus membership is more conditional and instrumental.

The Soviet organizational family—like the Mafia one at a national level—provides channels for the bubble-up of issues concerning turf, personnel, and policy. In the Soviet case, this flow interacts with the top-down flow of authority within the formal organization.

NOTES

1. Corporate climbers are told that "to succeed you need to be a team member. Let the boss know you are on his team; let the others in the department know you are one of them. The loner gets nowhere in business. Join a team" (Hegarty 1976).

2. But "the cool climbers, on the other hand, will become extra-ardent report writers to reduce the distance factor. They will find reasons to visit headquarters. And they will be extra-helpful when teams of inspectors from the home office come visiting" (Packard, 1962). Similarly, successful Soviet climbers establish ties with people in more central organizations. This was clear in the case history of a Soviet climber presented in Chapter 4, and will be discussed more fully later in this chapter.

3. The shape of local teams is revealed by examining groups of officials who are getting reprimanded in the press currently. For example, two specialists at

a plant criticized the dissertation of a department head after earlier being barred from further discussion. The specialists informed the Supreme Central Commission of the U.S.S.R. Council of Ministers, but they then suffered reprisals at the local level. This "persecution" was initiated by the deputy director of the scientific production association that included the plant, with the "connivance" of the party committee secretary, the "apathy" of the general director, and "tendentious attitude" of the chief engineer and chairman of the scientific-technical section "and other officials." The two were dismissed and given "biased references." As it turned out, the gorkom bureau reprimanded the director, who was relieved of his duties. The others were given marks on their party cards, and the raikom was ordered to follow up the investigation (*Pravda*, June 6, 1986, p. 2). This was a case of a group of managers at the plant and association level being involved in mutual protection. Other press articles reveal similar groups at higher organizational levels.

4. For example, the Sverdlovsk area specializes in heavy industry; it has produced a Sverdlovsk team that has placed its people in both industrial/political and more purely political types of appointments, including—over time—Kirilenko, Riabov, Ryshkov, Yeltsin (since demoted), and Kolbin.

5. Since the choice of staff subordinates is less constrained than the choice of line managers, staff will reflect an executive's orientation most clearly. For example, a minister has relative freedom in choosing his referents, but not his deputy ministers. This is because of the official need to obtain more approvals for line managers: There are a greater number of institutional and individual players who have an interest in the line appointments. One subject who had close dealings with a minister's referent noted that the latter was a political operator not especially involved in the technical work of the ministry. "N" served the personal needs of the minister as well as acting as his chief of staff. In the latter capacity, he was in charge of the minister's paper flow and ran the minister's secretariat. In his former capacity, "If the minister wanted to go to Switzerland, N would call the departments of the ministry and create some business in Switzerland. If the minister needed some furniture, he would call the council of ministers and arrange to get some furniture." N had followed the minister through his last three positions. Another subject had dealings with some ministerial referents and was impressed by their lack of technical knowledge. Going out to gather a choice tidbit to include in a speech they were preparing for the minister, the referents seemed to function merely as the minister's eyes and ears, as well as his drinking buddies. They were not capable of supplementing his thoughts on any technical issues. If these staffers were supplementary at all, this implies that the minister's job was itself more political than technical.

6. The tendency toward black-and-white thinking in Russian cognition also clashes with the rounding-out strategy. See Chapter 7.

7. Note that Gorbachev, for example, was apparently able to maintain good relations with a number of different factions during the late Brezhnev years.

8. Soviet managers may deliberately report plan underfulfillment once or twice a year to avoid this problem. The failure of the Schekino experiment, which allowed for greater flexibility in cutting costs while retaining some of the savings, (see Norr 1986) is, as I interpret the data, an example of institutional jealousies causing problems for a successful institution. See also Zinoviev 1984:

He calls this leveling process "communalism" or "communality," and devotes a great deal of attention to it.

9. Detouring competition through a superior moderates the tensions of "communalism" (envy, essentially) and of competition itself in horizontal relations. This is consistent with the idea of socialist competition, which in turn follows from the all-inclusive nature of the system. "Socialist competition" is competitiveness aimed not at achieving superiority, but at the common good— like boy scouts counting up their good deeds to win custody of the troop flag. Since everyone is supposed to be a member of—and a beneficiary of—the all-inclusive system, how can such competition produce losers? Ideologically, there is something wrong with the zero-sum aspect of competition. (But see Chapter 7 and Jowitt 1975 on the Soviets' zero-sum mentality.) Thus, the tension between inclusiveness and competition is resolved via the winner's identification with the larger supersystem (as opposed to subsystem), and the tendency of leaders to identify their own interests with that of the organization they lead—"La collective, c'est moi" (a source of corruption; see Klugman 1986).

10. Similarly, "if he [the U.S. manager] regards compromise as immoral concession and fears a harmony that brings certain side commitments with uncertain complications, he withdraws to his formal shelter and watches others find their way through ambiguity to dominate policy and take higher roles" (Dalton 1959).

11. This is in sharp contrast with the U.S. scene, in which tensions surrounding issues of autonomy can make vertical relations difficult (see Kram 1980), while horizontal competitiveness is softened by the factors mentioned earlier. In another cultural contrast, leaving the family of origin for the new nuclear family (U.S. style) implies a horizontal, peer orientation in contrast to a more traditional extended family loyalty, with its more vertical orientation. What are the psychological implications of the Russian patronymic?

12. This is a neat trick while one is trying to convince one's superior that one is "his man." In general, Soviet bureaucracy will be balanced a bit more to the loyalty side and a bit less to the independence side of this axis than Western corporations.

13. Clear boundaries for the Soviet Mafia family are also consistent with the culturally based cognitive pattern of extremely clear cognitive boundaries (see Chapter 7; Klugman 1986; and Inkeles 1968).

14. A sidelight: In 1947, Yuri Andropov was elected second secretary of the Karelian S.S.R., regarded as an appendage of Zhdanovite Leningrad. His boss— the first secretary—was tortured and imprisoned, and the replacement first secretary was shot a short time after. Andropov somehow came out with a top job in Moscow's central committee, apparently having the right allies outside the Zhdanov apparatus. He does not appear to have been on Zhdanov's team (Conquest 1983).

7. SOCIALIZED THINKING

Getting ahead in the Soviet Union requires certain social skills; and, in combination with the institutional structure of Soviet society, those skills reinforce a social view of the world. Groups—not individuals—tend to be seen as primary; group relations tend to be more important than problem solving; and, because the social sphere is all enveloping, relationships tend to be seen as zero sum. Thus, along with cultural and institutional influences, the socialization of Soviet executives molds their ways of thinking and perceiving. They are socialized to have social eyes.

MOBILE AND SOCIAL EXECUTIVES

Successful U.S. businessmen have been described as generally falling into two groups: mobile, "self-made men"; and "the birth elite" (Warner and Abegglan 1955). The former base their success more on technical than social skills, their major social skill being their ability to make and break working relationships. They are highly mobile—moving into new situations, establishing useful but limited relationships with those they have to deal with, and leaving when a better opportunity arises elsewhere. Mobile men often run into trouble if they get to the very top levels of management, because there they need social skills that they never had the opportunity to cultivate. The birth elite—in contrast—are very much embedded in their communities. They may serve on the boards of dozens of charitable organizations, for example, where they meet the childhood friends who are now their vendors, customers, and business associates.

Soviet executives combine some of the characteristics of both these U.S. types. They must be mobile—able to move into new situations and establish their competency. They cannot, in general, just rest in an inherited position of influence and rely on their social network to support them. But they must be intensely social, not just technically oriented.

Like the U.S. birth elite, Soviet executives rely on their social network but they have to build that network themselves, and partly on the basis of proving their competency and usefulness. They constantly reshape, expand, and refine their networks. Their primary skills are tact, trustworthiness, an ability to avoid the negative, knowing what is wanted, being regular guys (not haughty), and making no enemies. Their primary competency is in relating.

In part, the primacy of the social is a reflection of Russian culture, childrearing and early education (see Appendix A) but it also fits in with the politics of Soviet communism. After all, "the essence of socialist management [is] its diune goal of attaining production targets and educating the new man, the citizen, of consolidating socialist social relations" (Stolyarenko 1983). When shop heads and other managers give official reports to their superiors, they begin not by describing the economic activity of their unit—their production—but by describing the political work within the unit, the number of workers who went to the demonstration, and so on. This does not necessarily mean that their main interest as individuals is political, but it reflects the system's self-definition and its belief that adequate political conformity is a precondition for all else.

Thus, it is not just propaganda to say that each Soviet institution has two products: (1) its sociopolitical climate; and (2) its economic product. And while the factory manager may be only secondarily interested in the sociopolitical product, the first and most important interest of the party at all levels must be political stability and, therefore, the condition of the social system. Socialism is socially oriented.

The nature of a social orientation was illuminated for me at a dinner party where I happened to meet the personnel manager of a U.S. regional bank. He had formerly been the personnel manager of a large local bank that the regional bank had acquired. The acquiring bank had originally been comparable to the local bank, but had grown by absorbing a number of other banks, as well. The personnel manager's original employer—the local bank—seemed to him the more efficient organization. Too much energy at the bigger bank was taken up in gossip and office politics, instead of doing the job of banking. It was both surprising and ironic, he thought, that the less efficient institution had emerged as dominant.

I asked him to describe the leaders of the two institutions. The chief executive of the local bank, he said, had been task oriented, directing his attention inward—into his organization—in order to run a taut ship. In contrast, the chief executive of the regional bank was socially minded—active in all the industry associations—directing his attention outward toward the economic environment and industry trends. This orientation had led directly to his strategy of growth by acquisition.

Thus, the corporate culture and social structure of each institution was identical to the psychological and strategic stance of its leadership. And the inefficient, gossipy, and politically oriented bank survived and grew not in spite of, but because of, its social-mindedness.

We in the West are quite aware of the economic costs of the Soviet Union's social orientation. But perhaps we are not so aware of some of its noneconomic effects internally, or its effects and potential benefits externally. This chapter is devoted to looking at how the social orientation of socialism and the institutional experiences of bureaucratic climbers shape the thinking of Soviet leaders.

A SOCIAL AND GROUP-ORIENTED OUTLOOK

Soviet executives must be aware not only of the individuals in their environment, but of the groups—the systems of affiliations connecting the people around them. And from childhood on, the first non-family group to which they devote their attention is the group of their peers.

The majority of Russians have empathy with any group of which they are members. They immerse themselves in the group, and accept the group's control over their individual actions. Americans, on the other hand, feel that the group endangers the self (which they identify with the autonomy) of the individual. For the majority of Americans (at least in one study), the group was perceived to be a coercive force that deprives the individual of strength and integrity—either by threat, or by the individual's fear of isolation and rejection (Hanfmann and Getzels 1955, quoted by Valsiner 1984; see also Inkeles 1968). For Russians, the psychological theme of membership—being in the bosom of the group— is reinforced by the social system.

By regulating behavior through the punishment of scapegoats, the system reinforces identification with the group. Since the system includes rituals in which someone must be criticized, one protects oneself and others by choosing a safe object for criticism: the scapegoat—the last on the list. Even small deviations are punished: A critical remark, for example, can cause loss of a bonus or promotion. Such punishment clearly defines the limits of acceptable behavior, and thus the (official) group boundary. Therefore, a manager supplies the right number of people for demonstrations so as to affirm the manager's own loyalty. Also one avoids being last on the list (whether as a manager supplying demonstrators or a student picking potatoes) so as not to look like a shirker. For fear of being criticized or punished, one must carefully watch the behavior of one's peers and adhere to the group norms.

Group process will have an impact on decision making since, in group decision making, *group relations may be more important than decision content*. "Decision makers who realize the importance of interpersonal relations for their careers . . . can be expected to view decision-making situations as opportunities to demonstrate the proper behavior toward their colleagues—perhaps to the neglect of the decision problem itself" (Gaenslen 1986). Again, the system is social, and decisions will above all be aimed at regulating social relations.

Bureaucratically, people must sign off on each other—that is, take responsibility for each other (as, for example, in testifying to suitability to go abroad). They will be punished for their errors in judgment. Similarly, executives must sponsor subordinates, but their prestige will suffer if protégés fail. Thus, the official system forces people to be—and thus see themselves as—"linked together in life" (quoted in Berliner 1957).

The team, network, or family group is the unit of selection: People compete and affiliate for group membership, and groups compete and affiliate with one another. Thus, groups become the units of observation.

Groups are relied on to monitor and control their members, and an individual is only a representative of a group. Group membership is the most telling information about an individual. Family and friends reflect on a person as a *social* being. One's anketa is not just a Western-style résumé; it also includes information on one's relatives. And the higher the position, the more relatives that must be checked. Thus too, if people are primarily group representatives, it makes sense to punish the families and friends of dissidents or enemies of the people, not just the individuals themselves. This differs greatly from the Western emphasis on the individual and the view that the individual is the ultimate unit of social, economic and political analysis.

This difference in outlook was illustrated in Gorbachev's offhand suggestion that the United States, set aside a few of the 50 states for specified minorities. This was offered in response to his being confronted about human rights issues by some visiting members of Congress. Afterward, House Armed Services Committee Chairman Les Aspin commented that "[The Soviet leaders] don't understand that it's not a question of how do they treat Jews [as a group]. It's a question of how they treat the people who are not happy, a question of how they treat individual rights" (New York *Times*, April 18, 1987). But it is equally clear that the Americans did not really understand Gorbachev's proposal, which was to empower *groups* by giving them their own turf. "We have respect for our nationalities in this country," Gorbachev was quoted as saying, referring to the various Soviet republics and regions based on ethnic identity. "Why don't you have these autonomous areas?"

Soviet administration is based on quotas, and this is partly a product of group-mindedness (and partly an institutional factor—running an immense system is simplified by being able to use quotas as checks on performance). The Central Committee, for example, is apparently constituted by quota and by job slot, not by the selection of individuals. "The Central Committee . . . consists of a carefully defined set of job slots, in which the rank of any individual member of the elite depends on the status assigned to his job, or (in a few instances) on the imputed status of the social category of which he is a token representative" (Daniels 1976). So the Central Committee—with its membership either ex officio or by token representation of various groups, nationalities, and professions—is constituted on the basis of social role (official identity, or job slot) and group quota. Given this way of looking at things, why not a quota of U.S. governorships for specified minorities?

A ZERO-SUM OUTLOOK

A zero-sum game is one in which every player's gains are paid for out of someone else's losses; the players cannot all win together. Both Soviet bureaucracy in particular and Soviet social-mindedness in general foster a zero-sum outlook.

First, every bureaucracy fosters a zero-sum outlook by virtue of the fact that almost all relations are *within* the organization, and so subject to regulation from above. For example, a well-connected Soviet enterprise can obtain a smaller planned target from its ministry. But since the ministry's overall plan has been set, this advantage comes at the expense of another enterprise in the ministry that does not have as good contacts in Moscow (Berliner 1957). Also, "within each bureau, all activities are allocationally interdependent to some degree, since they have to be financed out of the bureau's single budget. This means that every part of a bureau is at least partly competitive with every other part. Therefore, it is quite possible for purely allocational conflicts to arise within a bureau as well as among different bureaus" (Downs 1967).[1]

The zero-sum nature of bureaucratic budgetary politics fits with a peasant society's notion of "*limited good*" (as described by Foster, quoted in Jowitt 1974). "Broad areas of peasant behavior are patterned in such fashion as to suggest that peasants view their social, economic, and natural universes—their total environment—as one in which all of the desired things in life such as . . . friendship . . . honor, respect, status, power, influence, security, and safety, exist in finite quantity and are always in short supply . . . hence it follows that an individual or a family can improve a position only at the expense of others" (ibid.). A society of genuine material scarcity also reinforces the notion of limited good.

Soviet administration-by-the-numbers (by official, quantitative reporting—however distorted in reality) further promotes a zero-sum outlook. First, because it is so easy to compare numbers, heavy reliance on statistical performance for evaluation itself leads to competition (Blau 1963). Added to this is the fact that social norms in the Soviet Union are set by scapegoating group outliers (whoever is at the bottom of a list), as opposed to having absolute standards that theoretically everyone could exceed. But since every list has a bottom, lifting oneself off the bottom automatically puts someone else in that unenviable position. Someone has to lose.

A zero-sum orientation also fits with the social orientation of Soviet society: If values are social, then they are also relative. Position, power, and prestige exist only in relation to others: If someone is higher, his or her counterpart is lower.[2] There are no absolute values that allow all to rise together. Thus, the social, cultural-historic, and institutional factors of the society all reinforce zero-sum thinking.

CONCRETE AND CATEGORICAL THINKING

Russians have a tendency toward black-and-white thinking and the creation of relatively few mental categories demarcated by distinct, well-defined boundaries. This is first established in childhood by a pattern—both within the family and in early education settings—of discipline by exclusion. Punishment by withdrawal of affection and ostracism creates a sense of undifferentiated badness that is in painfully clear contrast to a warm, enveloping maternal acceptance—a (submissive) sense of undifferentiated goodness. Russian parental discipline is quite different from Americans' ideas of appropriate disciplinary procedures—which emphasize drawing a distinction between the child, who is still loved, and the behavior, which is condemned. The American method begins a lifetime pattern of drawing distinctions; this creates a myriad of overlapping mental categories, which—by their very number—seem somewhat arbitrary and manipulable. In contrast, the Russian childrearing method begins a pattern of simple, inclusive mental categories, sharply distinguished. By virtue of both their paucity and the clarity of their definition, these categories seem concrete—even real. (See Appendix A for a fuller discussion.)

The Russian thought pattern is reinforced by a number of Soviet institutions. First, the socialization of Soviet children emphasizes in-group/out-group differences (Valsiner 1984). Like the scapegoating process described previously, this establishes very clear boundaries of what is permissible and acceptable, and what is not. The general pattern of group-mindedness and—later—the bureaucratic competition between cliques also reinforce a view in which group membership, and mental categories in general, are sharply defined.

As mentioned earlier, one subject told me that in the Soviet Union the first informal contact is the hardest to make. Once one has broken the ice, further contact becomes easier and easier. In the United States, it was this subject's experience that the reverse was true: The first contact was relatively easy, but it became progressively harder to cultivate the relationship. This exemplifies the pattern of Americans having permeable boundaries and multiple intermediate categories—degrees of friendship, for example—and Russians having rigid boundaries that define relatively few categories.

For Russians, friends are bosom buddies, period.[3] Everyone else is essentially an acquaintance or an alien. In a similar pattern expressed institutionally, Soviet diplomats cannot have personal correspondence with foreign nationals, even those of fraternal socialist countries. The boundary around Soviet citizenship is quite rigid.

The Soviets are apparently aware of this Russian tendency toward black-and-white thinking. Gromyko's Central Committee speech nominating Gorbachev as general secretary specifically mentioned that Gorbachev could rise above "the law of black and white." "There may be intermediate colors, intermediate links, and intermediate decisions," said Gromyko. "And Mikhail Sergeyivich [Gorbachev] is always able to come up with such decisions that correspond with the party line."

The sharpness of Russian boundaries produces—in group relations—a strong tendency for groups either to split into factions, or to cohere but secede from the larger system (that is, localism). These tendencies have to be controlled by social institutions: The social process of the collective prevents factionalism, and centralized controls prevent localism. These institutions perform the role that intermediate cognitive structures perform in Western society—preventing the breakdown of social relations into disjoint (that is, completely split) subsystems. *What is internalized by the individual in the West is externalized and institutionalized by society in the Soviet Union.*

In individuals, sharp boundaries show up in a public–private split (see Klugman 1986)—a clear separation between an internal, private self that may be shared with friends, and an official identity that determines public behavior. The public–private split is reinforced by the system's highly punitive stance toward disagreement and by the use of the social stigma of ostracism as a means of punishment from childhood on. This split allows for public compliance without private acceptance and without cognitive dissonance (since the high punishment provides sufficient justification for the split). (See the discussion in Jowitt 1983.)

Thought patterns tend to separate into concrete particularisms and high-level abstractions, with few intermediate categories to unite the two levels. (See Appendix A for elucidation of the origins of this split.) People, things, and policies tend to be categorized broadly, and then viewed in their uniqueness. Splitting thought into contrasting realms of abstract and concrete—high theory and practical engineering—Soviets start with the former (their big, well-defined categories) and move to the latter (particularism). An individual, for example, will be seen first as friend, acquaintance, or alien, and then viewed in all his or her uniqueness.

The concreteness of most Soviet thinking shows up first and foremost in the engineering perspective that they bring to most problems. While most fast-track U.S. managers have their undergraduate degrees in engineering or science (Jennings 1967), a high and increasing number of top-level U.S. managers have a master's, law, or Ph.D. degree (41 percent in 1976, according to Swinyard and Bond 1980). U.S. managerial training thus goes beyond its technical base. Contrast this training to the pure engineering training of Soviet managers, and most Soviet politicians too. (Most U.S. politicians are lawyers.) While U.S. management schools stress the ability to apply to the solution of problems whatever factual data can be remembered, Soviet management schools are engineeringlike in their approach: They emphasize a sound command of factual material. Thus, the Soviets are trained to be concrete and engineering minded, and oriented toward rote solutions (Granick 1961).

As a result of this culturewide training, even Soviet social scientists formalize their work until it, too, resembles engineering. Systems proposed for personnel evaluation, for example, take a typical formalistic engineering approach—as if social categories can be objectively rated. In the military, Soviet artillery manuals have nomograms to calculate the rate of shelling required to pin down various opponents according to their nationality: The Germans require the most shelling; then, the Americans; and down the line, to the Italians and Turks.

Balanced against this concrete and engineering-style approach is the very social way that Soviet managers and politicians have to get things done. Again, there is a split between two sharply contrasting approaches: Engineering-style rationality is the public value, while social skills are what makes the wheels go 'round.[4]

The cognitive flip side of Soviet concreteness and engineering-style problem solving is a level of abstraction so high that it has scarcely any connection to reality. When I interviewed one subject who had been a Soviet management consultant, we spent much time discussing his work in industrial consulting without getting to any concrete information at all. He tended toward the high level of generalization found in Soviet texts, alternated with storytelling. His stories were particularistic and were not offered to illustrate any general principles. He thus exemplified the split between the abstract and the concrete.

I questioned this subject about the high level of abstraction in Soviet books on management. He said that there were, of course, many concrete studies of individual institutions, but that these were printed in very low volume and were sitting on the shelves of the relevant factory directors and a few academics. These studies include psychological evaluations and assessments of the managerial style of every manager in the specified enterprise and recommendations on personnel reassignment or retraining, as well as recommendations on changes in procedures and management technique. They correspond, I suppose, to the reports that a management consultant might write for a Western corporation.

Meanwhile, Soviet management books are structural, classifying, abstract, and categorical. They are written in a highly abstract language that readers may then bring to bear on the particular and unique situations in which they are working. The books provide a context in which to place individual experiences—an outline to be filled in by the reader. Compared to Western books, Soviet management books lack a back-and-forth between example and theory. Apparently, to the Soviet author, there is no point in providing examples: Each particular situation is too unique to be worthwhile sharing. Soviet books provide a one-way street—from theory down.

DEDUCTIVE—NOT INDUCTIVE—THINKING

Both cultural and institutional factors predispose Soviet leaders to favor deductive—not inductive—thinking. This means that there is a nonconscious bias toward the analytic method of "scientific socialism"— reasoning from the general to the specific, from the abstract to the concrete, and thus from policy to reality.

This style of thought—top-down, deductive reasoning—is antithetical to the U.S. style of focusing first on the concrete and only then thinking about the context, inductively moving up levels of abstraction. A hypothetical (and perhaps hyperbolic) illustration comes to mind: An American would react to the Three Mile Island nuclear-reactor accident by first trying to contain the damage, then looking for implications regarding the safety of nuclear power, and finally thinking about ways to improve nuclear safety and/or decrease reliance on nuclear power. A Soviet decision maker would start thinking about the Chernobyl nuclear-reactor accident by studying worldwide trends in energy consumption, the future diminution of fossil fuels, the importance of energy in the Soviet economy and in trade, and the relations between the Soviet nuclear industry and the military. In light of these factors, he or she would decide the general approach to nuclear energy, and then the general approach to nuclear safety. Finally, our Soviet decision maker would discern what to do in the immediate situation of the nuclear accident at Chernobyl. Just as in the Soviet system of values the interests of the collective are higher than the interests of the individual, so in their system of thought the macrosystem takes precedence over the microsystem.

The institutional pressures that push Soviet thinking toward the deductive run as follows: Bureaucracy, in general, administers by seeing individual cases in terms of more general rules and policies. The top of the organization determines general policy, and each level below adds its own detail in applying that policy. The goal of lower level officials is to classify the situations with which they are presented so that they may bring the proper policy to bear. Lower officials call on top administrators to rethink policy only when unclassifiable or large, unforeseen events occur. In some sense, their goal is to bring reality into conformity with policy, top down.

For the individual climber—as discussed previously—the need to be useful and to anticipate the needs of the superior implies that it is useful for the junior official to tune into the larger system of the boss's world. In turn, this world depends on *the boss's boss's* world, and so on—right up the line to *Pravda*, the Politburo, and the general line of the party. Thus, the junior official places his or her career in context; and, since power starts at the top, that context must be described from the top down. (Note, however, that this unbroken chain of being depends on good party discipline. Each executive must be at risk, dependent on his or her superiors.)

A LONG TIME FRAME

A long-term perspective is both a part of and a result of the broad outlook required for success. Institutionally, the long-term planning, the long-term relationships, the necessity of multiple approvals, the slowness of the bureaucratic process, and the slow movement of bureaucratic careers all foster a much longer time perspective for Soviets than for Americans. Five-year plans, the necessity for multiple bureaucratic signoffs, and so on, all make executives used to long-drawn-out processes.

Culturally, a long time frame is reinforced by cognitive splitting: Time is either immediate or long term. The intermediate time span is less compelling. Thus, there is a tendency, on the one hand, to seek short-term gratification without regard to cost and, on the other, to plan for very long time spans. (This difference in time frame has been noted by many observers; for example, Leites 1952.)

INCREMENTALISM

All Soviet leaders come from within the system, and promotion from within favors incrementalist thinking.

All top officials have to work themselves upward through the hierarchy, presumably by repeatedly pleasing their superiors. Superiors usually approve of continuous development of their policies, rather than sharp breaks with tradition. Therefore, the screening process of upward movement tends to reject radicals and elevate a relatively homogenous group. . . . [A John Delorean who gets to the top of General Motors is rare indeed.] There is little doubt that 100 percent promotion from within tends to deemphasize new ideas and stress continuity. (Downs 1967)

Also Soviet officials learn patience in the course of developing their long time horizons, so they are comfortable with slow changes. Thus incremental—not radical—change will be favored.

Some cultural factors favor incrementalism. Russian childrearing creates, and Soviet institutions reinforce, a need for external discipline—a "moral corset"—instead of internalized controls (see Inkeles 1968; Klugman 1986). This creates a fear of loss of control (*bezporyadok*, or disorder), and this fear favors incrementalism.

A number of institutionally promoted behaviors also favor incrementalism. The avoidance of losing as a prime goal (first, don't be last; then, try to be first) and the dangers of making a mistake imply a tendency of the system to produce conservers (in the language of Downs 1967), and thus points to a difficulty with innovation. Risk avoidance implies leaving initiatives to superiors (a pattern that also fits the Soviet model of bowing before an intrusive, controlling authority): All initiative should come from above; all risk must be widely shared. Further, seeing things in black and white implies that any but small changes will probably be perceived as radical. Thus, only incremental change is tolerable or institutionally plausible. The Soviet system is like chess—punishing errors and rewarding careful, methodical play.[5]

LEGITIMACY

The authority of the Soviet regime feels (to its citizens) absolutely legitimate, as legitimate as managerial authority in Western corporations. This legitimacy is illuminated by examining another model of elite–mass relations: the alcoholic marriage (Klugman 1986). The sober spouse—the party or regime—controls impulses in general and attempts in particular to control the drunken spouse: the masses. In such relationships, neither participant for a moment doubts the supposed legitimacy and moral superiority of the sober spouse. As for legitimacy *within* the party and other hierarchies, leadership evolves toward meritocratic legitimacy (see Klugman 1986), as well as basing itself—essentially—on a justification of "might makes right."

The system is like a corporation in its internal governance. Western corporations—although bound by the surrounding legal system—can make and break their own rules in their internal governance. Internal corporate "rule books" are codifications of current procedures; they are not law, even within these same organizations. The rules can be changed without notice, applied, or overlooked, if management so deems. In this, they are like the Soviet constitution and Soviet law. Authority itself is not rule bound, but almost parental—based on a relationship—and therefore discretionary.

FALSIFICATIONS

Because discipline is never internalized but always socially imposed (see Appendix A and Klugman 1986), Soviet executives need have no moral compunctions about falsifications. Executives will falsify or not depending on the incentives offered them and the social norms that are established, especially by their superiors. If the system accepts and rewards falsification, such socially oriented people will have little internal hesitation about supplying what is required. *Truth is not objective; it is socially defined.*

Thus, unless top management puts a heavy emphasis on truth in reporting and rewards the bringer of bad tidings—instead of killing the messenger, as happens so often in every kind of organization—falsification will flourish. In most organizations, policies set at the top are contradicted from below only at great risk. Therefore, there will be a tendency not to knock official fantasies. Support your boss's ideas even if they are wrong, climbers are advised. Make them be right (Hegarty 1976). In return, at least in the Soviet case, the senior official will accept the junior's excuses for not having achieved the impossible—but official—goals.

Soviet leaders are used to portraying life and their own efforts in the style of "socialist realism." Like the school of literature, art, and music so named, they have portrayed "life as it should be" or "life as it is becoming," not life as it is. Only top management can change this corporate culture, and only then through unremitting, long-term effort: Increased discipline and truthfulness must percolate down through the system.

IMMERSION AND VIGILANCE

As illustrated by the local bank and the regional bank described earlier, organizations split their energies between their productive tasks—doing their jobs—and the social tasks that maintain their structure. Both Soviet organizations and Soviet leaders devote a great deal of energy to their social systems.

Soviet executives' personal relationships are both more engulfing and more inclusive than in the West; the stakes are higher; the emotions are heightened; the self-control is more conscious and manipulative; and the social skills required are even more ascendant over technical ones. Career success is much more political—based on interpersonal skills and relationships—in Soviet organizations than in the average Western organization (which is itself quite political).

The importance of personal relations—the primacy of the political—combined with the lack of alternatives outside the system means that one is always surrounded by the system, with no outside to escape to or relax in. Thus one feels enclosed, on display, and careful to avoid a negative. The world around oneself is tightly integrated; it is full of pitfalls, but with opportunities that must be continuously scanned for.

The process of getting ahead promotes an energetic (but not necessarily anxious) vigilance—a continuous scanning of the world for opportunities and dangers, not an inward focus on one's own task. This is part and parcel of the social-mindedness—the interpersonal, outward orientation—of Soviet leaders.

SUMMARY

Soviet executives base their mobility on their competence in developing and utilizing a social network. Their well-developed social skills and their success within a socially oriented system combine to reinforce a socially oriented view of the world. This view shows up both in a tendency to see groups (not individuals) as primary and in a zero-sum outlook. The sharp boundaries by which groups define their membership meanwhile reinforces a Russian tendency toward black-and-white, categorical thinking, while a social orientation means that group decision making will be aimed at protecting group cohesion more than at technical problem solving.

Bureaucratization itself reinforces an ideologically "proper" tendency to prefer deductive to inductive reasoning. Other cognitive effects of the Soviet social structure include promoting both a long time horizon and an incrementalist approach to problem solving.

NOTES

1. Hough has paid a great deal of attention to Soviet allocational politics, and has used such competition in support of his model of "institutional pluralism." See, for example, Hough 1977. Note also that increased mobility and opportunity would ameliorate this tendency.

2. This applies to competition *within* any organization, East or West. This effect is ameliorated in the West, however, by people's ability to go outside the organization, either for other jobs or for alternate, nonjob sources of identity.

3. One American I know—a professor of Russian history—has said that Russian friendships are stronger than American marriages. Then again, perhaps American friendships are stronger than American marriages.

4. The Soviet engineering perspective—along with centralization per se— reflects high needs for *control, uncertainty avoidance,* and *clear authority*. See Hofstede 1980a and b, for cross-cultural comparisons of uncertainty avoidance and "power-distance." These needs are part and parcel of the childrearing patterns that establish the cognitive patterns as well. See Appendix A.

5. This is in contrast to many aspects of the U.S. system—from entrepreneurship to baseball—in which one's best moments can redeem any previous errors.

PART III. PSYCHOLOGY AND ORGANIZATION: MANAGING THE SOVIET SYSTEM

Tracing careers sheds light on the structure of the Soviet system, its history, and its possible future. Chapter 8 compares Soviet career paths to those in Western corporations and uses this comparison to sort out the organizational role of the Communist party. Chapter 9 looks at changes in managerial style over the course of Soviet history, and discovers that these changes parallel the evolution that occurs in the development of all large organizations. It then shows that, in recent history, an "age lump"—itself a remnant of Stalinism—produced the stagnation of "Brezhnevism," in part because of the predictable effects of Brezhnev's personnel policies. Finally, Chapter 10 uses what is known of organizational behavior in Western organizations to examine the potential for a changed personnel policy making Soviet reform effective (within certain limits).

8. CAREER PATHS AND THE ORGANIZATIONAL ROLE OF THE PARTY

Studying which jobs in what particular suborganizations provide the best stepping-stones to success provides insight into the distribution of power within an organization. In the case of the Soviet system, our study of career building shows that the party's role is organizationally analogous to that of headquarters in a decentralized, multidivisional Western corporation. This, in turn, sheds some light on party–state relations.

U.S.S.R., INC.

The Soviet system may be viewed as a single organization. Western analysts recognize this explicitly when they use terms like "monoorganizational society" (Rigby 1977) and "USSR inc." (Meyer 1964). They recognize it implicitly in all the various models of Soviet reality, from that of "totalitarianism" to that of "institutional pluralism."

Early models that looked at the Soviet system as a bureaucracy stressed both its command possibilities (Meyer 1964 and 1965) and its orderly governance—its rational-technical aspects (Moore 1954). Following Weber—who originated the notion of bureaucracy—these descriptions implicitly used as their model the hierarchic, orderly, top-down, rule-driven Prussian army.

Other descriptions of bureaucracy, however, have focused on intraorganizational negotiation and conflict. (See the review of bureaucratic models in Hough 1977.) Hough's model of "institutional pluralism," for example, stresses bureaucratic (especially allocational) politics: Hough describes as pluralistic the multiplicity of suborganizations struggling for their place in the sun.

A corporatist model (Bunce and Echols 1980) allows for the interaction of top-down command and bubble-up suborganizational competition. Corporatism is defined as "a system of interest representation in which the constituent units are organized into a limited number of singular, compulsory, noncompetitive, hierarchically ordered and functionally differentiated categories recognized and licensed (if not created) by the state and granted a deliberate representational monopoly within their respective categories in exchange for observing certain controls on their selection of leaders and articulation of demands and supports" (Phillippe Schmitter, quoted in Bunce and Echols 1980). "In pluralist models, the emphasis is on conflict; in corporatism, consensus and cooperation" (Bunce and Echols 1980). Conflict is only reduced in corporatism, however—not eliminated. (This distinguishes the model from that of totalitarianism.) A corporatist system is activist, often paternalistic, explicitly goal oriented, and full of plans.

Private corporations are organized into hierarchically ordered noncompetitive constituent subunits; and the corporatist state is, in a sense, the private corporation writ large. Thus, corporatism produces a description of the Soviet system that is not so different from the earlier one (Meyer 1965) that compared the totality of the Soviet organizational structure to that of a "a giant Western business corporation . . . includ[ing] the thorough bureaucratization of management on all levels."[1]

THE PARTY AS HEADQUARTERS

Having used what is known about organizations to shed light on who climbs the Soviet apparat ladder, now let us use what we know about who climbs and how they do it to shed light on the Soviet system as an organization. First, what kinds of careers do people build in this organization?

Soviet careers are orderly progressions up an apparat ladder. "The party apparatchiki, the military, the heavy or light industry managers, the agronomists or agricultural experts in high positions, and the police are bureaucrats just as much as the officials [of the Soviet state apparatus] actually given this label by Western scholars" (Hough 1977). And bureaucrats have orderly, bureaucratic careers. There are no entrepreneurs, basketball players, or actors who enter politics late in life. The orderly careers of Soviet officials are much like those of men working their way up at AT&T or General Motors (both of which tend to promote from within).[2]

Mobility in U.S. corporations is high, with managers averaging about three years per job. Frequent switches in organizational level include 40 percent of switches going down in level—that is, from a corporate-level position to one at the division or group (cluster of divisions) level (Granick 1972). But these are not demotions: They are centrifugal promotions.

While working at corporate headquarters, executives get to know the people who make the ultimate personnel decisions, and they get to be known by these same people. This allows for both evaluation and socialization. To appoint those who have served at headquarters as executives in the divisional, peripheral suborganizations serves useful functions for the organization. Connections at headquarters are necessary to do the local managerial job properly. And it is important for headquarters to know and have confidence in the lower level leadership, and vice versa.[3]

Within Soviet industrial management, movement is unidirectionally up: People are not transferred from the ministry to the field (Granick 1972). But while movement from a ministry job to an enterprise is a demotion, movement from local party jobs to an enterprise is a standard promotional route: Managers often go from the local partkom to field management. For example, an official will move from a position at the raikom or gorkom to one as director of an enterprise subordinate to that raikom or gorkom. In fact, while the careers of Soviet leaders and managers pass through a variety of suborganizations, the most successful always pass—in some capacity—through the party.

At every level, in fact, a party assignment is like a headquarters assignment in a Western corporation, and the raikoms and obkoms are like divisional and group headquarters while the Central Committee is corporate headquarters. So just as a corporate-headquarters staff job often leads to a promotion to an executive position at a corporate division, or a divisional-headquarters staff job may lead to an executive position in a subordinate plant, a party job is "like a highway" that leads to an executive position in the industrial or state administrative hierarchy.

Within the Party hierarchy itself, a job in some party apparat will often lead to a higher job in a more peripheral apparat (for example, a gorkom instructor may become a raikom secretary), and a job at corporate headquarters—the Central Committee Secretariat—may lead to high-level appointments in some regional headquarters: the oblast and republic party organizations. The case history reported in Chapter 4 illustrated this in the young climber's move from a position as instructor in a republic komsomol central committee to one as gorkom komsomol first secretary. In general, *lower level positions in a central institution lead to higher positions in peripheral ones.*

The party—then—includes corporate, group, and divisional head-quarters, plus their local monitoring and control organizations. And the party—as headquarters—is the organization's unifier and coordinator. Thus, at the top of the organization, "a unified national perspective, and if at all possible a widely supported set of feasible and integrated domestic and foreign policies, is the officially stated and quite possibly the operative goal of most Politburo members. The Politburo is the only organ in the Soviet polity committed to formulating a long- and short-term conception of the common good and to making it prevail over group and individual interests and immediate pressures" (Hoffman and Laird 1982). More broadly, the party's role as the "decisive coordinator," "integrator," "regulator," "synthesizer," "adjuster," "mobilizer," and "energizer" of society[4] expresses the party's function as a headquarters ramified throughout the Soviet system.

THE CENTRALIZING ROLE OF HEADQUARTERS

The distributed (local and regional) party apparat serves a coordinating controlling (both in the sense of leading and checking up on), and *centralizing* function—imposing centrally determined values and mediating between central and peripheral needs. The party's centralizing role shows up in Central Committee membership, for example: While most state officials who are Central Committee members work in Moscow, party officials come from all around the country (Daniels 1976). This fits both with local party officials being more powerful than local govern-ment officials, and more generally with the party's centralizing role: local party officials are the dispersed representatives of central authority. The party is the glue holding together the various functions of the state—reconciling the social and the economic, and linking the center and the periphery.

The centralizing role of the party is manifested even on a more per-sonal level. For example, political activity affects the job assignments of graduates of universities and technicums, thus focusing the attention of the ambitious on centrally determined political values. A party control commission may be called in by one faction against another in an attempt to get central support in an intraorganizational struggle. Thus the party plays referee, and again imposes the values and needs of the center. The centralizing role of the mestkoms (the party and union committees of an enterprise) is revealed in the fact that mestkom officials are not subject to one-man removal by the enterprise director. Their dismissal requires confirmation by the relevant local social organizations. Thus, mestkom officials are to some degree representatives of the center at their enterprises, as well as representatives of their enterprises to the center.

The party's centralizing role is emphasized in Soviet organizational models. For example, in administrative scientist V. G. Afanas'ev's systems model, the party, *partinost'* (party-mindedness), and the unifying ideology act as centralizing influences—providing common goals and a common vocabulary for interpreting information and directives, and providing cohesion and unity (Schwartz 1974).

Various career moves of Soviet leaders can be seen as playing a centralizing and integrating role within the large Soviet superorganization. Andropov originally went to the KGB in order to restore party control to what had become—in the eyes of the leadership—a bit of a rogue organization. Eduard Shevardnadze's move to the Foreign Ministry can be seen similarly as reestablishing party connections with an organization that had become isolated and too self-involved in terms of its organizational culture and career patterns. Anatoly Dobrynin's move to the Central Committee Secretariat also served to reduce departmentalism and foster integration, centralization, and the headquarters role of the party.

Besides these moves there has been a recent return to the pattern of appointing regional and republican leaders who have passed through (that is, had jobs in) the Central Committee Secretariat. For example, the new first secretary of Kirgizia, Absamat Masaliyev, was until June 1985 the first secretary of Issyk-kul oblast (one of four oblasty in Kirgizia), but then served for five months at the CPSU Central Committee as an inspector before moving to his present post (CDSP 37:44:18). The new second secretary of Kirgizia had also served as a Central Committee inspector just previous to his appointment.[5] Such a career path again emphasizes the centralizing role of the Central Committee Secretariat as the headquarters of the whole Soviet system.

OPERATING OFFICERS AND EXECUTIVE OFFICERS

If the party is headquarters, what is the state? The state apparatus may be analogized, essentially, to the operations functions of a corporation, especially the production function.

Soviet industrial managers tend to be production specialists, not general managers in the Western sense. Thus, it is incorrect to compare U.S. corporate leaders to Soviet industrial managers. There are two big differences between U.S. and Soviet (industrial) management careers: The Soviet manager has had close contact with production problems on a shop level; and the main road to industrial management in the Soviet Union is through production and "line" operations (Granick 1961). Enterprise directors are trained for and oriented toward production (Ryapolov 1966). Meanwhile, slow promotion in the Soviet industrial hierarchy also narrows the industrial manager's focus (Granick 1972).[6]

It is Soviet political officials who are the general managers, with the production managers clearly subordinate. Putting the emphasis for economic managers on maximizing production, for example, instead of allowing them to make strategic trade-offs between maximization of output and other values—capital investment, human resources, and so on—allows Soviet political leaders to retain centrality of decision making. The Soviet planning system keeps strategic choice within the political apparatus (Granick 1972).[7]

Politically, industrial management is seen as the errand boy of the Communist party, merely working out the detailed implications of the party's decisions (Granick 1961). The industrial leader must have "political maturity—the ability to approach the resolution of particular economic tasks from the party position, from the position of the interests of the whole society" (Papulov 1985). This is to say that the industrial manager must know what headquarters wants.

But if party officials are the general managers, then there is nothing illegitimate about them taking an active role in managing any part of the overall organization.[8]

Thus, the intrusion of party officials into the affairs of their functional counterparts in the state bureaucracy is increasingly seen less as "petty tutelage," that is, unproductive interference, a transgression still condemned by party leaders, and more as a creative and compensatory endeavor made necessary in theoretical terms by the Party's growing role as developed socialism matures and in practical terms by the need to overcome inertia and to provide an integrative mechanism tying together both programmatic leadership and administrative flexibility. In many ways this new role is far from inconsistent with the time-honored functions of high-level party officials in the past; both regional party secretaries and apparatchiki in the branch and functional departments of the Central Committee have operated de facto in just this manner, understanding well—for their careers frequently depended on it—how to manipulate the bureaucracy and how to exploit the informal organizational network to obtain the necessary flexibility. What is different is the degree to which such skills are now touted as necessary, laudable, and, indeed, key in providing the sort of creative leadership necessary. (Kelley 1980a)[9]

At the regional and local levels—not just at the national level—broad managerial functions lie in the party apparatus. Regional party leaders may be, in a sense, specialized—their performance judged essentially on the production of key regional products. But this merely means that a whole region is essentially like a corporate division or corporate group (cluster of divisions).

Oblast and republic first secretaries are the general managers of divisions and groups; the Central Committee secretaries and Politburo, the general managers at the corporate level. Ryshkov is vice-president for production (he is not chief operating officer because too many operations other than production do not fall under his jurisdiction); Gorbachev is chief executive officer and chairman of the board; and so on. The point of these comparisons is not to be cute, but to point to the parallelism in organizational relationships that also helps explain—and is confirmed by—career paths. This analysis reveals, for example, that the nomenklatura system is standard corporate procedure.

SUMMARY

The party is the Soviet Union's central organization—its headquarters. The Central Committee Secretariat is the party's central organization. It is the headquarters of headquarters. These relations explain the role of party jobs in career tracks.

What, then, are the organizational roles of the CPSU? The party has the functions of personnel, policy formulation, strategic planning, and coordination across internal production boundaries—the centralizing role. The party also operates in the human relations sphere that is usually associated with the personnel function—morale/ideology, recreation, and so on. The strategic and coordinating functions as well as at least part of the personnel function are, of necessity, headquarters' activities.

Party organizations at lower levels have the role of representing headquarters (see Hough 1969). You might say that the secretary of the primary *partorg* (party organization) serves the industrial enterprise as vice-president for personnel and organizational development, as well as a kind of comptroller and officer for (some) strategic planning. The local party organs have the same roles, but the balance of their activities shifts more to their comptroller and organizational coordinating roles. Throughout the party, however, personnel (the determination of job placement and career advancement) is the key function: It underpins all the other powers.

NOTES

1. Granick (1961) makes a similar comparison, likening the Praesidium (now Politburo) to a U.S. board of directors, and the party to corporate shareholders. It seems to me that this is not quite right because, unlike mere shareholders, the party takes an active managerial role in allocation, strategy, personnel, as well as ideology, and so forth. In fact, one's party rank—and, in a sense, one's degree of ownership—is in general strictly related to the importance of one's managerial role. Aside from structural similarities between the Soviet state and a Western cooperation, however, there are other parallels. In a corporation, managerial authority is based on a claim of efficiency and rationality—a claim of knowing "the one best way" to organize work (Kanter 1977). This is not very different from the basis of the party's claim to manage the Soviet system. Also,

party officials are often in the position of ordering an economic organization to break a rule or violate a plan. They are governed not by strict legality, but by the spirit (not the letter) of the law (Hough 1969). Soviet law is like corporate "rules"—not like constitutionally based law. Like corporate handbooks, the procedures described are not truly binding. They just provide guidelines. To a large extent, managerial authority is discretionary.

2. Careers under Stalin cannot be said to have been truly orderly. Change that has occurred in the Soviet system over time is the subject of Chapter 9.

3. U.S. corporations use early rotation of managers through either or both divisional and company headquarters as both an evaluating and socializing force, reducing suboptimization (Granick 1972). In U.S. corporations, there is also a high level of switching between functions. Because of the brief time spent in each job, however, it is difficult to evaluate the performance of U.S. managers. Evaluation is therefore relatively subjective, and U.S. executives are correspondingly more sensitive to company politics than managers in—say—Britain or France (Granick 1972). There are some analysts who hold a contrary opinion on the utility of moving executives from headquarters staff to peripheral line positions:

In the problem of contralization and decentralization of authority, the existence of powerful corporate staffs [like partkom staffs at any level] is often a nonrational (and even irrational) response by chief executives to their anxiety, which is created by the need to control decisions at the group and even divisional level. The corporate staffs become the "training ground" for future group and divisional officers who, while responsible for profit centers, are also loyal to their benefactors in corporate management. (Zelaznik and kets de Vries 1975)

And "in organizations, hierarchical authority tends to drive out professional authority in direct relationship to the mobility of specialists from corporate staff to line jobs" (ibid.). This is to say that such movement makes the organization more political and less rational-technical—thus strengthening the importance of teams, networks, and families. This is also to say that such movement is centralizing in its effects.

4. These words are from a Soviet text quoted in Hoffman and Laird 1982. To verify the absolute and concrete accuracy of these descriptors of the party's role at the local and regional level, see Hough 1969.

5. Masiliyev made a speech at the province party congress denouncing his predecessor and charging, among other things, that his predecessor promoted personalism among subordinates—an issue that will be discussed in Chapter 10. See CDSP 38:5:9.

6. This also tends to restrict cooperation across organizational boundaries.

7. The U.S. satisficing model (planning "good enough" targets for managers to hit, without directly trying to maximize any production variable) leaves more room for managers to maneuver (Granick 1972).

8. I leave aside, for the moment, the issue of how much responsibility a good general manager should delegate. That is, what are the limits on the manager's appropriate interventions. This question will be discussed in depth in Chapter 9.

9. This party role as general manager is why Moore (1954) was wrong in thinking that, as the system became more rationalized, the party would recede

in importance in favor of the state. Instead, the party has incorporated managerial functions, uniting them with its political functions. In fact, its political functions correspond in part to the informal structures that underpin Western management. The informal and the political and the psychological are important in all management: Even U.S. corporations are not quite as rational-technical as Moore might have believed.

9. MANAGERIAL EVOLUTION AND BREZHNEVISM

Steve Wozniak and Steve Jobs started the Apple Computer Company in a garage. As the company grew, Wozniak withdrew from management and took a role in research. It had been his idea to build personal computers in the first place; but he was primarily a computer designer, not a manager. The company thrived selling to the home and educational markets, but then ran into trouble. As it tried to enter the business market, the Macintosh division—Jobs's darling—was duplicating many activities of the older Apple II division, and the company as a whole seemed without overall direction. The board of directors eventually pushed Jobs aside in favor of John Sculley, a marketer from the Pepsico Company who had no background whatsoever in computers. He was a professional manager.

Organizations need different kinds of managers as they change and grow. The person who can found and build a great organizational empire—whether Apple Computer, the Ford Motor Company, or the Soviet Union—is not usually the appropriate person to run it after it is built. The skills and the personality of the entrepreneur and the professional manager are too different. Thus, over time, organizations change both their managerial personnel and their managerial style.

Such a change in the Soviet Union—from a highly charged, personalistic, and political atmosphere toward a more rational, technocratic order—was predicted as much as 35 years ago (Moore 1954). What happened? Is the Soviet system really evolving in this direction—and if so, why so slowly? In order to answer these questions, we must begin by looking at the style of empire builders, and at the forces that eventually make them obsolete.

THE ENTREPRENEURIAL MANAGER

The entrepreneurial manager is characterized by personal involvement in all parts of the organization: The organization belongs to the entrepreneur, who—really—wishes that he could do every job himself. "The implicit delegation contract between [the entrepreneurial manager] and his subordinates is that he reserves the right to influence directly any decisions that are of importance or interest to him, regardless of the organization level of these decisions. The entrepreneurial manager's subordinates acknowledge his right to make decisions in any area and at any level" (Tashakori 1980). "Although each subordinate manager may structure his area in a regular hierarchical manner, he knows that the entrepreneurial manager reserves the right to go around him and to make decisions at any level" (ibid.).

Entrepreneurial managers "equate their personal interest with the firm's interest" (ibid.). This creates a kind of personalism in which authority "resides in the man rather than solely in the post he holds" (Granick 1954). (This last description was offered for the Soviet system, in particular.)

The entrepreneurial manager tends not to trust subordinates, and this lack of trust undermines their independence. "Since the owner-founder does not trust his subordinates, he usually either makes the major operations decisions facing the company or has a large input in them. The consequence of this is to discourage independent decision making on the part of the executives" (Tashakori 1980).

There is little or no delegation of authority, and decision making is personalistic; so there can be no true organizational planning. In general, entrepreneurial managers have no plans or else constantly change plans. Alternatively, in their zeal for control, they overly and contradictorily specify plans; then they have to resolve the contradictions by resorting to ad hoc decision making. (Sound familiar?)

In trying to run the empire alone, the entrepreneurial manager strains his or her own skills to the breaking point. "His inability to delegate authority weakens the quality of management" (Zelaznik and Kets de Vries 1975). The entrepreneur is personally the main coordinating mechanism; so, as complexity grows, he becomes overloaded (Chandler 1962).

Unfortunately, entrepreneurial managers seldom if ever change their style to accommodate the organization's need for a different, more professional style.

The ambivalent, paternalistic attitudes of the entrepreneur become a burden to the company as soon as the organization's structure demands sophistication.

The need for greater systematization places new demands on the entrepreneur, demands he may be unable to meet. At this point, the situation is ripe for the professional manager. . . . But this process is not automatic; many years of frustration . . . can elapse before it is completed. The entrepreneur is usually unwilling to give up his powerful position to provide for succession. (Zelaznik and Kets de Vries 1975).

Any influence that might threaten [the entrepreneur's] total control over the enterprise could trigger irrational acts. Sharing power, authority, and responsibility becomes difficult. He will resist any intrusion into his autonomy and dominance. . . . The entrepreneur tends to see acts by other individuals connected with the enterprise as attempts to remove him from control. Entrepreneurs, therefore, resist planning for management succession. (ibid.)

But, since, "the essential reshaping of administrative structure nearly always has to wait for a change in the top command" (Chandler 1962), this means awaiting the entrepreneurial manager's death or forced retirement.

The entrepreneurial style—its potential for empire building and its unfortunate possibilities—all show up quite clearly in the career of Henry Ford.

Fundamental to Henry Ford's misrule was a systematic, deliberate and conscious attempt to run the billion-dollar business without managers. The secret police that spied on all Ford executives served to inform Henry Ford of any attempt on the part of one of his executives to make a decision. When they seemed to acquire managerial authority or responsibility of their own, they were generally fired. And one of the chief reasons why Harry Bennett, Ford's police chief, rose during these years to almost supreme power in the organization was that he could never be anything but the old man's creature. (Drucker 1954)

The Ford company gradually moved toward professional management, but it took a few "generations" of management—and of Fords. Only gradually did the company incorporate the idea of delegating responsibility: Ford's grandson, Henry Ford II, liked to end disputes by saying, "It's my name over the door"; and Henry II fired Lee Iaccoca because he did not like the latter's independence. Now—finally—Ford (the company) is being run by professional managers.

THE PROFESSIONAL MANAGER

In comparison to entrepreneurial managers, professional managers have a cooler—somewhat distant—executive style. They make realistic plans; they delegate responsibilities; and they have more trust in their subordinates. "The predominant attribute of professional management is the delegation contract between the professional manager and his subordinates. The subordinates have the right to make decisions in their own areas as long as they act and perform in accordance to plan" (Tashakori 1980). The professional manager's job is to *assist* those below in reaching their objectives, while pushing decisions down to the lowest level appropriate (Drucker 1954). As one subordinate said of his professional-style superior: "[His] overall philosophy is to put people in charge of areas and leave it up to them to run their area in accordance with the basic overall plan. If there is a problem, he'll get involved in discussions. Otherwise, you're left to run your own part of the business in your own way" (quoted in Tashakori 1980). Thus, in practice, "the core characteristic of professional management is the professional manager's involvement in operations decisions by exception (that is to say, when there is a deviation from plan) rather than on a routine basis" (ibid.). To quote the management charter of General Electric's lamp division (a pacesetter in these matters): "All authority not expressly and in writing reserved to higher management is granted to lower management" (in Drucker 1954).

Looking at social evolution in abstract terms, "the advanced technology of the twentieth century necessitates information feedback and specialized skills, which are incompatible with an authority structure resting on blind obedience to orders issued through a chain of command. As a result, authority becomes depersonalized, and impersonal mechanisms of control displace old-fashioned discipline and command authority" (Blau and Meyer 1971, quoted in Hough 1973). *Voilà*—the professional manager.

THE EVOLUTION OF SOVIET MANAGEMENT

Within that huge organization that is the Soviet system, the Communist party itself—with its petty tutelage of state institutions—has in general taken the role of entrepreneurial manager. The party has delegated operational authority to various state organs; but it then watches over the shoulders of the responsible managers, and intrudes at every level.

Similarly, the Soviet state institutions have used an entrepreneurial style in managing their own areas of responsibility. The fact that a manager cannot get along without law violations is only proof that there are too many laws and not enough delegation. One study in Kalinnin Province showed that each leader received 200 director's orders and instructions a year. When polled, the leaders said that the problem with the director's orders was that they were impossible to fulfill, or that they were formulated in too general a manner (Antoniuk and Mochenov 1984c). Remember: Entrepreneurial managers often overly and contradictorily plan in their zeal for control.

The stress of complexity on the Soviets' hierarchic, pyramidal administrative system has been noted by Soviet management analysts. "With the growing size and complexity of the Soviet economy . . . [there is a] need to separate strategic and coordinating functions from operating management and control. According to Milner [in a book on managerial organization], . . . *both strategic and operational functions are concentrated at the highest level of management. Consequently, the command channels become overloaded* as problems are constantly referred upward in the hierarchy for resolution. Decisions are delayed and their quality is reduced" (Cocks 1980, emphasis added). The problem of command overload results from the party's entrepreneurial style of management, and would be ameliorated by a more professional style of delegation.

The Soviet political elite historically recruited entrepreneurial-style managers—"persons who are less open-minded and more authoritarian than corporate executives in the United States" (Meyer 1965). However, "with its growing heterogeneity and maturity, the Soviet political system too will have increasing need for negotiators and bargainers, for urbane and bland manipulators and persuaders rather than local and provincial replicas of the despotic man of steel who imposed his will on a reluctant and recalcitrant peasant population" (ibid.). But the "accomplishment [of industrialization] is likely to lead Soviet society out of one variety of totalitarianism into another: While the adoption of a crash program of industrialization requires the application of Stalinism, the totalitarianism of achieved industrialism conforms, roughly, to the modern corporation as a form of government" (Meyer 1964).[1]

But such an evolution of the Soviet system toward professional management—toward the rational and technocratic from a highly charged, personalistic, and political atmosphere—was predicted as much as 35 years ago (Moore 1954). Why—if it is happening at all—is it happening so slowly?[2]

It is my contention that this evolution is indeed occurring, albeit slowly. First, professionalization has occurred within the party itself. Since management requires more than overseeing (what—in a corporation—would be called) operations, *the party has not withered away in favor of technocratic state officials* (as Moore 1954 suggested). Instead, *party leaders themselves have become—as a group—technically more competent* (see Hough 1980 and Bialer 1980), *but only to the degree required for their general managerial functions*. Also, at the top of the party leadership, there has recently been a further shift in professional backgrounds from production engineers to lawyers and policemen/politicians—the latter presumably having more sophisticated people skills.

This is not to say that previous generations of executives did not rise on the basis of personal politics and social skills. They did. It is rather to say that the new generation of leaders will have a smoother, cooler, and (for reasons to be discussed) somewhat less personal style than their predecessors (albeit still quite personal in comparison to Western executives).

Professional managers are less authoritarian than their entrepreneur-style predecessors. Formerly, bosses ruled with *klyatvi, krigi, i kulaki* (curses, shouts, and fists). Nowadays, we have a Soviet management book with three pages on why and how not to be emotional, and why giving unnecessary offense is *nikulturni* (uncultured) (Stolyarenko 1983). The text quotes Lenin to the effect that given good class consciousness and discipline, leadership is like conducting an orchestra: It requires mild cues only (ibid.). Another Soviet text (Vendrov 1969) stresses the importance of good manners in avoiding conflicts. The authoritarian style of leadership—Soviet managers are informed—uses "administrative methods of influencing subordinates. The leader-autocrat does not consult his subordinates, takes decisions individually, [his] tone of address with subordinates is categorical, in the form of an order, [he] rejects initiatives, often turns to sanctions" (Papulov 1985). In contrast, the democratic style "is characterized by a combination of scientific principles of leadership with the maximal utilization of the initiative and creativity of subordinates, and the wide attraction of collective members to management. The tone of address of the leader to subordinates is comradely, inviting cooperation" (ibid.). Leaders must be able to command without "power methods" (ibid.).

Soviet managers are thus learning about delegation. They should never insist on doing what subordinates can do just as well. Trust your subordinates, they are told. Don't fear that they'll seem better than you (Vendrov 1969). (Note, however, that this reference is from 1969. Soviet management advisers have been saying these things for quite a while without very much happening in the way of true change. More on why, later.)

Both academics and politicians know that "the personnel of enterprises must be freed from the habit of waiting for or requiring instructions from above on the questions that now come within their competence" (a Soviet professor quoted in Hardt and Frankel 1971). Gruzinov—another Soviet professor—argued in 1979 that "the point basically is to achieve a sound and efficient balance in the distribution of powers and responsibilities between the centralized leadership and units further down the organization ladder . . . so that some initiative and independence can be preserved at the base" (quoted in Hoffman and Laird 1982). "It should become a hard and fast rule that decisions be made where (i.e. at the level on which) the most information exists about the given question, and where one may be assured that they will be implemented most competently" (ibid.). This sounds remarkably like what Peter Drucker (1954) wrote 25 years earlier about organizing U.S. management (see the description of the professional manager, above).

In arguing for more delegation of responsibility, Gruzinov was specifically writing about the control of foreign trade. This delegation would not be a loss of power for the state, he asserted, but would aid the center in "developing strategies for foreign trade policy and for improving business relations with industry." It is worth noting that Gruzinov was demoted within a few years of writing this, having lost the trade debate to more traditional proposals. It is also worth noting, however, that Gorbachev implemented decentralizing proposals in the field of foreign trade eight years after Gruzinov's recommendation.

More generally, in April 1985, Gorbachev "spoke of the need to release managers from the fetters of superfluous instructions, arguing that economic management was now at a level where accountability to higher organs could be decisively decreased" (Brown 1985). Since Gorbachev was in Moscow only six and a half years before becoming general secretary, he presumably remembers the experience of trying to be productive in the provinces (ibid.).

With regard to relations with his own subordinates, "[Gorbachev] listens also to specialist advisers and to his subordinates. British politicians who had extensive dealings with Gorbachev [in December 1984] observed that he had an easy relationship with the group he led. There was neither bullying from the one side nor obsequiousness from the other. Members of the group with something to say felt free to speak up, though there was never any doubt about Gorbachev's ultimate authority" (ibid.). Thus, he demonstrates how successful leaders create a virtuous circle: Delegating and empowering employees to be productive, they enhance their own productivity and thus gain more authority to delegate (see Kanter 1979).

"All historical epochs formulate their own conceptions of the leader's personality whose traits are conditioned objectively and are in keeping with the needs of society's development" (Stolyarenko 1983). In general, *the evolution of Soviet leaders is reflected in a shift from "command" to "leadership" competences.* This means a "shift from coercive to manipulative skills. . . . Behaviorally, the shift in competence is reflected in new styles of leadership" (Jowitt 1974). The new leaders "are rationalists, men who are well-trained, authoritarian but still appreciative of the need to receive expert information and to structure situations so as to elicit that information and support. They are 'win-oriented,' not neutral pragmatists or technocrats. They tend to be sober individuals with a penchant toward the puritanical. They contrast with the rather hedonistic apparatchik new-class cadre" (Jowitt 1975). (The "hedonistic apparatchik new-class cadre" refers to the Brezhnev generation, of which more later.)

The new type of leader is not the technocrat nor the traditional apparatchik, but a member of the "managerial political cadre." This new leader is distinguished by

two competences: first, his relatively high level of technical expertise and/or experience and second, and perhaps more importantly, his manipulative skills in sociopolitical settings. Unlike the technocrat and the [Brezhnev-generation] apparatchik, the manager is a political actor sensitive to the social–personal dimensions of a situation and possessed of a capacity and willingness to manipulate the social and personal dimensions of a situation to achieve his goals. It is this competence, a leadership competence, that distinguishes the political manager from both the command-oriented apparatchik and the rule-oriented technocrat. (Jowitt 1975).

If this description of political skills sounds familiar, it should—because these are precisely the skills that we have seen to be requisite for climbing the bureaucratic ladder. It is at this juncture, however, that we must begin to deal with history—the organizational and stylistic changes that have occurred over time—because the ladder-climbing process described in earlier sections of this book characterizes only one phase of Soviet history: All the stories and examples are relatively recent, coming essentially from the Brezhnev period—the period of the rise of the current generation of leaders.

But even during this recent period, the evolutionary changes described above have been easiest only in the lower echelons of the party leadership. Only gradually have they made themselves felt at higher levels.

Like any complex organization, the Soviet Union needed (and needs) to evolve to a different kind of management. But the evolutionary process has been slowed down by the size and isolation of the huge Soviet organization, and the fact that managers cannot be brought in from the outside but must rise up under their more entrepreneurial predecessors. The strongest factor in retarding evolutionary change, though, has been that entrepreneurial managers neither change their style nor let go of their power and positions. They have to die or be forcibly retired.

THE LEGACY OF ENTREPRENEUR STALIN

The ultimate entrepreneurial manager was the man who truly built and unified the Soviet system as we know it; Josef Stalin. Henry Ford's managerial style—with its intrusiveness and level skipping, its personalism, its paranoid fear of independent action, and its powerful secret police—was not very different from Stalin's. It was just applied to a much smaller and much more limited organization.

Stalin—like Ford—assigned his subordinates responsibilities, but then intruded—skipping levels of authority to become involved in all manner of decisions and debates. But Stalin had a much larger field of inquiry than Ford: linguistics, agriculture, and whatever else caught his interest. His secret police made Ford's look penny ante. His personal identification with his organization—the Soviet Union—was even greater than Ford's, to the point that Stalin personified and embodied the Soviet Union through his well-known cult of personality. He trusted no one. And most of all, he brooked no independence.

The purge of 1938–39, for example, included among its targets "the independent Red Directors who apparently were slow to accept Stalin's sovereignty over the economy. Lazar Kaganovitch characterized the thrust of the purge in industry in the following terms: 'In 1937 and 1938 the leading personnel of heavy industry were thoroughly renewed . . . in some branches it was found necessary to remove several layers.' However, he continued, ' . . . *we now have cadres who will perform . . . any tasks assigned to them by comrade Stalin'* " (Hardt and Frankel 1971, emphasis added).

The elimination of independent thinkers or those with any independent base for their authority extended throughout the whole Soviet system. It was especially thorough and ruthless within the Communist party itself, where almost all of the victors of the revolution (who attended the Seventeenth Party Congress—the "congress of victors") were removed, imprisoned, or executed to make way for Stalin's own creatures. No subordinate could have an independent notion. Whatever the arena, Stalin—like Ford—had a better idea.

After Stalin's death, the struggle between Georgy Malenkov and Nikita Khrushchev pitted a technocrat against a leader who was more like what we have called the "managerial political cadre." The latter—more the manipulator and politician—won. Khrushchev's criticism of the party—and of Stalin, in particular—and his struggle against the party bureaucracy in some ways moved the system away from unquestioning authoritarianism. (One of my subjects, you may recall, dated the beginning of the acceptability of "careful criticism" to the period immediately following Khrushchev's secret anti-Stalin speech.) The reduction in terror and paranoia and the almost constitutional rise in authority by the Central Committee in 1957 were shifts away from the extreme concentration of authority represented by Stalin and toward more respect for those below the top leaders—at least down to the level of Central Committee members.

Khrushchev, however, rose up under Stalin; and his leadership smacked of Stalin's style even as he himself criticized the memory of the boss. Khrushchev's adventurism, voluntarism, compaignism, and criminalization of failure were all remnants of the entrepreneurial style that he had experienced and utilized before attaining the position of first secretary. His rather willful imposition of various ideas—from the maize campaign to the great reorganizations that he forced on the party—were hardly the mark of professional management. His unrealistic planning—as if not just art and literature, but also economics were subject to the dictates of socialist realism—made professional "management by exception" an impossibility.

Having experienced the physical insecurity of the Stalin years, Soviet executives were in no mood for the job insecurity of Khrushchev's reorganizations. Remember that, in the Soviet Union, position is everything—except life itself. Thus, whereas the entrepreneurial and terrifying Stalin had to die to leave office, the somewhat less entrepreneurial and certainly less terrifying Khrushchev was forcibly retired. His replacement as first or general secretary of the Communist party was Leonid Brezhnev.

"BREZHNEVISM"

The Brezhnev generation of leaders were still heavily influenced by their many years under Stalin—both in terms of their own managerial style and in terms of their wish for, finally, some security and comfort. With Brezhnev's policy of "stability of cadres" and "trust in cadres," they attained that security.

The key fact about Khrushchev's successors, though, was their relative youth. Their seniors having been killed or imprisoned by Stalin, the Brezhnev generation had achieved high posts at a very young age, while Stalin was still alive. Having experienced tremendous insecurity along with their tremendous mobility, they filled all the top organizational levels with cadres of approximately the same age. And then they all grew old together.

The stagnation and corruption of the late Brezhnev years is not—as some say—intrinsic to the Soviet system, but was the result of both the policy of stability of cadres and the demographic synchronization of elites produced by the purges of the 1930s. Because of their predisposition to stability, bureaucracies require periodic succession at the top if they are to adapt to their environment: Without frequent succession, bureaucracies tend to lose the degree of flexibility that they need (Grusky 1961). Thus, systemic performance eventually suffers when there is a lack of leadership turnover.

Filling the Soviet Union's executive levels with people of the same age produced an "age lump" (Downs 1967), and the age lump—without any external organization to impose discipline—did the rest. An age lump appears in a Western organization when the organization reaches a plateau following a period of rapid growth. During the period of growth, a great number of young managers are brought on board. When growth slows, however, "there is a squeeze on the members of the age lump regarding promotions because so many of them attain the necessary qualifications all at once. Not all who are objectively suitable for promotion to the few high-level posts can be shifted upwards. Hence relatively low-level jobs continue to be occupied by very senior people" (ibid.). The more ambitious—the so-called climbers—leave the organization at that point unless they have no alternatives. But "a high proportion of the bureau's membership tends to be changed into conservers because of increasing age and the frustration of ambitions for promotion. In any organization, officials tend to become conservers as they get older if they are not in the mainstream of promotion to the top. Hence the whole bureau tends to become more conserver-dominated as members of this lump become older" (ibid.).

Low-opportunity personnel—people with little or no hope of advancement—have the behavioral stigmata of "the stuck": They minimize risk, show little initiative, tend toward ritualistic comformity, jealously guard their domains of responsibility, and oversupervise their subordinates (Kanter 1977). Quoting one young manager: "A person who has stabilized [in other words, is going nowhere] feels less secure. . . . So you won't take risks. When you set goals for your department, you set them low. You won't put your neck on the block. If you find out you did something wrong, you panic and try to cover your tracks." The only way you can go is down, so you protect yourself. Similarly, a personnel specialist commented on static hierarchies: "Managers aren't developing people, they are expecting of them. They won't try anything new, even if it might mean an improvement. All they want are enough results to prove they've met their targets. If they can't get results, then they sharpen their pencils so they can get them on paper" (Kanter 1977). Also, they want preapproval from every potentially relevant person, thus slowing all decisions and projects (ibid.; see also Kanter and Stein 1979; and Gouldner 1954).

People who are stymied in their careers feel powerless and constrict those below them, who in turn become less productive—causing more stagnation, and so on, in a vicious circle (Kanter 1979). Low power and low advancement–potential managers favor "more directive, rigid, and authoritarian techniques of leadership, seeking control over subordinates. Subordinates are their primary frame of reference, and they find it important to 'lord it over' group members. They also do not help talented members of the group get ahead (perhaps finding them too threatening) and select immediate assistants of mediocre rather than outstanding talent. . . . [They] are extremely authoritarian and paternalistic" (Kanter 1977). They do not delegate much; they control communication in and out of their departments; and they interfere in the operational work of their subordinates. (This they have in common with entrepreneurial managers.)

Such stuck managers guard their own domains jealously, and worry about their own welfare and that of their department to the exclusion of the welfare of the organization as a whole ("suboptimization"). Their peer groups are oriented toward protection and reassurance of their members. Also, their low career mobility is correlated with low commitment to the organization since, in general, one's belief in organizational fairness is proportional to one's own chances of promotion. Thus, they are concerned only with basic survival and extrinsic rewards: the economic or social payoff of the job for themselves as individuals (Kanter 1977).

As they grow old together, conservers are interested only in security and the avoidance of conflict.

The search for security and the avoidance of high risks establish the climate for consensus leadership. The style itself, however, is not born of a rational, carefully thought out approach. It is reflexive, a product of tradition, an attachment to certain ideals that nourish belief in oneself, the group, the corporation. . . . The [consensus] style is self-perpetuating and resists change. (Zelaznik and Kets de Vries 1975)

This search for conflict-free consensus in a context in which every manager has no chance to advance, is guarding a particular domain, and has job security, leads to each manager essentially being left to run his own show in his own way (and, usually, for his own benefit). Just as in Western universities—where tenure is granted to promote greater freedom of expression and winds up allowing for less self-control (Williams, Sjoberg and Sjoberg 1980)—tenure is decentralizing in the sense of loosening controls.[3] This produces a diversity of interests, with each manager pursuing his self-interest and each bureaucracy cultivating its own garden. (This is what Hough saw as "institutional pluralism"; see Hough 1977.)

Given tenure, there are few or no meritocratic consequences to one's behavior; and so, quality of work doesn't matter much. This means that subordinates tend to be chosen on a more personalistic than meritocratic basis. Thus, people are rewarded for attitudes instead of (or as much as) skills, and loyalty instead of (or as much as) talent. The whole reward system is structured to induce personal loyalty. This is necessary so that subordinates will collude in their boss's "front" and so help maintain their security.[4]

Similarly, in U.S. nonprofit organizations, people expect security in trade for their low mobility and low salaries. Since it is also hard to measure productivity in these organizations, issues of loyalty and personal relations predominate. "People polish attitudes instead of performance" (Kennedy 1980).

The disadvantages of such personalism in personnel policy are similar to the disadvantages of nepotism and tribalism (Downs 1967): Relatives enjoy great leeway regarding nonvital issues since it is so difficult to replace them with equally loyal officials, and nepotism discourages ambitious nonrelatives. Thus, organizational performance suffers.

In John DeLorean's opinion, centralization at General Motors (which made it more Soviet-like than some decentralized U.S. corporations) and the practice of managers being promoted on the basis of personal associations led to the increasing involvement of GM central management in operations to the neglect of long-term strategic planning. For example, the engineering policy group spent its time designing bumpers, and missed the 1970s move toward small cars. Top managers protected their own positions by promoting mediocre underlings—a practice DeLorean called "promotion of the unobvious choice"—thereby ensuring that the new manager was totally dependent on the patron. DeLorean's attempts to evade the oversupervision inherent in the system—for example, in his unapproved but successful introduction of the "muscle car" at Pontiac—led to increased supervision, his being viewed as a non–team player, and his eventual decision to leave (Wright 1979). Thus, initiative is forced out of such an organization.

In general, the corruption, lack of initiative, and other various possibilities for organizational pathology are no different in the Soviet system than in other organizations. For every example of Soviet corruption, misuse of resources, crazy incentives, and so on, I came across a similar case in some Western corporation or bureaucracy. Both institutional differences and cultural differences, however, make Soviet organizational pathology more difficult to counteract or control: There are no outside police organizations and no institutional checks and balances, on the one hand, and no (or few) internalized psychological controls, on the other (see Klugman 1986).

The bureaucrat or "minimum man" who is externally oriented toward pleasing and coordinating with others in the group, who values consensus above all else, who "functions like radar . . . search[ing] for contact with people on the outside" (Zelaznik and Kets de Vries 1975) replaced the more self-directed, dominating "maximum man"—the inner-directed entrepreneur. While Khrushchev was transitional, Brezhnev was the true minimum man.[5]

Brezhnev's minimalism is not belied by his "emergence as the preeminent figure within the hierarchy [which] must be read with some caution. . . . His initial selection for the post of general secretary is best understood as the result of high-level deliberations among Khrushchev's opponents who chose him as the most generally acceptable candidate; there is little to indicate that he was himself the prime mover of the plot that ousted Khrushchev in 1964, nor did he incautiously overplay his hand to consolidate power in the immediate post-coup period" (Kelley

1980a). While Brezhnev had all of the people skills required of the professional manager, he lacked the initiative, goals, energy, and willingness to maintain discipline ever at the cost of losing his reputation for warmth.

Or perhaps he just lacked an appropriate mandate: Having been elevated to implement a policy of stability of cadres, how could he impose discipline? Tenure took away his disciplinary sticks, even if he had wanted sticks. On the other hand—with no dismissals, and given the age lump—there were few promotions to offer. Thus, tenure and the age lump also took away the carrots that could induce people to work in the overall organization's interest.

Eventually, Soviet leaders became aware of the debilitating effects of the trust-in-cadres policy. By the time of the Twenty-fourth Party Congress in 1971, the themes were balanced between "trust" and "discipline," and Brezhnev spoke of how "trust in and respect for people is combined with principled exactingness toward them" (quoted in Kelley 1980a). "Competence" emerged as a key in the evaluation of cadres, but an unwillingness to impose discipline undermined this rhetoric. Ultimately, the various reform proposals advanced (mostly by Aleksei Kosygin) in the 1960s and 1970s—all aimed at a more professional management of the economy—came a cropper on the regime's unwillingness to "kick ass."

SUMMARY

The managerial style of the Soviet system has been moving from its entrepreneurial past into a professional future, but the extremes of Stalinism left a remnant—an age lump—that slowed the system's evolution. Only with the passing of the Brezhnev generation—the last to gain power in the entrepreneurial days under Stalin—could professional management appear at the highest levels of Soviet leadership.

NOTES

1. In a similar vein, "any pressure for rapid political change that is applied by the emerging managerial elite is much more likely to be directed toward the establishment of a technocratic order than toward the creation of a liberal democracy" (Azrael 1966).

2. One question raised by this approach is whether such phenomena are comparable across cultures. I think so: First, the notion of managerial evolution applied in this context is not so different from the pure modernization arguments that have been applied cross-culturally (e.g., Gerschenkron 1962). And, after all, "organizational systems are *cultural* answers to the problems encountered by human beings in achieving their collective ends" (Crozier 1973, emphasis added). Crozier added that, in analyzing these cultural answers, "two central concepts are power and uncertainty." In fact, this relationship between power

and the control of uncertainty is readily applied to organizations of all kinds (Pfeffer 1981), uniting interorganizational and cross-cultural comparisons. One cross-cultural analysis of organizational behavior within a multinational company spread across 40 nations found that three of the four key dimensions distinguishing the various national styles were "power-distance" or authoritarianism, "uncertainty avoidance," and collectivism–individualism (Hofstede 1980a and b). Russians would—I assume, in keeping with Inkeles's findings (1968)—score significantly higher than Americans on power-distance, uncertainty avoidance, and collectivism. (I do not know how to do the comparison on the fourth dimension: "masculinity–femininity.") These differences should imply that Soviet modernization will take somewhat different forms than in the United States—specifically implying less pluralism, stronger and more comprehensive authority, and more centralized control. This is in keeping with the structure of a mono-organizational society, which is to say that the evolutionary process will occur within culturally determined forms.

3. See Klugman (1986) on the decentralizing deterioration of discipline under stability of cadres, and Jowitt (1983) on "neotraditional degeneration" and the growth of informal and corrupt practices since Stalin.

4. In Western corporations, this description applies to secretaries (the kind that type), not to executives (Kanter 1977).

5. This last "comparison can be illustrated nicely by examining, as Jerry Hough has done, the content of accolades addressed to the two leaders at the peak of their powers. In 1961, at the Twenty-Second Party Congress, 'almost no one spoke of [Khrushchev] with real affection, and the words of praise stressed his "tireless energy," "revolutionary fervor," "daring," "decisiveness," "principles" and "demanding" nature, and so forth. The words "smelnyy" (bold) and "smelost" (boldness) appeared with particular frequency' [Hough 1976]. In contrast, at the Twenty-Fifth Party Congress in 1976, the strongest emphasis in the effusive praise for Brezhnev was placed upon such personal qualities as 'deep humanity, considerateness, and attentiveness to people,' as well as his modesty. In particular, it was often said that Brezhnev has 'established comradeliness, trust, and a respectful relation to people in the party,' has created 'a good atmosphere for work,' a 'situation in which people can breathe easily, work well, and live peacefully'; 'has an ability to establish an atmosphere of trust, respect, and dedication to the standards among people' and 'to coordinate (nalazhivat) strong and friendly common work by a large number of people'; under his leadership, 'the Central Committee consistently raises the role of the local party organs, widely consults with them, alternatively examines initiatives and proposals from the localities' " (Hough 1976, being quoted in Bunce and Echols 1980).

10. PERSONNEL POLICY AND ECONOMIC REFORM

The bureau will experience a crisis of continuity when the age lump arrives at the normal retirement age. Almost all of the upper echelons will suddenly be vacated by members of the group that will have dominated the bureau's policies for many years. As a result, the bureau will go through a time of troubles as its remaining members struggle for control over its policies and resources.

A. Downs, 1967

The forces for old habits and against change are strong in many organizations. The reason that Citicorp, Morgan and others have been able to renew themselves continuously without turmoil is they have a host of bureaucracy busters in their systems. To shake up the status quo, Citicorp and Morgan reorganize with great regularity and constantly move people around.

R. H. Waterman,
interviewed in the *New York Times*,
March 31, 1987

The problems that have beset the Soviet system are not unique. Other organizations have struggled with the consequences of age lumps, over-centralization, and bureaucratization. This chapter further analyzes the Soviet dilemma in light of the experience of other organizations; it looks at both the possibilities for reform and the organizational and psychological sources of opposition to it, and defines the role that personnel policy—discipline, compensation, promotion, and job rotation—might play in improving systemic performance.

CENTRALIZATION AND DELEGATION

"Stability of cadres" led to a pathological form of decentralization in which executives pursued their individual interests instead of the interests of the overall system. At the same time, the official economic incentives in the Soviet Union have encouraged "suboptimization": "Soviet enterprise managers pursue the interests of their individual enterprises rather than that of the larger organization of which the enterprise is only a part" (Granick 1972).

Suboptimization has been in part a result of the strategy that Soviet authorities have used to keep decision making highly centralized: the establishment of objective indicators, which local managers are supposed to maximize. By picking objective indicators, the central authorities restrict the scope of local decision making, and focus the local mangers' attention on the centrally chosen variables.

However, the verticality of the controls makes horizontal, interinstitutional relations difficult. Coordination is thus centralized; but, as discussed in the preceding chapter, it overloads the command system. Because of this overload, the indicators chosen for monitoring must be to some degree crude. Thus, they can never provide the kind of guidance provided by markets in the West: The crudity of the indicators guarantees that maximizing them is not, in general, truly the best use of local resources. But local managers will maximize those variables whether or not it is in the interest of the overall organization. (If the indicator is tons of product produced, for example, they will produce heavy products. Also, quality—which is hard to measure—has traditionally been slighted in favor of quantity.) Thus, while decision making has been centralized, the incentives established to maintain this centralization themselves promote suboptimization—a perverse kind of decentralization.

Meanwhile, planning from the achieved level—"the ratchet principle"—is another aspect of the attempt to maximize enterprise output. It too has debilitating effects, specifically undermining innovation and attempts to improve efficiency (see, for example, Norr 1986), because of the unwillingness of managers to sacrifice current output in order to modernize. Thus, the planning process forces the local manager to pursue goals that are both short term at the expense of the long term, and localistic at the expense of the national interest.

Why haven't the party organs—which, after all, have a centralizing and coordinating role—been able to prevent suboptimization? The fact is that the local party secretaries have been judged in large part on the basis of the economic performance of their regions—often on the performance of the one main industry or agricultural activity in the area (Hough 1969 and 1971). This invites the same kind of suboptimizing behavior from local party officials, for all that they are supposed to serve a centralizing function. To control this tendency, the central authorities must closely manage their local division chiefs (the local and regional party secretaries), implying still further centralization of authority within the party itself. Thus, authority is closely held in corporate headquarters—that is, in the Central Committee Secretariat and Politburo.

But, again, such a high degree of centralization is clumsy. As Gorbachev said to the Central Committee: "We must realize that the time when management consisted of orders, bans and calls has gone. It is now clear to everybody that such methods can no longer be employed, for they are simply ineffective" (New York *Times*, June 26, 1987).

Suboptimization implies that the system is—in terms of its performance—not centralized or coordinated enough. But the overly centralized, entrepreneurial Soviet style of leadership is already overloading the decision makers, resulting in poor efficiency. The solution is clear: While heretofore the system has centralized decision making in a way that fostered decentralized motivations (suboptimization), to improve its functioning it needs to do the reverse. *The system must centralize motivation, while it delegates decision making.*[1]

What must be delegated is operational—not strategic—authority. Such delegation, therefore, does not mean that top executives are giving up any power—far from it. Instead, they are making their authority more effective by focusing it. In Western corporations it has become clear that delegating more responsibility via a decentralized, divisional structure can shorten lines of communication, reduce levels of management, and thus actually increase the ability of top management to run its organization. In 1946, for example, General Electric undertook such a reorganization, reducing it hierarchies from a starting point of 20–25 levels between the chief executive and the workers to an end point of only 7–9 levels (Downing 1967).

Applied to the Soviet Union, this kind of reform is *not*—as some have suggested—"an uneasy mixture of conservative and reformist elements" (Gustafson and Mann 1986). Gorbachev does *not* need to "break decisively with the centralizing, mobilizational style of the past." (ibid.). He needs to keep strategic functions centralized while delegating operational responsibilities, and establish a centralizing structure of incentives and discipline.

The party itself could delegate more authority to its lower organs, for example. Within enterprises, the primary party organization has at least theoretically the capacity to perform some of the roles of what Kanter has called a "parallel organization" (Kanter 1979 and 1983). Such "parallel structures" are "flat, flexible, but formal problem-solving and governance organizations that serve to supplement bureaucracy and exist side by side with it, not to replace it" (Stein and Kanter 1980). The parallel organization provides a setting for cross-hierarchical task forces for problem solving. The parallel organization is a structure outside of, but complementary to, the industrial hierarchy and the formal assignment of jobs. The best examples of successful parallel organizations are the "quality circles" used in Japanese management. Parallel organizations have been a potent force for change in organizations that have set them up, but they require receptiveness on the part of higher-ups to the ideas of the worker activists who are mobilized by the program. This kind of function is what the primary party organization was supposed to do all along (see Hough 1969), but it is possible that it could actually work if the primary party organization were strengthened within a party more interested in delegating operational authority.

Some attempts have been made to use the party organizations in this way. In the Leningrad association called Pozitron, for example, sociologists have been investigating the "moral-psychological" climate of the work collectives, including issues such as the formation of subgroups, laxity, indifference, indiscipline, and conflicts. Under the advice of the sociologists, one section of the Mezon factory undertook a number of recommended tasks, including seminars with *partgruporgs* (party group organizations—suborganizations within the broader party organization of the enterprise and association) "designed to strengthen party influence in the brigades." The partorg "rallied the collective." Workers' views were solicited, leading to many suggestions for improving the "moral-psychological" climate. In the Kirov factory, the partkom organized thrice monthly meetings of sections with their partgruporgs to analyze conditions. At Lenpoligrafmash, the partkom instituted *politdni* (political days), with meetings on preset topics and with plant leaders meeting with each collective (Ershov 1986).

Is this just propagandistic nonsense, with people dozing off in the meetings? Whatever one may think of the language with which these meeting are described, they might actually be playing the role of parallel organizations, quality circles, and so on, with similar kinds of motivational or problem-solving benefits for the organization. Even if they are not doing all this yet, they might in the future, if the partorgs are given sufficient responsibility and authority.

Alternatively, workers' councils or other new structures established by the "democratization" campaign might serve the same function. To the degree that the regime uses such groups instead of the existing party structure, this implies a distrust of the party apparat and/or a belief that workers are so turned off to the party that they won't respond to it for such mobilization.

More broadly, the issue of suboptimization and the need for delegation within the government and the economy are potentially addressed by a number of structural changes that have been proposed. Here we will briefly examine the possibilities for structural change and explore the potential role of personnel policy in helping or hindering such change.

The announced plans for reform allow (in their vague way) for a much greater degree of delegation. They include the idea of making the planning organizations more purely strategic—not operational—in their authority. Similarly, they hope ultimately to devolve control of pricing from the central authorities, and devolve most managerial responsibilities from the ministries to the production associations and individual enterprises. This shift—if it happens—will be a clear systemic change from entrepreneurial to professional management.

Coordination under the new reforms is to be left, (in part, at least) to an internal market: Enterprises will negotiate direct—horizontal—contracts with one another. But horizontal relations have been difficult in the past. They have either been too cohesive or not cohesive enough. For individuals, these poles correspond to "clan nepotism" at the cohesive extreme, and factional conflict at the other end of the spectrum. For interorganizational relations, they correspond to localism on the one hand, and poor coordination on the other.

These problems have in part been a reflection of the lack of intermediate institutional structures to regulate interinstitutional relations. All horizontal relations were (supposed to be) indirect, flowing vertically through higher authorities. In fact, the science and production associations were formed, in part, to make external (interenterprise) relations internal. "Instead of being guided by its own special interests and parochial perspectives, each unit is to be motivated by common objectives, by 'only one concept: ours.' The associational forms are seen as means by which to transform 'awkward external cooperation into harmonious intrafirm cooperation' " (Cocks 1976). The proposed reform's direct interfirm contracts will supply the missing intermediate institutions— agreements that will not directly involve the central authorities, but will presumably have recourse to enforcement by them.

ORGANIZATIONAL RESISTANCE TO REFORM

In general, decisions to flatten pyramidal organizational structures are made in order to shift decision making downward and to secure wider participation and commitment. The underlying effect of such shifts, however, is to squeeze senior and middle management and reduce their power—thus creating a natural opposition.

In fact, when—in particular—it is a new leadership making such a reorganization, there can be "confusion between what is good for the organization and what is necessary for the chief executive and his staff (given the problems of developing confident relationships with people who, at the outset, are not dependent upon the chief executive exclusively for their power base and autonomy)" (Zelaznik and Kets de Vries 1975). Many a reorganization really serves only to bind people to the new chief executive, although the reorganization cannot publicly be explained as such (ibid.). This is to say that what looks like reorganization may be just a power grab by the new chief executive and crew. Thus, the resistance to change by those senior and middle managers being squeezed out may have some justification, or a least a handy rationalization.

In the case of the Soviet Union, there are now a number of factors promoting "bureaucratic sabotage"—defined as the resistance of the permanent staff of a bureaucracy to the policies of their superior, especially one who is new to the office. First of all, such sabotage is a characteristic feature of changes in bureaucratic leadership. In the general case, the resistance comes from the old staff having developed understandings of which the newcomer is ignorant (Gouldner 1952). In the Soviet case, the old staff have developed understandings of which the newcomer disapproves.

Furthermore, for all the changes at the top, the Soviet bureaucracy is still filled with officeholders who have grown comfortable and secure with both their positions and the old system of which they are a part. Their lack of mobility has reinforced their tendency to become conservers. And "if [conservers] are numerous but do not occupy key posts, a bureau may adopt changes in principle; but its leaders will have trouble implementing them" (Downs 1967).

Soviet executives are practiced in defending themselves from the dictates of higher authority. Each enterprise manager, "in order to be always prepared to defend himself, issues a tremendous number of written orders and directives. It is completely immaterial that no one carries them out. What is important is that they can be used for defense in case of a plant investigation" (Ryapolov 1966). Recall also the anticrime campaign in which a friend of one of my subjects participated as a student: It was certainly productive in promoting careers, if not in stopping crime. For years, economic and political managers have been submitting glowing reports describing how they complied with the demands made on them, while in fact doing as they pleased and paying only lip service.

In the face of demands for change—and short of outright falsification—managers can also practice "negative timing."

[The executive] initiates action, but the process of expedition is retarded. He is considering, studying, and planning for the problem; there are difficulties to be overcome and possible ramifications which must be considered. He is always in the process of doing something but never quite does it, or finally he takes action when it is actually too late. In this way the executive escapes the charge of dereliction, and at the same time the . . . program "dies on the vine." (Martin and Sims 1956).

In dealing with such opposition, a new leader generally resorts to formalized controls and the replacement of strategic personnel. The leader makes new appointments, and the new appointees are then obligated—which establishes extraformal ties that can be drawn on to achieve the new leader's goals (Gouldner 1952). This process is ongoing in the Soviet case. What is now required is for the new high-level appointees to appoint new subordinates of their own, and so on down the line. This process of change is a difficult struggle.

"It takes a powerful leader to be willing to risk short-term deprivations in order to bring about desired long-term outcomes" (Kantor 1979); and if his or her individual authority is not great enough, the leader must find or create as large a coalition as possible to support the new policies. This is because even partial opposition can undermine complex and interdependent reforms. "Making a decision in a context in which there is enough opposition so that implementation in an interdependent set of actors is problematic, is doomed by implementation problems. Thus, in formal organizations instead of the observation of the principle of the minimum winning coalition size, what is observed more often is the maximum possible coalition size principle" (Pfeffer 1981). In the Soviet case, such a maximum coalition—if it is to exist and work at all—must somehow form around the conjunction of mobilization and discipline (a traditional and ideologically nonthreatening theme), and economic restructuring (a more radical and ideologically risky idea).

All this takes enormous time and effort to implement. As of this writing, Roger Smith has taken six years to restructure General Motors, hopes to see some results soon, and still isn't done. And the Soviet Union is a lot bigger and more complex then GM. As Mikhail Gorbachev has said: "Those who think that we can restructure in a month or two are naive! This has taken shape over years and will demand massive efforts and titanic labors" (*New York Times*, December 22, 1986). One of these titanic labors will be overcoming the kind of opposition described above. This will require the imposition of discipline—which is to say, the end of "trust in cadres."

PSYCHOLOGICAL RESISTANCE TO REFORM

There is another and deeper source of resistance to Soviet reform—one that has its roots in the Russian style of childrearing (see Appendix A). Russian psychological patterns revolve around issues of control and dependency, and current organizational structures are adapted to this psychology.

In the face of decentralizing reform, both central authorities and local managers will tend to experience a fear of disconnection and a sense of disorientation. Exclusion, isolation, and disconnection are—after all—a form of punishment in Russian society.[2] A central planner who is given responsibility for a sector or industry will feel enormous anxiety if he or she cannot guide the charge in the only way the planner knows how. To give the ministries a purely advisory role—focused on strategy— would relieve them of this anxiety, but in fact the "state contracts" that they must administer tie them back into responsibility for industry performance. Similarly, local managers will certainly be anxious if they are judged on their performance and influenced in their careers by people who cannot supply guidance on exactly how to perform. If local management is disconnected from central control, both groups will tend to find ways to reconnect.

After all, Soviet executives have gotten to their positions of authority within the existing system; and, as much as they might complain about various constraints, they are security minded. They most likely want to do better within the system they know, with an incremental increase in their own authority—rather than shift to an unfamiliar system in which they might not succeed. Workers, too, fear unemployment and so are chary of reform. So it is not just the central elite that is threatened by major reform, it is every participant in Soviet industry.

Traditionally, psychological security for Russians flows from gratified dependency, external control, and a sense of membership, as well as feelings of mastery and the privilege of intrusive authority for those who have incorporated a need to be controlling. Servility up and arrogance down has meant that everyone was secure within the hierarchy.

Given this setting, there are only two ways to improve job performance and reduce corruption: One is to help the populace internalize psychological controls, instead of having control imposed; the other is to tighten external controls. But the former strategy requires a major cultural shift; it can occur only slowly, and only under conditions in which the latter strategy has been cunningly applied. (See Chapter 11 for a discussion of the psychological consequences of increasing discipline while decentralizing authority.) Thus, the system must in some ways tighten the "moral corset" of external control via discipline campaigns and decreased job security—effecting "a meritocratic permanent purge."

Furthermore, central authority must be more impersonal than heretofore. Personalism undermines identification with the system. Personal authority creates personal loyalties, instead of systemic loyalty. It promotes local networks, suboptimization, self-serving behavior by superiors, and flattery and bribery by inferiors. It gives cause for resentment in inferiors, and thus leads to poor discipline. It prevents the appropriate delegation of authority.

Personal authority is undisciplined authority. To promote discipline without resorting to terror, authority itself must be disciplined. Personal ties and personal loyalties must no longer be the sine qua non of success, nor can they any longer provide immunity to performance-based discipline.

DISCIPLINE

As Gorbachev said in a speech in Leningrad on May 17, 1985:

Those who do not intend to adjust and who are an obstacle to solving these new tasks must simply get out of the way—get out of the way, not be a hindrance. We cannot regard the interests of one person as being higher than the interests of society as a whole. We are for observing Leninist norms in the selection, placing, and education of cadres. . . . [Lenin] taught that one has to assess people in accordance with their political, businesslike, and moral qualities. (FBIS, May 22, 1985)

More simply, the Central Committee resolution of January 28, 1987, favored "the infusion of new blood into the leadership and the replacement of leaders who have proved no match for new tasks or compromised themselves by improper conduct" (*New York Times*, January 29, 1987).

But who is to guard the guardians? Who will administer this discipline? And what is to prevent the appointment of new leaders on the same personalistic bases as their predecessors?

In part, discipline must be top down, passed down the party hierarchy. But because of the necessity of cooperative relationships between superiors and subordinates, there are limits to discipline within a hierarchy. Also, as mentioned earlier, "colleagues within a single promotional hierarchy usually avoid making enemies of each other through excessive conflict. Each knows he might some day be in a position where the other's decisions could seriously affect his own welfare" (Downs 1967). Thus, because of intertwining career paths, the party's ability to discipline the state is almost as limited as its ability to discipline itself.

One organizational strategy to deal with this problem is to encourage accuracy in communications by giving overlapping responsibility to different bureaus—or monitoring agencies—that have separate career paths. The system needs a separate organization—a KGB, for example—to do its monitoring. This does not imply that such an organization must avail itself of the KGB's traditional methods. On the other hand, it is surely not accidental (as the Soviets like to say) that, in this time of the reimposition of discipline, there have of late been so many KGB and police alumni in the Politburo, as well as party officials formerly exiled into diplomatic assignments.

Glasnost' has received much attention in the West as an apparent liberalization, but it is also a disciplinary tool. In part, glasnost' is a form of using lower level people as fronts for criticizing competitors, and specifically using the press as a parallel organization (separate hierarchy)—like the KGB—to expose activities that the top authorities wish to root out. (It also represents increased generalized trust—a theme to which we will return.)

In fact, glasnost'—as an au courant political term—goes back to the early 1970s, but was apparently confined to narrow official circles—with the term used to refer only to the consultative policy process of the Brezhnev years. To quote from a paper on Soviet administration written in 1973:

"Today the Soviet call for "criticism and self-criticism" is perhaps stronger than ever, but the official watchword is glasnost'—greater *intra-party* publicity, openness, and frankness about contemporary accomplishments and shortcomings. At CPSU meetings especially, a spirit of cooperative problem-solving—free of personal recriminations, self-serving and bombast—is now strongly encouraged and expected. . . . Significantly, the call for glasnost' seems to be accompanied by freer discussion of alternative methods of policy implementation and—more cautiously and subtly—of alternative policy-making procedures and alternative policies. (Hoffman 1973, emphasis added)

This sounds much like what has been described here as "careful criticism." Nowadays, glasnost' has been expanded to allow the press to function as a monitoring agency, and nonparty people to express their wishes and criticisms.

Whatever the mechanism of discovering poor performance, suboptimization, foot dragging, and personal self-seeking, however, the practitioners of these deviations will have to be punished or removed. This vulnerability has consequences: "A mid-level official in a trade ministry recently confided to an American friend over dinner that, for the first time in his life, he was scared about his job" (*New York Times*, March 8, 1987). Perhaps this mid-level official will work a littler harder—or just butter up his boss more—as a result. Which course he takes depends in part on the style of that boss, on that boss's boss, and on that official's reading of his own future possibilities.

Discipline can make a difference in economic performance. A series of high-level firings in the Railroad Ministry, for example, were the opening shots in a series of measures designed to improve the discipline of managers. These changes were characterized in *GUDOK*, the railroad newspaper, as "measures for improving the style and methods of work, increasing the responsibility of cadres, and raising the level of economic activity" (quoted in Kontorovich 1985). Included were restrictions limiting revisions of the plan. This cut both ways: While insisting that managers meet their plans, it restricted the authority of planners to alter them. Thus, both planners and managers had to negotiate more realistic plans in the first place.

There were, in fact, measurable improvements in the performance of the railroad system. However, it is important to note that, along with disciplinary changes, more responsibility was delegated to lower level managers. If efficiency is to improve, *delegation and discipline must go hand in hand*.

Do the current shake-ups in personnel represent a systemic change or just a new cast of characters? In other words, will the new broom keep sweeping clean? To evaluate this, we must look for the meritocratic ouster (that is, for poor performance) of officials appointed under Gorbachev. (Surely, they cannot all become successes.) This would imply that he is not just bringing in his own Soviet Mafia family, but is genuinely interested in performance. Gorbachev's criticisms of Gosplan Chairman Nikolai Talyzin and Gosnab Chairman Lev Voronin in a speech to the Central Committee on June 25, 1987, may be the example that we are looking for. However, both of these figures are associated with Prime Minister Ryzhkov, who may himself be lukewarm about Gorbachev's plans for the economy (*New York Times*, June 26, 1987). Whether Yeltsin's ouster as Moscow party chief and candidate Politburo member is an example of meritocratic discipline is also subject to debate. It thus remains for the future to find clear examples of Gorbachev firing his own appointees on a meritocratic basis. Until that time, his appointments must be seen as political (in the personal sense) as much as—or more than—meritocratic (while recognizing that good performance requires good political skills).

INCENTIVES: COMPENSATION

Discipline is not enough, however. More carrots are needed, not just more sticks. While the policy of stability of cadres removed the stick of dismissal, the lack of opportunities in a stagnant hierarchy removed the carrot of possible promotion; so neither was available to centralize motivation. The only carrots around came from localism and corruption. Increased mobility and opportunity should make a difference, but how might incentives be structured so as to centralize motivation and prevent suboptimization?

First, the compensation system can be changed. In U.S. corporations, bonuses are partly deferred salary and partly performance based. Significantly, they are tied to corporate—not divisional—profits. Thus, they do not foster suboptimization. These bonuses have some tendency to overemphasize current profits, but top people do get stock options to encourage them to take a long-range view.

In Soviet industry, bonuses are up to 40–60 percent of base salaries. Fulfillment of the plan is generally required to get any bonus at all, so there has been an enormous difference between just missing and just achieving the plan. Soviet bonuses extend much farther down into the ranks of lower management than in U.S. industry, and thus have unified all levels of management around their desire to suboptimize. And bonuses depend on the results of the individual subunit, factory, and so on, further encouraging suboptimization. Moreover, bonuses are based on short-term results, and are paid immediately—not spread out, like in U.S. companies—and therefore foster short-term suboptimization and avoidance of long-term investment. Also, the lack of promotional opportunities even more strongly focuses managers on bonuses (Granick 1973).

In general, the Soviet bonus structure seems aimed at inducing intensity of effort, even if this effort can be only crudely directed by the centrally formulated criteria (Granick 1961 and 1972). "American firms, to the contrary, seem to take effort for granted"(ibid.).

Objective bonuses mean that the central planners have not delegated any responsibility for choosing priorities. While U.S. managers have to hit the plan on certain indicators, they are not expected to maximize. As long as they hit their targets, they are free to devote spare resources to secondary priorities of their choice (Granick 1972).

While objective criteria do maintain centralization, they also reflect the engineering mentality described earlier. In part because of this mentality, it has been hard to recognize and acknowledge the system's inability to specify sufficiently useful success criteria. This desire for engineering-style "objectivity" also shows up in Soviet management literature regarding the development and evaluation of cadres. Attestatsia (certification examinations) and objective evaluation of personnel is strongly valued, at least by academics (but even they include an "objective" factor of political maturity).

Although the Soviet system officially minimizes subjectivity, it creeps in through the backdoor deals that are made while negotiating about the plan and obtaining materials, through the falsification of statistics, and so forth. Seeking objectivity has been part of an attempt to escape the power of the entangling, personalistic networks that have in fact determined promotions and rewards. Thus, *the system has been split between the objectivity of performance measures and the extremely personalistic maneuvering by which targets have been set, manipulated, and achieved.*

Objectivity—when it is not being personalistically manipulated—often degenerates into mechanistic approaches. This mechanistic approach was the essential basis of the dissatisfaction expressed about bonus criteria during research conducted at three enterprises. Among these groups were named the following: inadequate connection between bo-

nuses and real results of work and attitude toward work; equal distribution of bonuses among workers, occasionally as a result of the bonus
criteria; receipt of bonuses "in turn" (*po ocheredi*), as a result of unofficially
set-up practices; dependence of bonus on plan fulfillment by another
collective, rather than one's own; workers' unfamiliarity with regulations
on bonuses; ineffectual control by social organizations over activity of
leadership on distribution of bonuses; and the limited number of individuals taking part in decision making on bonuses (Antoniuk and Mochenov 1984a). Note that their criticisms reveal that the workers have been
experiencing the demotivating effects of equal pay for unequal work.
Part of the solution must be increased wage differentiation (see *Pravda*,
February 17, 1987).

The proposed reforms apparently delegate to enterprise and association management the determination of compensation, including bonuses. These managers (including the mestkom officials) will have their
motivations—and, thus, their attendant need to perform economically—
centralized by "self-financing." They will presumably use their power
of the purse to encourage better work. They themselves have an incentive to reward higher productivity by increasing wage differentiation.

Determining compensation locally—closer to the actual performance
of work—theoretically allows compensation to be fine-tuned. Allowing
more discretion in these decisions—making compensation to some degree subjective—is itself centralizing, tying the workers to the ultimate
goal of efficient performance. Thus, delegating responsibility for determining compensation can help to centralize motivation.

INCENTIVES: MERITOCRATIC VERTICAL MOBILITY

Bonuses in particular, and compensation in general, would be less
dominant a motivator (especially for executives) if there were higher
mobility—more chance for promotion. But the widespread possibility of
rapid promotion implies a need to retire or demote upper level occu-
pants.

Opening slots for promotion is required, to increase mobility and opportunity. Thus, a policy of mandatory retirement and/or an up-or-out
policy at middle or mid–upper levels is needed. (Such a policy was
proposed in the Central Committee's "theses" to the June 1988 party
conference.) These policies would produce a constant stream of job open-
ings; up-or-out is used in the U.S. armed forces for precisely this reason.
These personnel policy changes—demotion for nonperformance, increased job rotation (discussed below), and a retirement policy—would
be a coherent, modern, and more differentiated version of Khruschev's
personnel policies and reorganizations.[3]

The appearance of *voluntary* retirements at high levels would also signal major change, but of a different sort. They would suggest a broadening of personal identity beyond "official identity" (Jowitt 1983)—a pluralism of the heart.

Another "bureaucracy buster" is reorganization for its own sake: Reorganizations break up rigidities in bureaucracies, and improve performance for a while—although rigidity eventually sets in again (Downs 1967). This fact—along with the need for increased mobility for Soviet executives—implies that a so-called *treadmill of reforms* plus a *meritocratic version of a permanent purge* may be important and valuable organizational strategies.

But what is "meritocratic"? Indeed, the system does need increased executive mobility, and it does need promotion more on merit than connections; but, as we have seen earlier, this is a slippery thing to evaluate, given that people skills are increasingly more important than technical skills as one rises higher in an organizational hierarchy. The new rhetoric—with its denunciation of "clan nepotism," "cliquishness," and "favoritism"—is perhaps just as much aimed at replacing the old clans—new clans for old—as it is at personalistic management per se.

To make a real difference and for the system to ultimately benefit, the new clans must be based not on pure personal loyalty, but on professional, "cool" people skills in which mutual utility depends on getting the job done. In all organizations, both efficiency and loyalty count. The balance between the two can shift, however, and it clearly needs to do so in the Soviet Union.

Workers and managers are, in fact, aware of how personalism has distorted the promotion process. The survey at three enterprises—cited above—showed that reasons for dissatisfaction with promotion prospects were: absence of objective, accurate, reliable, and widely known criteria for promotion; too weak a connection between promotion prospects and real production successes, attitude toward work, and real qualifications and capabilities; absence of an operative, differentiated, open list of existing vacancies in various sections; absence of planned, systematic work for preparing engineers for promotion; not a close enough connection between the existing mechanism for attestation (certification by testing) of engineering–technical workers and prospects for promotion; inadequate reflection of work success in the job characterizations of the attestation commission; and the absence of workers on attestation commissions who are familiar with the jobs that they are evaluating (Antoniuk and Mochenov 1984a).

One approach to limiting personalism and the appointment of cronies is to involve more people in managerial personnel decisions. Thus, managers and party organizers are told that, whereas the selection and placement of cadres is the primary party organizations' most important work, they must overcome the "subjective approach" by sharing responsibility for cadre policy between the party organization and the industrial administration. The practice of discussing the administration's cadre proposals at partkom (party committee) and *partburo* (party bureau) meetings before taking action is important in this respect.

Attempts to resolve cadre questions by circumventing the party organizations leads to mistakes and distortions in work, brings serious harm to cadres' education, lowers their responsibility before the collective, [and] gives rise to careerism and servility. . . . Thus, it is important that work with cadres in the enterprise be conducted publicly, and that the community actively takes part in dealing with questions of their [cadres'] promotion or transfer. (Anonymous 1979b).

There is a strong emphasis in Soviet management writings on openness about cadre policy, objectivity, and formal processes as opposed to personalistic, ad hoc deal making. This emphasis is apparently a reaction to the kind of personalism that has permeated the system, and is an attempt to formalize and objectify the process—in part, with a typically Soviet engineering type of approach—in order to avoid appointments on a private-personal basis.

Objectivity is apparently measured by widespread agreement on the appropriateness of an appointment. This can be achieved—at least in part—by having a more public process for the selection of cadres. "If only the leadership of the enterprise is involved in the promotion to the reserve [list of future executive candidates] or appointment to a leadership post, it is unlikely that we can exclude cases where it [the promotion] turns out to be non-objective." Also, "knowing that he was recommended only by the leader, and not the collective, not the social organizations, a particular worker may, willingly or unwillingly, begin to feel a sense of dependency on that leader" (Shakhovoi 1985). Everyone must be convinced that the entire process is entirely objective. Therefore for the most part, matters should be dealt with in open meetings (Anonymous 1979a).

While the Soviet systems for personnel evaluation stress the opinions of the party in particular, in the United States it is the opinion of the party's analog—divisional or corporate headquarters—that counts. In fact, in the United States a constant reevaluation of managers acts as a substitute for centralization. While the rapid job rotation that is characteristic of Western organizations limits the period of time over which a candidate's actual performance can be judged, the corporate planning process involves the candidate in ongoing consultations with headquarters. This implies that his or her contributions to planning for the unit—not just execution of the plan—is key for promotion. "Through its promotional decisions, [headquarters] provides a constant guidance as to the sort of managerial activity which is desired" (Granick 1972). Thus, headquarters' strong participation in promotion policy centralizes motivation. Involving the partorg even more directly and explicitly in cadre policy will have the same effect, provided that the partorg itself has had its motivations centralized.

In order to avoid subjective factors in cadre selection, there are proposals for various formalized methods of evaluation involving commissions of anonymous experts, and so on (Popov 1976). Rational criteria for personnel selection have included psychological tests and competitions (Miller 1976). (But conservatives say that such procedures should be restricted to technical and midlevel personnel, not top management.)[4] For example, there is the "Engineer's Examination," which "evaluates achievements and shortcomings of captains of production according to a specific method, which allows the consideration more of a well-rounded and, most important, more objective characterization of a person" (*Pravda*, February 1, 1972). The evaluation is not purely technical, however, as categories rated include "organization skills, knowledge of work, striving toward raising his level of qualification and [significantly] ability to cooperate with social organizations [that is, the party and trade union]."

A law was adopted on attestatsia in 1974, and revised in 1979. In the early 1970s, after the introduction of attestatsia, there was—according to critics—too much focus on education and technical knowledge. There was not enough input from the collective, and not enough information on a candidate's "ability to work with people"—which is so very important. After the 1979 revision, evaluators were supposed to place more stress on practical and personal qualities (Shakhovoi 1985). Also, there is a repeated emphasis on the importance of fairness in making assessments (Golubkov and Fatkin 1984).

Thus, there has been some recognition of the limitations of strictly objective, target-based evaluations: "In carrying out work on the selection and placement of managing cadres, the evaluation of their practical and personal qualities are of greater importance than the evaluation of their work and results" (Shakhovoi 1985). After all, many secondary factors can influence production results. Further, the type of work that one may be doing at the time of the assessment may not require those personal qualities that will be needed higher up. By looking at personal and practical qualities, the evaluation can try to predict future performance (ibid.). In its evaluation, the partorg is therefore advised to consider ideological tempering, political maturity, competency, the ability to work with people, comrades' opinions, social responsibilities, education, age, and character (Anonymous 1979b).

In fact, *the importance of political consciousness* has been stressed in all of the proposed evaluation procedures: The leader must be ideologically mature, politically aware, a convinced Marxist-Leninist, and must realize in practice the idea of the unity of politics and economics. He or she must consult with the collective and respect collegiality in decision making, involving all: the partorgs, unions, and so on (Kruk 1973). The required qualifications include "political literacy, conscientiousness, and organizational capabilities" (Shakhovoi 1985). A sample list of categories for formal evaluation of a manager include major headings for "moral-political" and "ability to lead collective and individual employees," as well as "ability to organize self" and "knowledge." Under "moral-political," the subheadings include: "puts societal interests above personal," "participation in social life," "moral stability—firmness," "sense of responsibility for assigned tasks," "capability to build correct relations with social organizations," "striving to raise ideological-political level," and others (Popov 1976). While Westerners may see these criteria as a cover for the party's political manipulation, we must remember the importance of people skills for high-level management. These sociopolitical criteria may in fact be the relevant people-skill criteria in the Soviet context.

This means that meritocratic selection is not the same thing as establishing a civil service, since civil service is supposedly based on technical qualifications only—not political ones. Instead, the criteria of the sociopolitical attestatsia formalize and bureaucratize a party-boss or machine style of politics. The difference between the past and future will reside in the different values and management styles of the bosses and their machines.

Instead of promoting from within an organization, *bringing in new leadership "from the side" (from the other organizations) or "from above" (centrifugal promotion)* is another way to avoid personalism and the formation of cliques. And there are certain other advantages for the leader from above: He or she has been in close contact with workers and managers at a higher level.

But, say Soviet analysts, there are problems with a promotion from "outside." The newly installed leader is likely to be slow to pick up the reins, and his or her presence may create ill-feeling among those in the organization who thought that they themselves deserved the post. There is much that is strange to the leader from outside. There are different traditions of the collective, for example. Thus, it is supposedly always better to promote from the organization's own promotion reserve than from the side or from above.[5]

The reserve cadre from within the organization knows the nooks and crannies of the collective, its idiosyncrasies, ways, and so on. The reserve cadre doesn't need time to adapt.

Selection of cadres from the side is fully justified only when there is a need for a completely new approach to the carrying-out of managerial tasks at the enterprise, a fundamental restructuring of the organization of production and sometimes even the interrelations of the collective. In that case the leader from the side is free from the existing conservative views of the traditional habits and ways and methods employed at the given enterprise in the resolution of managerial tasks. (Shakhovoi 1985).

Other writers similarly emphasize the importance of the stability of the collective (see Stolyarenko 1983).

Western writers see similar advantages to promotion from within: "organizational socialization"; more accurate evaluation of candidates from within; a continuous process for selecting the best management; and direct rewards as an incentive to current employees (Stein 1976). The advantages of hiring from the outside, on the other hand, include access to new perspectives. In the West, "hire-ins" are in fact more frequent at the lowest and most senior levels, and less common at middle levels (Stein 1976).

The utility of all proposals for improving mobility must rise and fall on *giving up the policy of stability of cadres,* however, and on the imposition of economic discipline. After all, these Soviet proposals for rationalizing cadre policy have been studied and called for since the early 1970s without much effect.

Opening up positions in the hierarchy is not necessarily very easy, though. While the party's puritans will be comfortable in ousting the corrupt, it will be harder for them to get rid of those who share their values but have reached their level of incompetence. Mechanistic approaches that force promotions and demotions have been tried in the past, and failed for lack of conviction.[6]

It's hard to demote people: Mandatory retirement or up-or-out is mechanistic, but has the advantage that the ousted don't remain around to make their successors feel uncomfortable. In sum, the issue of how to maintain a meritocratic permanent purge will be central to perking up economic performance.

HORIZONTAL (LATERAL) MOBILITY—JOB ROTATION

Transferring someone to another organization is easier than demoting the person. Such transfers, however, may serve a variety of purposes other than quietly getting rid of personnel who have not worked out.

Frequent job rotation—moving personnel through a variety of suborganizations and functions—is in fact a fixture of corporate America. This is because it broadens experience, breaks up cliques, reduces direct personal competition, and reduces the efficacy of noncorporate commitments by creating strong boundaries around the organization (Kanter 1977). Transfers in some corporations are so frequent that, for example, corporate wives say that "IBM" stands for "I've Been Moved."

In U.S. corporations, there has been a strong relationship between mobility and competency. "The requirements of many, if not most, managerial positions can be learned in a year and a half or less. Mobile executives have an 80/20 orientation toward most positions. By this is meant that 20 percent of any job counts for 80 percent of the learning. If they can master the 80 percent and move on to another job, the learning curve is constantly rising" (Jennings 1967). Thus, "the men moving to the top today are compression products. They have ranged far and moved up fast and have had compressed into them an intensive and varied set of experiences in a very short period of time" (ibid.).

In the Soviet Union, moving people around between jobs has been used in the past to deal with the "family circle" problem—the formation of local "rings" of officials who protect and support one another for their own (as opposed to the system's) benefit (Granick 1972). Such, at least, was the case made for job rotation under Stalin.

Under Khrushchev, the role of job rotation was less clear. Writing in 1965, Meyer suggested that the then high rate of turnover of personnel in the party elite was not a Stalinist method of eliminating potential competitors, but was standard organizational procedure. He argued that the "frequent rotation of executive personnel is a routine in many other bureaucratic structures" because it gives "aspirants for highest office the greatest possible variety of experience and as much chance as possible to prove their worth. It is a training and recruitment device for screening national leaders, even though it may also be part of political maneuvering and power plays" (Meyer 1965). In retrospect, however, it looks as if Khrushchev's shake-ups were meant to increase his own, centralized, power at the expense of the divisional chiefs (regional first secretaries) on whose support he has depended earlier, in 1957.

Brezhnev sharply reduced the shifting of officials from one assignment to another (Hoffman and Laird 1982) as part of his commitment to stability of cadres. As described in Chapter 9, this was in reaction to the insecurity created by Stalin and—to a lesser degree—Khrushchev.

But such stability will not be seen as desirable by the Gorbachev generation. That generation—now assuming power—has been frustrated under Brezhnev, and is more secure by virtue of not having experienced the terror of the 1930s. In fact, they are resurrecting job rotation as an anticorruption device: In his speech to the Twenty-seventh Party Congress in 1986, Secretary Ligachev stressed the need to station cadres around the country in order to avoid the poisoning effects of localism (CDSP 38:10:8).

But job rotation—even if instituted solely for anticorruption reasons— will have a number of other effects. For example, regular job rotation implies a need to avoid overly personalized loyalty. This is because, when there is rapid succession, authority is being transferred for the subordinates as much as for the rotated executives, as well as for those executives themselves vis-à-vis their own superiors. In such a situation, it is functional to attach loyalty somewhat more impersonally to the rules, rather than to specific managers (Gouldner 1952). Also, the need to fit into new teams again and again is conducive to the development of good social-psychological (people) skills, bland affability, and impersonalism.[7]

Furthermore, importing outsiders into organizations increases the rate of innovation (Downs 1967). And—consistent with Ligachev's proposal—job rotation produces more detached views of each job, thus decreasing the advocacy of parochial interests (ibid.).

Soviet leaders are to some degree aware of these effects. Speaking in support of Ligachev's proposals, K. Makharov, first secretary of the Tadzhikistan Communist party, said that

In recent years collective decision-making had been ignored in our republic too; cadres were promoted according to the principles of personal loyalty, which led some executives into violations of statutory requirements and the norms of our morality. . . . We believe that the interrepublic exchange of cadres that Comrade Yegor Kuzmin Ligachev, Secretary of the CPSU-CC, talked about so convincingly is introducing a new businesslike approach into the activity of the Party committees. This course makes it possible to energetically rid ourselves of stagnation and manifestations of national narrow-mindedness and parochialism. (CDSP 38:10:14).

All of this means that increased job rotation will help bring more professional management to the Soviet Union. Rotation will undermine the prevalence of fixed "teams" and "families" (such as Brezhnev's Dnepropetrovsk "Mafia"), and favor a blander, interchangeable style of team player.[8] The negative effects of personnel turnover on the cohesion of collectives can thus be compensated for by mangers' improved psychological skills and bland affability—more interchangeability among managers.

Job rotation will have another effect by allowing—ultimately, indeed demanding—a multiple sponsorship process for personnel selection. Job rotation provides exposure to many senior managers, and thus the opportunity to develop multiple relationships with superiors (Kanter 1977). Because the pyramid narrows so quickly in U.S. corporations, and given that job rotation exposes candidates to multiple superiors, the higher up one goes, the more one needs multiple sponsorship—not just support from one's boss (ibid.). After job rotation has been implemented for a while in the Soviet Union, those candidates for promotion who have multiple sponsorship will be much stronger than single-sponsored candidates.

In a stagnant hierarchy without many prospects for mobility, subordinates rise only at the expense of their superiors: In some sense, they are natural competitors. This possible competition between superior and subordinate is one basis for the lack of delegation, as well as the demand for intense personal loyalty on the part of the subordinate (who thus denies any dishonorable intentions; (see Klugman 1986).

Once the hierarchy is no longer stagnant, however, the relationship between subordinate and superior is changed. If the superior has the potential and desire for mobility and if the prospects for mobility depend on performance, then the superior must optimally utilize the potentials of the subordinates. Furthermore, in a context of increased job rotation and multiple sponsorship, developing competent subordinates increases the prestige of the superior by showing an ability to develop organizational resources. It also increases the superior's influence by putting an ally in a useful position (Kram 1980). (This latter effect has been true all along.) Thus, the sponsorship system exerts disciplinary pressure on the senior as well as the junior, since the senior must be careful not to sponsor a failure or deviant. Otherwise, when that incompetent is transferred to his or her next position and messes up, it will reflect poorly on the sponsor (ibid.).

A strict hierarchy plus strong boundaries—no job rotation—have heretofore meant a total dependence on one's immediate supervisor, or perhaps one's supervisor's supervisor, unless one were lucky enough to have a ruka. This dependence has strongly reinforced the personalism and localism of the system. But the "promotion of the unobvious choice"—that is, of a mediocre or unqualified candidate (Wright 1979; see also Pfeffer 1981)—so as to earn that person's undying loyalty and strengthen one's coalition is less desirable if one needs strong subordinates, and if one's own prestige is dependent on their performance after they are eventually transferred. Thus, job rotation and multiple sponsorship promote truer meritocratic evaluation, which tends to weaken personalistic coalitions. By allowing for multiple sponsorship, job rotation again reinforces greater impersonalism and more professionalism.

Multiple sponsorship already exists to some degree. It was probably important, for example, in the appointment of Kolbin—who had connections with both the Sverdlovsk group and Shevardnadze—to lead the party in Kazakstan, as described in Chapter 6. The notion of multiple sponsorship is certainly congenial to the Soviet system—14 people had to sign off on one of my interviewees before he could go abroad—but it requires job rotation to allow it to be applied in the workplace.

SUMMARY

In spite of both organizational and psychological opposition, structural reform can produce a better performing organization by delegating responsibility and centralizing motivations. Personnel policy can help attain the latter—motivational—goal. The key elements of the new personnel policy must be improved discipline, local determination of compensation, meritocratic vertical mobility, and increased horizontal mobility—that is, job rotation.

If the Soviet system is indeed evolving toward more professional management and if it does in fact implement personnel policies along the lines suggested above, certain predictions can be made about the emerging and future generations of Soviet leaders; who they will be, how they will make decisions, and how they might view the world outside the Soviet Union. These topics comprise the next—and final—part of this book.

NOTES

1. In the West, the "invisible hand" of the market—by imposing "market discipline"—provides the mechanism for "invisibly" centralizing motivations across the economy as a whole. Within organizations, however, there are the same issues of suboptimization and its avoidance.

2. See Klugman (1986) for a fuller discussion of the issues in this section.

3. In regard to the possibility of such a retirement policy, it is interesting to note that Gorbachev has yet to appoint a full Politburo member younger than himself.

4. There have also been attempts to apply a similar certification process to whole enterprises (as opposed to individuals), assessing the "level of organization and technology" (Koriushkin 1986).

5. In regard to the promotion reserve system: "At each enterprise or association the administration together with the social organizations (party, union, komsomol) attentively survey reports on potential candidates for promotion to leadership positions. After exacting discussion of the candidatures, and coordination of them with the party organs, a reserve list is made up" (Shakhovoi 1985). Unfortunately, Soviet managers suboptimize even in forming their promotion reserve. "Usually, the reserve for the post of director and main engineers is composed of workers recommended by the leaders of one or another enterprise or association. However, since they are not interested in the departure of good specialists and organizers to other organizations, sometimes less than the best candidates are nominated for the reserve" (ibid.).

6. "Pul'sar," for example—proposed in 1970 (see *Literaturnaia Gazeta* 36, 1970, and *Literaturnaia Gazeta* 21, 1971)—was to be a system of cleansing "pulsations" in the cadre selections system: Leaders at all levels would be "periodically checked according to definite criteria. On the basis of such assessments a certain quantity of the best workers at each level of management would be regularly (say every year or two) obligatorily raised to the next level (or put on promotion reserve), and some percent of the weak [managers] similarly obligatorily would be reduced in responsibility." Although readers discussed the idea (some liked the mechanistic approach, while others thought it artificial and formalistic), the

program was nowhere truly implemented. In some enterprises, it was distorted into a system for giving the bonuses of the lowest 20 percent to those in the highest 20 percent of the ratings.

7. "The trend toward depersonalization of authority in organizations is still in its early stages. . . . Competent specialists tend to be consulted by colleagues and superiors, and the resulting greater frequency of social interaction concerning the work contributes to coordination, further reducing the need for commands" (Blau and Meyer 1971, in Hough 1973).

8. See Kanter 1977; see also Hough 1969 on party officials as broker/negotiators.

PART IV. INDIVIDUAL PSYCHOLOGY AND INSTITUTIONAL BEHAVIOR

Professionalization of the Soviet executive style is producing certain systemic trends in the present, and should allow us to predict other trends for the future. Chapter 11, "The New Soviet Man and the Soviet Future," looks at the future implications of professionalization and the other topics under study here. Chapter 12, "Psychological Models of International Relations," tries to imagine how the psychological phenomena revealed here might apply to Soviet perceptions of foreign affairs.

11. THE NEW SOVIET MAN AND THE SOVIET FUTURE

THE MANAGERS OF THE FUTURE

A selection process is at work, shaping the population of Soviet executives. Delegation of responsibility, increased discipline, pressure for merit selection, job rotation, and multiple sponsorship—assuming that they are fully and truly implemented—will all select against those who degrade their team through too much nepotism or patronage, and will instead reward utilitarianism and a more impersonal kind of loyalty. The conflict between the Soviet future and the Soviet past "may be viewed symbolically as one between rules and patrons..., between contracts and blat..., and between merit and pile (connections)" (Jowitt 1974). Even if performance or merit is based on people skills—not technical ones—those skills are increasingly *managerial, not personal-political;* and although this difference may be subtle at times, it is nonetheless real. What will be rewarded is more a matter of teamability than personal loyalty; it is mutual utility more in terms of economic performance than of direct personal benefit.

Other factors should also promote a more impersonal approach, specifically executives' increasing levels of technical and professional education.

A number of studies have pointed to an increasing professionalism—higher education and specialized career paths—among elites (see Bialer, 1980; Hough, 1980), but they do not address the question of whether advancement occurs on a personal or impersonal basis. Candidates may be better qualified as a group, but choices for promotion could still be based on personal loyalty. It can be expected, however, that professionally trained people will over time put more and more emphasis on professional, impersonal qualifications. (Klugman 1986)

Heretofore, personnel selection has been split between—on the one hand—intensely personal informal mechanisms and—on the other hand—formal attempts at an objective, engineering-style selection process. The tension between these two approaches can be reduced by using more impersonal but still socially based evaluations. Because of both their teamability and their effectiveness, the same people who are good informal team or network members should rate high in a formal process centered on widespread (and therefore somewhat impersonal) consultation concerning their social-political qualifications.

Remember, though, that selection pressure does its work on populations, not on individuals; an individual with the "right" qualities may not succeed, and one with the "wrong" ones may succeed spectacularly. Luck counts.

Statistically—however—over the population, there will be a gradual shift. What will emerge is an elite of professional managers (both industrial managers and political executives) characterized by chameleon-like flexibility, strong teamability, interchangeability, bland affability, technical-economic competency, greater commitment to the system, and more willingness to delegate. These changes, in general—and the willingness to delegate, in particular—represent an evolutionary shift in the culture-based psychology of the Soviet system.

The newly emerging managers will not be smarter or intrinsically more talented than their predecessors: Professional smarts and talent are not greater than entrepreneurial smarts and talent—just different. The new managers, however, by virtue of their professional style will be better adapted to the greater complexity of the modern Soviet state, and therefore should be able to make it perform better. And a psychology rooted in peasant culture will shift to one more adapted to modernity.

THE PSYCHOLOGY OF DISCIPLINE AND DELEGATION

Soviet reform is obviously going to have its winners and losers—those who will benefit materially or politically; and those whose positions will be lost, and along with their positions their official perquisites and even their ability to engage in blat. We might assume that the potential winners are the supporters of reform, while the potential losers are opponents; but this raises the question: How can we identify the potential winners and losers? And how can they identify themselves?

In general, the answers to these questions are not obvious. Presumably, the corrupt are more liable to prosecution, and are therefore among the potential losers. But anyone else in the system might win or lose, get promoted or demoted, or—these days—even start a small business.[1]

How do people decide whether to be supporters or opponents of reform? Most simply, they decide on the basis of whether they like the idea, whether it appeals to them, whether they are more comforted by the traditional system or the new one that seems to be emerging. But those who are more comfortable with the loosening-up of controls, the greater delegation of responsibility, and the increased freedom of (useful) expression will presumably—by virtue of that comfort—be better able to take advantage of the new opportunities. Thus, the potential winners self-identify on the basis of their psychological/emotional comfort with the reform process; the potential losers self-identify by their discomfort.

Delegation is not divestiture, however; and the new managers and politicians who succeed in the Soviet system will not be independent entrepreneurs any more than they will be old-time ward heelers and wheeler-dealers. The shift in the makeup of the new managers is slight— slightly more technocratic, slightly less personalistic, more willing to delegate, and less willing to intrude. They will still be members of a huge organization, and their values will still revolve around dependency and control: dependency in their seeking the approval of their superiors; control in their functioning in a managerial hierarchy. They will still desire membership: They want their success within the organization, not as outsiders.

For the new elite, however, these values are—again—a bit more impersonal. Their dependency is less on some specific boss and more spread among multiple sponsors—less on individuals and more on the organization. Their control is exercised less through direct petty tutelage around the details of operations, and more through indirect (but realistic) goal setting and management by exception. This shift is real, but it is not radical. It is not revolutionary, but evolutionary.

The impact of increased delegation is to select for the marginally more autonomous and self-contained members of the managerial population, while the impact of increased discipline is to select for the more controlled and goal driven. Psychologically, reform tightens the moral corset with its discipline. At the same time, the necessity of maintaining the disciplinary standards while functioning with less intrusive supervision selects for people who have to some degree internalized the system's values. These are the people on whom the tighter moral corset will not chafe.

Thus the combination of discipline and delegation gradually selects for people who don't need the moral corset so much in the first place. It pushes the managers and executives of the Soviet system toward internalization of the system's values.

HOMOGENIZATION

Job rotation, multiple sponsorship, and the necessity for out-place-ment of team members onto other teams imply a selection not just among individuals, but among teams. Recall once more the story of the raikom secretary taking his protégé to show at the gorkom. Everybody has to read each other and fit together—the protégé, the sponsoring raikom secretary, and the gorkom secretary. With more horizontal movement in the system, that sort of fitting-together will spread and encourage interchangeability among teams. And as the individual managers be-come more interchangeable, so will the teams themselves become more uniform and homogeneous. Team, network, and "family" boundaries will be widened and to some degree blurred by both the mixing process of job rotation and the growing impersonalism of the system.

While rotation will connect the system better horizontally, discipline will connect it better vertically—centralizing motivation even as respon-sibility is delegated downward. We have already noted the necessity of tuning one's antennae upward to see the needs and desires of superiors. The stronger the carrots and sticks brought to bear on those superiors, the more the superiors themselves will also be attuned upward—their eyes focused on fulfilling centrally determined demands. Thus—in un-derstanding one's boss's world—the further up one is able to see, the better. (This does not apply under conditions of stability of cadres, since tenure eliminates the necessity of doing anything special to please some-one up the chain. However, more realistically speaking, the old system meant staying in the higher-ups' good graces on a personalistic—per-haps corrupt—basis.) If there is strong discipline, being attuned up the chain of command—right up to the general party line—will be selected for at every level.

But one's immediate boss is still most important; and if one is not connected well enough there, it could mean the end of one's career. If one's own boss is out of tune, it is necessary to somehow get out from under. (If one can't get out from under—tough luck.) For example, the immediate predecessor of Gorbachev in Stavropol kraikom was on his way down. Gorbachev's connections at higher levels—presumably with Politburo member and former Stavropol first secretary Fëdor Kulakov—allowed him to survive working under a failing boss. Thus, personal networks and organizational families will still be useful, but they too—in seeking mutual utility under the new rules of the game—will select their members relatively less on who's the best drinking buddy and relatively more on who can help get the job done.

This does not imply the end of faction and struggle: There will still be teams, networks, and families. But there will be more shared characteristics and similarities in managerial style across all these groups, as well as the growth of a broader, systemic loyalty.

COMMITMENT AND MOTIVATION

In the recent past, organizational stagnation and low opportunity have produced cynicism, not systemic loyalty. But for all that members of the elite may have been maintaining "divided selves"—outward conformity and inward disaffection; communist faces and who knows what kind of hearts—their inner doubts or cynicism have been exceedingly well controlled. Otherwise, if acted out either consciously or unconsciously, such feelings surely would have impeded the progress of their careers.

A certain scientist—on being nominated to become deputy director of his institute—said to a party meeting that he was now joining the party "because I have to." Apparently, he was a very proud man. He said what he said in an attempt to maintain his pride while in the very act of submission. Being a scientist—and appointed more than most on purely technical grounds—he got away with this. No apparatchik would say such a thing: The very idea is contradictory.

For the "man on the make," compliance itself—because it is chosen— becomes a form of control: Freedom is the recognition of necessity. In choosing to play the game, one's apparent loss of autonomy is willing, or even eager. The outer, social self engages almost all one's energies.

What has guided and shaped this outer self? Protégés surely tend to identify with their sponsors, their teams, their networks, their organizational families, and their institutions. Also, self-perception theory would say that, even in "putting on" characteristics, the apparatchik will tend to identify with those characteristics. In the past, though, all these identifications have been essentially localistic and personalistic. What has been missing is an operational basis for identification with the greater whole or total organization—system patriotism, if you will— which would centralize motivation and counter suboptimization and self-seeking.

But choosing personnel more on the basis of competency and less on personal ties, and in a context of repeatedly shuffled work teams (because of job rotation), will encourage systemic—as opposed to personal—loyalties. This is true for a number of reasons:

1. "The greater the vertical mobility within an organization, the stronger the identification of the individual with the organization" (Stone 1952).

2. More general as opposed to specific supervision—meaning more delegation to subordinates, more participation by them in decisions, and giving them a

higher sense of authority—plus more employee versus production orientation all produce greater identification with the organization (ibid.).

3. Frequent changes in supervisors and subordinates requires a more impersonal, diffuse loyalty.

4. In a more meritocratic system, talented individuals feel more assured of success, and thus feel more committed to the system.

5. A more vigorous and optimistic outlook for the system itself promotes idealism and identification with the organization.

On the other hand, better motivation in subordinates allows their superiors to comfortably delegate more responsibility. Soviet researchers—for example—are less administered than U.S. ones, but still produce substantial results (Kaplan 1970). Thus, there is the possibility of a self-reinforcing, virtuous (as opposed to vicious) circle in which professionalism and delegation can grow because of improving (centralization of) motivation, while motivation is improved by increases in professionalism and delegation.

TRUST, GOAL CONSENSUS, AND ECONOMIC EFFICIENCY

There are a number of signs of increasing generalized trust within the system: decreased bombast; glasnost'; the publicizing of accidents; public announcement of riots in Alma-Ata, Armenia, and Azerbaijan; and so on. This kind of systemic trust—the widespread sharing of information formerly kept confidential—does not represent an increase in the trustworthiness of any individuals in particular. Instead, it is as if the whole society were a bit more trusting of its members in general.

The lack of personal trust interferes with delegation, and "managers who cannot trust others usually attempt to over-control them. They substitute control for trust" (Jennings 1967). "But most executives find great advantage in giving subordinates wide latitude and they derive great gains from the creativity that usually ensues" (ibid.).[2] Thus, in a setting of increased job rotation and impersonalism in which managers must repeatedly form new relationships with one another, economic performance should be helped by the increasing level of generalized trust.

The phenomenon of increased general trust may be seen as an outgrowth of the post-Stalin experience. But it is not just a result of rulers taking power who made their careers after Stalin's death. In some sense, it is a late benefit of Stalinism. After all, the children raised in the 1930s and 1940s grew up with their parents' anxiety. Recall the subject who told me about his friend's father's advice: Never take initiative; never be at the head of a group. The care and the calculation of the current generation of leaders—their assertion of membership and belonging, and therefore of reliability—have become automatic and unconscious; such traits need no gross demonstration now. The whole society having gone through the upheavals of the 1930s—and then the war—who among the survivors can be suspect?

The knee-jerk ideological bombast—which was ingrained in the Brezhnev generation as a ritual incantation to ward off the secret police—is no longer necessary. There are no more traitors, wreckers, and saboteurs—only the venal and the inefficient. Thus, too, competition is no longer to the death. Losers are just losers—not enemies of the people.

The new leaders—for all that they might disagree with one another about going slower or faster, or decentralizing more or less—have a fair degree of goal consensus arising out of their common experiences. They have all had the experience of being children growing up in a context of fear and tumult. They learned that the world was dangerous, and that they had to be very careful. They were the best and the brightest and the most controlled and the most conformist. They were young—early in their budding careers—when they were subject to the dizzying changes, hopes, and failed idealism of Khrushchev. They moved into positions of authority only to be stifled and frustrated by intrusive superiors with inferior educations, and to feel shackled by the stagnation of Brezhnevism. This set of experiences has led to a shared belief in control and management, as well as an "I can do better!"technocratic attitude (for those who were not themselves corrupted). They want to manage the system better; and they are ready to believe that this requires better discipline, better incentives, and better delegation.

In organizations, personal trust and loyalty can cease being pivotal issues and can then be taken more for granted, when there exists a high degree of consensus about the functions and tasks of management (Kanter 1977). In such situations, there can be less stress on social conformity (ibid.), and thus less ideological bombast, more representation of women and other groups, and so on.

Greater goal consensus means that top officials can both be more powerful and delegate more authority. "Cultural and goal homogeneity within a bureau reduces the total volume of messages required therein" (Downs 1967), thus reducing the overload on communication channels and on central decision makers. Greater goal consensus reduces conflicts among bureau members, and thus improves coordination. This reduces "authority leakage"—the difference between what top leaders think they are ordering and what the bureaucracy many levels down actually ends up doing (ibid.). Reduced authority leakage means increased power for top officials, which means in turn that leaders can cut back on explicit controls, reports, and performance checks. This is the essence of greater delegation to subordinates. This is why "strong goal consensus is a vital part of any true decentralization of authority" (Downs 1967).

Systemically, Soviet suborganizations have not been able to trust or rely on each other. Because of problems with supplies, for example, each ministry has been willing to pay the price of its own high-cost production in order to achieve independence. Thus, each ministry acts like an independent nation engaging in "foreign" trade in its dealings with other ministries. And this pattern is reproduced by individual plants, which in turn strive to become autarkic principalities within the ministerial "nation" (Granick 1961).

Caught in a bureaucratic web of mutual dependency, and given the unreliability of those on whom one is dependent, every entity—individual enterprise, or ministry—experiences a tremendous push toward autarky. Every factory has its "dwarf workshops" producing high-cost spare parts that cannot be obtained reliably from the original manufacturers of the factory equipment. The transport ministry must have its own steel mills. There are 7,000 tons of nails shipped both into and out of Leningrad every year because the nail factories are subordinate to different ministries. Ministries, associations, enterprises, and individuals—all unable to rely on official arrangements—either do for themselves or rely on unofficial arrangements. This can never be very efficient.

Thus, increased trust and mutual dependability, combined with a more realistic strategic-planning process and more delegation of operational responsibility, have the potential to produce an enormous increase in Soviet industrial efficiency by eliminating duplicative efforts. Also, as we have previously seen, managerial and organizational measures aimed at personnel policy (which are already in the process of implementation) have a much greater potential than many people think for improving managerial—and thus economic—performance.

The basic political features of the system define the limits of trust, however. Everyone understands that, at base, glasnost' applies to "how we do"—not "what we do." The basic tenet of the monoorganizational society remains the idea of a centrally managed society, however well authority might be delegated. Underneath any attempts to decentralize the organizational structure, essential unity is to be maintained.

Thus we are discussing reform—not revolution—and all the changes detailed above need not encroach on the basic organizational features of the Soviet system. Again, I must emphasize that appropriate delegation of authority does not diminish—but increases—the power of those at the top. For example—as previously discussed—when General Electric went to a decentralized, divisional structure, central authority was effectively strengthened, not weakened. And, for all that its table of organization changed, GE remained GE. Similarly, the Soviet system can function better and still be—in essence—a managed, monoorganizational society under the leadership of the Communist party. Incremental change can be effective.[3]

The potential economic efficiency of the Soviet system is to some degree limited, however—by politics.[4] After all, "the essence of *socialist* management is its diune goal of attaining production targets and educating the new man, the citizen, of consolidating socialist social relations" (Stolyarenko 1983, emphasis added). The second of these two goals is sociopolitical—not economic—and so limits the system's ability to pursue the purely economic goal of productivity. Also, as long as the system is essentially monoorganizational, all markets will be internal ones, and pricing policy will remain a significant problem—albeit somewhat alleviated to the degree that reforms really allow for direct horizontal relations between factories and (ultimately) between producers and consumers.

Still, managerial reforms of the sort discussed above should be able to produce significant results. But *the primary product of the collective is its political atmosphere;* secondary is its economic product. The first report at meetings is on the political product; the second report, on the economic one. On its own terms, the Soviet system should be judged primarily in social—not economic—terms.

NONIDEOLOGICAL REALITY

Josef Stalin may have thought that genetics were subject to ideological analysis; Nikita Krushchev, that plant physiology—for example, the climate required to grow corn—was whatever he wished it to be; and Leonid Brezhnev and Konstantin Chernenko, that it was economic to run rivers backward. But the Soviet Union cannot afford such decision making. Decisions can no longer be based on "socialist" realism instead of the ordinary kind.

The technological imperatives of good management exert continuous pressure in the direction of reality and truth. Better delegation of responsibility means more trust in—and openness to—the feedback of subordinates. And meritocratic, performance-based evaluation means that results are what count. Attaining those results requires realistic knowledge and planning. Even Brezhnev knew—at least in theory—the necessity of a nonideological reality: "We must put an end to subjectivism," he said, and "guard against extremes, proceeding in a rational economic manner, taking all aspects and implications of each measure into account" (quoted in Bunce and Echols 1980). In a more impersonal system, questions like where to grow corn or whether to concentrate on modernizing current industrial facilities instead of building new capacity should be less political questions than rational-technical ones, albeit that such decisions will have political implications for the advocates and beneficiaries of various policies.

Thus, over time, Soviet society should develop more truthful habits. The emerging manager will incorporate (if not internalize) truthful habits as the socially appropriate shell permeates deeper and deeper, and the split-off, hidden, inner self diminishes even more.[5] Alternately, as discussed previously, the system will select for those who have already internalized its values to some degree.

One type of more rational, nonideological planning showed up as early as the late 1960s, when there was "explicit recognition of the need for 'objectivity' in the obligations [of socialist competition]" (Hough 1969). This meant, for example, that a shipyard refused a newspaper's exhortation to take on the "obligation" to finish a ship ahead of schedule, because doing so would have disrupted work on other projects. In earlier times, such paltry considerations of efficiency would have been given short shrift in the face of revolutionary ardor.

But rationality and reality are not always obvious. The Brezhnev years were characterized by debates among specialists aimed at discovering policy rationality. There were "first, a greater emphasis on knowledge and scientific analysis in policymaking; second, a greater use of specialists and experts in the policy process; third, more realistic policymaking [compared to Khrushchev]; and fourth, greater stability and evenness in policy outputs" (Bunce and Echols 1980).

Without discipline, however, the Brezhnev years saw only a modest improvement in realism. Subject #20—an economist—met many people at the ministries and planning commission "who thought things would happen because they said so." Whenever the subject presented an economic input–output balance, the officials would demand changes that were physically impossible—requiring the appearance of materials that seemed not to require production, but came as if by magic into the plan. Only with great difficulty could the officials be persuaded of the reality of economic constraints.[6] Leftover officials have been denounced in the press for their "alienation from reality," and Gorbachev even described the situation in a speech to the Central Committee on January 17, 1987: "The world of day-to-day realities and that of make-believe well-being were increasingly parting ways" (quoted in the *New York Times*, January 28, 1987).

The planning process has thus suffered from slow, weak feedbacks and great distance between planners and those with operational responsibility. Ministers and planners have been "protected" from harsh realities. These are precisely the conditions conducive to "superman planning" (Downs 1967)—unrealistic exaggeration of capabilities. Delegation, better truthfulness, and thus better feedbacks to planners—

combined with devolution of operational planning to lower levels and restricting the central organs to strategic planning—will lead to more realism among economic managers at every level.

Whether glasnost' itself represents increased realism is unclear. Glasnost' does bring with it a related kind of progress, however, in that it legitimizes more open policy debates—bringing them aboveground to a greater extent than the purely specialist debates encouraged under the Brezhnev regime. The cost of suppressing explicit policy debates and attempting to depoliticize the appearance of decision procedures is that politics goes underground—bringing on a (perhaps unconscious) slanting of criteria and information (Pfeffer 1981). Thus, the supposedly objective economic-planning process under Brezhnev became riddled with under-the-table, personalistic deal making to alter plan targets, supplies, and so on. An open advocacy process is more likely to help the facts see the light of day. This is one benefit of widening the "marketplace of ideas."

It is difficult to speculate on what it will mean if nonideological reality extends even further into economics and then on into sociology and psychology. Perhaps the policy of glasnost' and the democratization campaign—viewed as motivational techniques—represent such an extension.

Ideology will always have its own appropriate realm, however: values and meanings. What society deems important, what it pursues, what constitutes success or failure, what is appropriate behavior, how one should treat one's fellows, what determines the rights of individuals and the obligations of group members, and whether rights should be political or economic—all of these and similar questions lie in the realm of ideology. They have no objective answers; they are socially determined.

THE REAL NEW SOVIET MAN

Improved motivation and greater identification with the system as a whole, along with the selection of cadres who have internalized more of the system's values, will tend to heal the Soviet citizen's (or at least, the successful Soviet executive's) inner splits. The individual will be less alienated, diminishing the split between the private and the public self (see Klugman 1986). Outer splits will also be moderated: Peer relations will be easier, if somewhat more impersonal. Team, network, and organizational family will be more integrated into the whole.

As this individual rises in the more professionally managed organization, he or she—like officials everywhere—will become more intensely and personally involved in work—which will encourage a further increase in identification with the system (Downs 1967; also Kanter and

Stein 1979, and numerous others). Climbers will—of necessity—be competent. They will have highly attuned social antennae to read the desires and needs of superiors and to understand the broad system in which they work, as well as good people-skills to work well with peers and to find and use good subordinates.

In sum, the successful Soviet executive will more and more resemble the fabled "new Soviet man." I shall call this emerging type the "real new Soviet man" by analogy to "real socialism"—a term used to distinguish what exists in the Soviet Union from theoretical socialism.

The *real* new Soviet man might not be so terribly idealistic as that paragon of socialist virtue, the new Soviet man; but he is as acutely socially aware and socially responsive and—at base—almost as fully identified with the system. And if that system does indeed begin both to perform better and to offer the emerging new man greater opportunities for advancement, then he might even be idealistic, into the bargain.

How does the real new Soviet man differ from the West's "organization man"? The real new Soviet man is appropriately rewarded for what William Whyte (1956) criticized in the West's corporate organization man—the renunciation of individualism in exchange for a "soothing" sense of belonging and security. ("He not only works for the organization; he belongs to it.") The real new man tends to be homogeneous throughout the Soviet system, while the variety of Western organizations—with their different subcultures—calls for some variety in organization men. Thus, the real new man is more ideologically uniform, as well as more uniformly ideological than the organization man.

Most strikingly, however, the real new man belongs to his organization even more fully than the organization man does. This is because the new man's organization—the Soviet system—is itself more encompassing, more a total institution. By the same token, the real new man is broader than the organization man because his interests must encompass areas left to a variety of organizations and individuals in the West.

NOTES

1. The business opportunities now available represent the system's "spinning off" of small-scale services (repair, restaurants, and so on) and small-scale consumer-oriented production (tailoring, for instance). The scale of these operations has never been appropriate for centralized management: Even in the West, the major centralized form for such businesses is a system of franchises.

2. See also Tashakori (1983) on the trust required for the professional style of management; and Gouldner (1952) on trust and delegation.

3. Thus, too, the Soviet Union will ultimately remain a sequential processor at heart, while the United States functions as a multiple parallel processor. This suggests reason for Western optimism.

4. This is also the conclusion of many Western analysts (for example, Rumer 1986).

5. Nonideological reality is for the social organism in some ways analogous to psychoanalytic theorist Heinz Hartmann's notion of the individual's conflict-free ego.

6. Subject #20 compared the thinking of these officials to the story of Trishkin's kaftan. Trishkin—the subject of a cycle of folktales—had a jacket with only one sleeve. The poor condition of his jacket was kept secret, however, because he always turned only one side toward whomever he was talking with—switching his one sleeve from arm to arm as required. Note also Potëmkin's villages—mere facades set up to look like prosperous towns from a distance.

12.   PSYCHOLOGICAL MODELS OF INTERNATIONAL RELATIONS

RELATIONSHIPS, INTERNATIONAL AND OTHERWISE

Why did the Soviet Union invade Afghanistan? Was it—in the minds of Soviet leaders—a defensive maneuver arising from their fear of a grand encirclement in which China allies with Europe and the United States? Or was it just an easy, opportunistic land grab by "power hungry S.O.B.'s out to rule the world" (to quote a former U.S. congressman)? Or are both of these theories missing something important?

Too often, below the surface, analysis of Soviet behavior rests on some Westerner or some alienated ex-Soviet thinking, "Who would I have to be—how would I have to feel—to act that way?" This sort of analysis usually leads to a variant on the two themes mentioned above: Soviet defensiveness, even paranoia; and Soviet aggressiveness and raw power-seeking.

In the hope that analyzing Soviet behavior can be more than—implicitly—a projective test for Westerners, I would like to attempt a different kind of analysis, one that is explicitly psychological. Putting my projections on the table, I want to imagine empathically the workings of the minds of Soviet leaders.

I want to look at them as a group. This is both because of our limited knowledge of them as individuals, and my belief that they can best be studied as a group or type because of the strong forces that shape them and make them fit the system. In a sense, I am accepting the validity of the "official identity" of Soviet executives: Knowing their roles in the system, we know the most important things about them.

We know, for example, something about what they experienced earlier in their lives, how they got to their positions of power, and how the individuals and organizations in their lives related to one another. Their ideas of how the world works have been formed in the Soviet context, and this context is much more enclosed and predictable than, say, the U.S. one. This is because of the monoorganizational nature of the Soviet system: People experience basically the same setup wherever they come from in the Soviet Union, and whatever kind of work they do.

So, Soviet leaders all come from similar backgrounds and worked themselves up through the same kinds of bureaucracies, using essentially the same techniques. Thus, if we can deduce anyone's world view, we should be able to deduce that of Soviet leaders—the most highly socialized group (no pun intended) in a highly socialized society.

What I would like to hypothesize about these leaders is that their notions of relations between nations will be based—unconsciously—on their experiences of relations between individuals and between organizations. This idea has two bases: one about relationships, per se; and the other about Soviet leaders.

First, a relationship is a relationship is a relationship. Two entities of any kind may interact in a number of ways: They may be complementary or symmetric, close or distant, competitive or cooperative, or some mixture—depending on the issues involved. Relations may be channeled through certain activities, issues, or institutions, and not others.

Cultural and social factors determine the channels and themes through which relationships express themselves, and these descriptors apply to both individuals and institutions. For example, compared to the corresponding U.S. relationships, Soviet authority relationships are more vertical and more controlling, while Soviet peer relationships are more encompassing and more enveloping—or, on the other hand, more undependable or even rejecting and hostile (see Appendix A). These characterizations are as true of relationships between Soviet institutions as they are of relationships between Soviet individuals. To take another example, Americans are more concerned about issues of autonomy, while Russians are more concerned about membership and acceptability. Or, to put it differently, Americans are more individualistic; Russians, more collectivistic. These tendencies are reflected in relations among both individuals and institutions: in the integration of Soviet society with its lack of independent institutions, and in the deep closeness of Russian friendships, on the one hand; and in U.S. institutional pluralism and the intermediate gradations of American interpersonal relationships, on the other.

Soviet leaders do not come to power with any extensive experience or knowledge of the outside world. They rise in a domestic apparatus, dealing with Soviet institutions and Soviet citizens. In a purely Soviet context, they form their ideas about how the world works and about how individuals and organizations relate to one another.

The second basis for my hypothesis is the fact that Soviet leaders are very social guys. They are not introspective, philosophical loners who might develop idiosyncratic ideas. I said above that Soviet leaders are the most socialized group in a highly socialized society, and they are; but this does not only imply that they might be analyzable because they are so embedded in their system. It also implies that they are very social in their thinking: Their mental categories are social and relational. And their mental categories presumably apply to relationships of all kinds, including relationships between nations.

THE INDIVIDUAL'S EXPERIENCE

As I have already described, the primacy of the political plus the lack of alternatives outside the system means that the Soviet executive is always surrounded by the system, with no outside to escape to or relax in. Thus, he or she feels enclosed (in both positive and negative senses), on display, and careful to avoid a negative.

The Soviet world of officialdom is tightly integrated: Everything is connected to everything else. Life is full of pitfalls, but with opportunities that must be continuously scanned for—especially via close attention to superiors. Occasionally an official can knock out a potential competitor, but the utmost care must be taken in such dangerous maneuvers. In the meantime, the official works with all his skills, both technical and social—fulfilling the world's demands, seeking to improve his position, maintaining good working relations—but always looking for competitors' weaknesses to exploit at a strategic moment. All this is very personal and specific—not diluted even in part through an impersonal marketplace.

How careful one has to be! One must make no errors; one must not lose what one has; and one must avoid the negative in one's remarks and one's life. As in chess, success is governed by the careful and methodical avoidance of error and the exploitation of opportunities as they arise. This is in contrast with Western entrepreneurship, in which one's best moments may more than make up for numerous errors. It fits with Soviet officials having a conserver attitude and being risk averse.

The conscious focus on and importance of social relations going back to at least secondary school—in a context of unconscious social immersion from the time of sitting on mother's knee, and preschool age—must have some lasting effect in establishing a calculating, careful, defensive, and extroverted attention. What chords are struck in the graduate of the sociopolitical attestatsia who is now a Soviet diplomat when he is listening to some attack, criticism, or demand?

The palpable reality and importance of both one's immediate social system and its embedding in the broader social sphere reinforce the importance of relationships. There is no independence, and—worse—isolation is punishment (see Appendix A).

THE COMMUNITY OF NATIONS

Given this experience, Soviet leaders should tend to see international affairs in terms of all-encompassing relationships among nations. They will view the world as an integrated whole—not as a collection of discrete entities. Everything will be seen as connected to and affecting everything else.

More specifically, Soviet leaders will tend to view international relations as a social(-political) system—a system of interrelated ongoing relationships that is truly a community of nations. This is in contrast to the U.S. tendency to see the world as a collection of autonomous entities. This difference shows up, for example, in conflicting meanings for "peace." While in the West the word *peace* has connotations of isolated tranquillity and a live-and-let-live philosophy, the Russian *mir*—identical to the words for "village community" and "world"—connotes harmonious, coordinated togetherness.

Symbols are important, because symbols carry social meanings. Procedures are important, because procedure—who goes first; who gets invited to sit at the table—embodies a relationship. "Meaningless" treaties of friendship, for example, have symbolic and relational meaning. They are exactly equivalent to expressions of friendship made over the dinner table: They are communications in an ongoing exchange—not laws or guarantees of future behavior or intent—and they can be made sincerely or manipulatively. They are a part of a relationship.

The "words" and the "music" are both essential aspects of interpersonal communications, and they can simultaneously send entirely different messages—the words being the manifest content of communications, while the music is its tone or emotional coloring. Similarly, the rhetoric of Soviet international communications is taken internally to be of great significance (which is not necessarily to say, of great sincerity), and Western rhetoric is closely examined in the Soviet Union for its hints about the nature of the U.S.–Soviet relationship. In fact, the training of Soviet officials as Kremlinologists—always looking for hints about official and unofficial wishes and intentions—might lead them to send signals too subtle for Western ears, and to find clues to Western intentions and feelings even when none are there, let alone intended.

When the Soviets were asked to reduce the size of their U.N. mission, they protested, but then quietly allowed their staffing levels to diminish.

They would not (at that time) officially accept the lower level, however. This would mean being too subservient within the relationship. Their unofficial compliance gave the United States a choice either to accept the unofficial move and help them save face, or to demand official compliance and thus stress the authority issue in the relationship.

Every move that is made on either side defines the relationship—and the U.N. staffing levels matter far less than the symbolism of the behavior. Most actions, in fact, will matter less for what they are concretely than as symbolic communication.

To the Soviets, every action is—or is seen to be—an answer to the question, Who are we to each other these days? Arms control, for example, is less about weapons than about relationships. Every question— every interaction—is at base political and social.

But exactly what relationships are involved in arms control, for example? Not just U.S.–Soviet, but also U.S.–European, Euro–Soviet, and Sino–Soviet relations—to mention just the most important. Everything— remember—is connected. Like a social system, the international system is seen as dynamic, ever changing both in its external realities (the "objective conditions") and its social jockeying for position.

MODEL RELATIONSHIPS

What kinds of relationships do Soviet leaders see as predominating in the social system of nations? There are no arm's-length relations, but instead a mutual involvement in which one maneuvers for position— much like the bureaucratic social system in which they spend all their lives.

Vertical dependency is quite familiar, and provides the model for Soviet relations with its dependencies in Eastern Europe and its more distant dependencies in Southeast Asia and the Caribbean. Such relations—like Russian parental relations and Soviet authority relations— tend to be intrusive and paternalistic. (But increases in delegation of authority at home imply increases in autonomy for the Eastern European dependencies.)

Horizontal intimacy in a true peer relationship is uncomfortable except in two forms, one of which is krugovaya poruka—involvement based on a shared fear of a superior authority (mutual covering). This stands in contrast to the voluntary cooperation of independent peers. Generally, "cooperation and coordination are simply not the norm between agencies of government in any country, least of all the USSR. Integration cannot spring forth spontaneously" (Cocks 1976). In fact, most horizontal relations within the Soviet system take the shape they have in reaction to the presence of a higher authority. Horizontal cooperation cannot be trusted unless it is enforced by a superior or is mutually incriminating, and thus exists because of fear of a superior.

But without an external authority like a world government imposing itself on the Soviet Union and other nations, krugovaya poruka is not a possibility for the Soviet Union in its external relations. Soviet leaders might perceive certain relations among Eastern European countries as krugovaya poruka, however.

An unusual variant of krugovaya poruka is possible for the Soviet Union in the international sphere, though. If the United States were to suggest a true condominium to the Soviets—a joint codomination of the world—they would understand and accept this idea. This would be a case of superiors uniting against or over a host of inferiors. This is not to say that would be the end of U.S.–Soviet competition or maneuvering for advantage—just that such a relationship would be congenial to the Soviets.

The other stable and intimate peer relationship is deep mutual involvement and support: More than mere alliance in international terms, this would look like federation. Perhaps this is the idealized model of the relations among Union republics. I believe that the leadership's psychological boundary around Soviet identity is too strong, however, to make this model worth further consideration in the international arena.

What of the proverbial "businesslike" relations? What are they, to the Soviets? In actual Soviet experience, businesslike relations are *not* objective, cool, and distant—as we might think—but involve an ongoing relationship. After all, impersonal, legalistic relations are—in the Soviet experience—totally unreliable in the absence of a personal relationship.

But what of the business relationship, then? This relationship is not usually a true alliance—a virtual melding of interests analogous to Russian friendship—and it cannot be out-and-out hostility, either. To the Soviets, businesslike describes a complex relationship typical of mutually involved peers—a mixture of cohesion and conflict.

According to one official Soviet source on the character of interpersonal relations in the labor collective, "trust, sympathy, and friendliness permit tighter *businesslike* contacts and improve the collective's work" (Antoniuk and Mochenov 1984b, emphasis added). Thus, Soviet businesslike relations are to some degree blatlike. If these relations are like business at all, they are like the long-standing relationships between Japanese corporations and their networks of dependent subcontractors and long-established suppliers, bankers, and so on. Linkage between various aspects of a complex relationship seems quite natural and understandable.

But there are tensions within the collective, and within businesslike relations. "Communalism" (Zinoviev 1984) implies a tendency for a group to cohere and secede from the surrounding system on the one hand, or to split into hostile factions on the other. Thus, if people or institutions are mutually dependent, they either establish a blatlike relationship or their relations deteriorate into competition. Still, relations can partake of both blatlike cooperation and partially suppressed competition at the same time. We have seen how people cooperate in their working relationships while gathering ammunition in the form of damaging information—waiting for the opportunity to slip in the knife. This simultaneous combination of two extremes does not equal a bland middle.

Communalism is controlled within the work collective by the tension between—on the one hand—competition for the goodies that the collective can provide and—on the other hand—the necessity for cooperation. This cooperation is important both to do the collective's work and to establish a strong position within the collective's social system (and thereby get those same goodies). People are at one and the same time aware of competition, mutual vulnerability, and mutual necessity.

Thus, the Soviet experience of businesslike is quite different from the arm's-length, competitive, but no-hard-feelings businesslike style expressed, for example, in the idea of bidding out every subcontract. Such a procedure interposes an impersonal marketplace between relational players, maintaining their sense of separateness and independence. The fact that, in most business dealings in the West, either party can walk away from the table—that they don't have to deal with one another— moderates the intensity of the social process. Western labor–management relations, on the other hand—with both its strong competitive tensions and its mutual necessity—captures the underside of Soviet businesslike relations.

While "businesslike" should thus connote complex, long-term mutual engagement, the Soviets are most likely aware that in the West the word implies a cool, rational exchange; and they may play on these meanings. The nature of businesslike relations within the Soviet system is changing, however; it is becoming more impersonal—elbow's, if not arm's, length. This should mean that the Soviet notion of businesslike will come to resemble the Western one somewhat more than it does now.

An alternative reading of the Russian word for "businesslike" would focus on its root del, which means "matters" or "things." Thus, businesslike could mean a concrete engineering approach to issues—attempting to ignore or deny the existence of social or political issues. This shows up, for example, in discussions with Soviets when they take an attitude that boils down to, "If you want peace, what's the problem?" Or as Pravda has put it: "People realize increasingly clearly where the watershed lies between the two main political courses—the policy of peace and the line of preparing for war" (Pravda, February 21, 1985, quoted in Stewart 1986). Looks like a pretty simple choice, yes? In this interpretation businesslike implies a black-and-white, stark relationship that is without the softening effect of social relations, and with undercurrents of hostility if there be any disagreement whatsoever.

Since in some sense the United States and the Soviet Union must deal with one another, U.S.–Soviet relations more closely resemble (at least in that way) the Soviet idea of mutually involved businesslike than the U.S. one.The two nations are engaged in enforced relationship. But it is not enforced by anyone or anything other than circumstances. The international system has no higher authority to enforce horizontal relations. Thus the U.S.–Soviet relationship must be viewed by the Soviets as inherently unstable, and "coexistence" in their view does not mean stability in the international system. This is in contrast with U.S. beliefs in invisible hands, automatic regulation, and a tendency of most systems toward equilibrium.

THE INTERNATIONAL SYSTEM AS A BUREAUCRACY

Given the richness of even businesslike relations, the social system of nations is quite complex. There are relationships of authority and dependency, and of cooperation and competition—all interlocking and mutually interdependent. Relationships count more than concrete affairs. Nations maneuver for advantage in terms of both concrete resources and capabilities, and for social position and community support. Maneuvering in the international system involves a keen awareness of the perceptions and desires of the other players, and the flexibility to present oneself in an attractive fashion. This is all very familiar to the Soviet bureaucratic player. This model leads to a number of conclusions:

Competition

To a modern Soviet leader, international relations looks like a partially structured bureaucracy. I say partially structured because it has no dominant superior and because it has even fewer, less codified, and less enforceable rules than Soviet bureaucracy. Détente, for example, looks in retrospect like bureaucratic competition—competition constrained by a structure of mutual engagement. The direct relations between the two super nations were blatlike—an exchanging of favors—while in other arenas the competition continued. Like bureaucratic competition, détente was not a cease-fire, but just a channeling of aggression into subterranean channels.

Soviet leaders learn to hide their aggression even as they vent it; they learn to be indirect. Criticism is potentially dangerous because it can lead to the critic being scapegoated, and because it is in general valuable to avoid looking aggressive and thus making more enemies. Only at the proper moment will Soviet leaders be overtly aggressive. But if it is at all possible, they want to look like they have clean hands throughout the process; and this is done by having an untraceable "front."

Bureaucratic competition is often conducted by means of fronts. Statements or suggestions too dangerous, or too self-seeking in appearance, can only be made by third parties. In enterprises, I was told, certain criticisms can only be made by workers, not by managers. This pattern repeats itself at even the highest levels of Soviet bureaucracy. Early in Gorbachev's tenure there was criticism of former Politburo members Viktor Grishin and Dinmukhamed Kunayev in the Soviet press, for example, prior to their removal from office. Criticism from on high did not initiate the process.

This is the same pattern that characterizes the Soviet use of fronts internationally—both front organizations and subordinate countries acting as fronts. So, while the use of stalking-horses is universal bureaucratic politics, the Soviet Union generalizes the procedure to international relations.

Relational Power

Power in a bureaucracy is relational—not absolute. It is measured in terms of the other players; what one can get them to do, and what others can do against one's wishes. It is played out in many areas, in terms of the bureau's external functions as well as its internal governance, personnel policy, and so on. Power may shift from moment to moment, according to the relationships between the players.

Similarly, the correlation of forces—the basic Soviet concept for looking at international competition—is relational, multidimensional, and dynamic. It encompasses social, economic, political, and military capabilities. It is abstract and interactive between the players: It can only be gauged by looking at both parties simultaneously. The corresponding Western concept—the "balance of power"—looks static by contrast. Usually, it is concretely military, and seems to represent an independent toting up of forces on the two separate sides. It is as if the Western idea of competition is based on the notion of two independent players in an impersonal marketplace, while the Soviet idea of competition is based on the notion of two mutually interactive players embedded in the same social system.

Embeddedness

Feeling embedded, however, raises fears of dependency. Others may have what one needs; but one wants autarky, since dependency is tremendously dangerous. Thus, the Soviets have enormous ambivalence about international trade because they fear manipulation. They could live without the grain, if they had to. In fact, they did live without it—at least, without grain from the United States.

Feeling embedded is a familiar feeling, though, and this is a kind of social system in which they are used to maneuvering. Recall the story related earlier about the local bank acquired by a regional bank: The local bank was more efficient and run by an inward-looking manager, while the regional that acquired the local had a more social atmosphere and was run by an externally oriented, social manager. This story should imply that the Soviets will give more attention than Americans do to the international implications of policy choices, will have more awareness of the global social environment, and will pay more attention to international organizations. (Note, for example, recent Soviet moves toward enhancing the status of—and their involvement in—the United Nations.)

Flexibility

The bureaucratic social model of international relations is a fairly accurate representation of how the world works. A cooler, more professional and goal-directed style will cause some shifting in Soviet leaders' attitudes toward foreign affairs as much as domestic ones. But the cultural factors and the institutional experiences of making their way within one big organization mean that Soviet leaders will continue to maneuver internationally in their bureaucratic-social way.

And in this maneuvering, the new Soviet leaders seem to have better social antennae than their predecessors. These improved antennae have shown themselves in two ways, one of which is in greater sensitivity to Western audiences' reactions. Just before the German elections in which the deployment of the U.S.-in-Nato Pershing II nuclear missiles was in question—when the center-right coalition apparently had a lead—Andrei Gromyko (then still foreign minister) made offensive and threatening remarks. This did not help the German left parties at the polls. These days, it appears that Soviet behavior and public rhetoric are much more carefully and successfully calibrated for their public relations value. Soviet behavior is more socially attuned than ever.

This is also true of domestic public relations. Gorbachev plays to multiple audiences—wooing the intellectuals with cultural liberalization, while delivering nose-to-the-grindstone sermons to the masses.

In keeping with Gromyko's observation that Gorbachev is not bound up by "the law of black and white," the second improvement in Soviet perceptions of the social system of nations lies in transcending the "two camps" model of the world. In a February 1985 speech, Gorbachev said that "while the Soviet Union attaches great significance to the normalization of relations with the United States, we never forget for a minute that the world is not limited to that country alone but is a much bigger place"(*Pravda*, February 21, 1985, quoted in Stewart 1986). Similarly, in a May 1985 interview: "The Soviet Union has never looked at the world in the context of U.S.–USSR relations alone" (*Pravda* May 20, 1985, quoted in Stewart 1986).

While the U.S.–Soviet relationship is not diminished in importance, it is placed in a broader context in which other international relationships may be quite important. This makes for both a more accurate if more complex model of international relations, and for the possibility of improved relations with some of the other players—who might now be getting more attention from the Soviet Union. These relations may be valuable both in themselves and in terms of the pressures they bring to bear on the U.S.–Soviet relationship. New approaches to Europe and Asia will tend to be seen by U.S. analysts in the East–West context, but consideration should be given to non–two-camp hypotheses.

How does the United States look—in the eyes of the Soviets—as an international bureaucratic player? Strong, physical, and a bit crazy, I suspect. More than anything, Soviets value control. They play chess while Americans play football. The Cuban missile crisis with its implicit threat of a U.S.-initiated if Soviet-provoked war, the 1973 military alert ordered by President Richard Nixon in reaction to war in the Middle East, Nixon's "madman theory" that the Soviets need to see the U.S. president as a bit crazy in order to be deterred, the U.S. policy to use nuclear weapons first if necessary to defend Europe or other interests, the design of the U.S. military establishment as what looks like an escalation machine, and—on a lesser scale—the to-and-fro in U.S. trade policy with the Soviet Union, all contribute to the idea that the United States is anything but reliable. Then too, what are they to make of the U.S. political process? It's either a sham—a conspiracy and a mystification—or it's a frightening form of unpredictable near-chaos. If the Soviets have indeed pursued nuclear superiority, it is at least in part because they trust their own control more than anyone else's.

U.S.–SOVIET RELATIONS

What of U.S.–Soviet relations? If we view them as a form of bureaucratic-style competition within the social system of nations, it implies that there may be the possibility of some kinds of cooperation mixed into the competition. What there cannot be is relaxation.

The relationship will be reminiscent of the tense relationship of peers in the work collective—partaking of competition, mutual dependency, and mutual vulnerability. The West needs to accept the tension in this relationship. It must accept that a relationship with the Soviet Union must be a long-term, complex, somewhat frustrating affair without easy solutions. Like any bureaucratic competition, it will be tortuous and tricky, full of indirection, and with periods of calm. As in bureaucratic competition, certain kinds of destructive behaviors are possible, and these can only be constrained by a higher authority—which does not exist in the international sphere. That is the bad news.

The good news is that the Soviets are used to such relationships and will be relatively comfortable allowing it to go on the way it is. They will not seek dramatic resolutions unless they are either mortally threatened or they have a clear and relatively risk-free opportunity. The crudity of military competition is too risky and uncongenial for these bureaucratic players. Having learned to channel their aggression in very indirect ways, they will tend to compete more politically than militarily. (The Brezhnev generation grew up in rougher times.)

Without a dominant superior, however, such a system of social competition is unstable—always ready to tip one way or the other. The Soviets will be continually looking for things to tip their way, and continually afraid of it tipping the other way. That the tension will remain is thus the bad news as well as the good.

One danger in such a tense relationship is that of ignoring the possibilities for constructive engagement and focusing too exclusively on the competitive aspects of the relationship. No matter what, there will inevitably be large elements of competition in the relationship. Focusing on it exclusively, however, would serve only to amplify the competition. Albeit that the United States and the Soviet Union are not married, they must live together. And, as in a marriage, it may be that "Who's winning?" is not always the most productive question to ask. The U.S.–Soviet relationship needs to be managed—not solved.

APPENDIX A

BRINGING UP IVAN:
The Psychological Effects of Russian Childrearing and Soviet Early Education

The economic system of planning and management was character-ized by stress on detailed output targets and by proliferation of instructions not only on details of what should be done and when, but also how it should be done and according to what sequence of procedures, and following what detailed timetables.

Seweryn Bialer[1]

In Murmansk, at Kindergarten-Nursery No. 101, I saw one group of toddlers where the tea tables were perfectly set up for all the dolls. When the children started to play, large women in white gowns enveloped one child after another and guided them, in warm tones, where to sit, how to sit, how to handle the dolls, how to play in general.

Hedrick Smith[2]

PARENT AND CHILD

Even on warm spring days, Russian children are wrapped in layer on layer of clothing. And their care in general is as warm, enveloping, and restraining as their style of dress.[3]

Children are given the best of what is available: A child —though thoroughly unappreciative—will get a family's last bit of caviar. In a country with a scarcity of consumer goods, "there are huge children's stores overflowing with well-made, colorful, and relatively inexpensive toys."[4] Urban, middle-class parents usually have one child[5] and such parents shower their only child with attention. In professional, career-centered families where both parents work, the child

spends the greatest part of its time in the care of a grandmother or (less frequently) a local nursery; but these caretakers, too, share the culture's pattern
of treating children with great tenderness and intense attention.

In the Russian home, parents and children are enmeshed together in an
intense, enveloping relationship. Children get little chance to be independent
or explore off on their own. "Letting go of their children is something Russians
find hard. The first day of school . . . [for example, is reminiscent] of Americans
sending children off to camp for their first prolonged absence rather than the
mere surrender of youngsters for a few hours."[6] In fact, all partings are quite
emotional for Russians. This is a result of the intensity of their involvements:
People are either totally together, or they feel totally apart.

Along with the hothouse warmth of Russian parenting comes a great protec-
tiveness (to Western eyes, overprotectiveness), and intrusive control. This control is not necessarily a form of discipline; only children (that is, those without
siblings), especially, are in fact often "spoiled" by extreme permissiveness. "A
Moscow kindergarten director asserted that one major justification for Soviet
kindergartens was to socialize 'only' children spoiled at home."[7] Control is
used—then—not to inhibit misbehavior or unruliness, but to guide and shape
the child in a way that is at once caring, protective, intrusive, and in some case
infantilizing. The layers of wrapping applied to infants (swaddling) and the
clothing of Russian children of all ages are at once warm, enveloping, and
restraining: They inhibit movement. Many toddlers are toilet trained by the time
they are 18 months old (versus 2–3 years of age in the United States). When
three- and four-year-olds are taken out on a walk with their parents, they are
strapped into harnesses attached to leashes. Children are included in adult
gatherings, but kept close to their parents—making them passive spectators.
Teenagers are discouraged from doing chores, or having jobs to earn money.
Childhood, in general, becomes a training ground for passive dependency and
compliance with an intrusive authority.

Everyone—not just a parent—is eligible to play the role of parental authority.

The official theory, expressed in every manual about child care, is that everybody is
responsible for assuring that youngsters are brought up properly. Neglect or mistreatment
of any child thus becomes everybody's business. And the theory, reinforced by a dem-
onstrative love of children, is so broadly interpreted that free advice and even criticism,
handed out to complete strangers, is considered perfectly normal, when it might be
resented as meddling in other people's affairs under similar circumstances in the United
States.[8]

In fact, there is a general, countrywide license to give advice and admonish-
ments even to adults. Anyone may play parent to anyone else. Well-meaning
busybodies are accepted and, in general, obeyed. Strangers will tell a man to
put on a coat if they feel he is dressed too lightly. While waiting at the Moscow
airport, Andrei Gromyko—then foreign minister, and known for his forbidding
style—took the time to admonish a Soviet diplomat for going hatless.[9]

But "while Russians tend to overprotect and overpraise their children, . . . as
the principle form of discipline they withhold their love and approval. In fact,
Russian childcare manuals suggest just such withdrawals of affection—tempo-
rarily but demonstratively—as the basic form of punishment."[10] Thus, the very

warmth of the parent–child relationship is what is risked by resisting parental control.

But punishment by rejection promotes a split emotional world: On one side is the total warmth of submissive belonging, while on the other is the frightening isolation of being thrown out into the cold. In or out—there is no middle ground.

Parenting manuals in the United States discourage such discipline because, they say, it makes the misbehaved child feel that *he* (or *she*) is bad. Instead, they suggest that a distinction be drawn between the child and the bad behavior. Condemning the behavior, but not the child, creates a relationship of partial rejection within a context of affection. Thus, American parenting creates complex boundaries and degrees of affiliation—not just total merger-acceptance or total separation-rejection.[11]

Americans draw—and teach their children to draw—endless distinctions: They always want to know where to draw the line. Drawing so many lines means that no line in particular is as important, thick, and well defined as the one big line drawn by Russians at the boundary of social acceptability. That line separates the "us" from the "others"; it is the skin of the social organism.

Russians do have more than just the social organism as a whole with which to identify. Nonetheless, they draw fewer and heavier lines than Americans. For example, "Russians in their personal relations draw a sharp distinction between the inner ring of trusted friends and all outsiders, [just as] in their national feelings they distinguish sharply between their clan, their nation, and all others. Words like nash (our) and chuzhoi (other, foreign, alien) crop up constantly in both propaganda and conversation." At every level—family, friendship circle, industrial enterprise, and nation—these words "have immense force in delineating friend and foe and in fixing attitudes, for Russians think in terms of only two sides—for and against."[12]

TEACHER AND COLLECTIVE

In Soviet early education, "free play" is not a desirable activity; it may occur, but only because there are not enough "upbringers" at the nursery. Instead, play is supposed to be directed and controlled for a moralistic or didactic purpose. In kindergartens,

"the children learn to play and work together, even to look after disciplining each other, under the warm but firm maternalism of the 'upbringers.' In Murmansk, at Kindergarten-Nursery No. 101, . . . one group of toddlers . . . [played at] tea tables perfectly set up for all the dolls. When the children started to play, large women in white gowns enveloped one child after another and guided them, in warm tones, where to sit, how to sit, how to handle the dolls, how to play in general. . . . The children could hardly move without some instruction. . . . At Moscow Kindergarten-Nursery No. 104, the director described . . . how older children play scenario games where the teacher manages them from start to finish, arranging the games to teach the ethic of collective cooperation. And if a child was selfish or misbehaved badly? . . . The punishment, she said, is usually exclusion from the game and ostracism from the group.[13]

Just as nursery school teachers precisely guide their charges, so the central educational authorities guide the teachers, spelling out in detail how they are expected to get the children to behave. Two- and three-year-olds, for example, are supposed to notice missing buttons, to wash their hands if dirty, to use napkins, and to button up their coats by themselves.[14] These demands are not always met, but they set a tone by their very existence.

Conformity to detailed and explicit expectations is the rule. Children's art, for example, is copied identically from models, and must be realistically colored: A class will draw pictures of daisies and every picture will show the flower in the same position, with the same five petals, in the same colors, and with the same three leaves on the stem. (This rigid conformism diminishes outside the urban areas of Russia, and is still looser in the non-Russian parts of the U.S.S.R. Latvian and Georgian children produce art that is more varied and individual than that produced by youngsters in Moscow and Leningrad.)

An American whose child spent time in a Soviet kindergarten remarked on the artwork: "Twenty little children made clay rabbits and every one of them is the same size, the same shape, the same position. You couldn't tell Scott's from Masha's or Misha's!"[15] But that is precisely the point! The (typically American) fixations on ownership and individuality are being suppressed in favor of the values of fitting in, sameness, membership, and acceptance of intrusive, parental-style authority.

In the higher grades, teachers use an authoritarian, lecture style of teaching. They dominate the classroom, with little or no student participation. For the most part, the students don't even ask questions; they are passive. Science, math, reading, and penmanship are stressed; and students are tested on rote learning. No learning games, no spelling bees, no discussions or digressions—drill and memory work are emphasized; neatness counts; and no originality is called for. In fact, originality can be detrimental to success.[16]

Parents are enlisted in the educational process by group meetings at the school. There—in front of all the parents—the teachers offer a critique of each child. This procedure embodies the ideal of collective responsibility for childrearing, and puts social pressure on parents to get their children to perform—and conform.

Political indoctrination starts early. Teachers' manuals specify that two- and three-year-olds be taught to recognize, love, and respect Lenin's portraits; four- and five-year-olds, to decorate paintings of Lenin with ribbons and flowers on holidays; and six-year-olds, to lay flowers at his statue in their hometown. Some six-year-olds can name Communist party officials down to the district party secretary—equivalent to naming the president, governor, and mayor (more than any six-year-old Americans in my acquaintance can do). The Octobrists and the Pioneers—the Soviet versions of the Cub Scouts–Brownies and the Boy Scouts–Girl Scouts—get increasing doses of politics as they get older. The most frequent theme of Soviet children's literature is Soviet patriotism, which is called the "embodiment of collectivism," and the "prime virtue." The other important virtues in children's books are "love of work" and "discipline"—that is, submission to authority.

In many ways, the Soviet educational system treats its children the way U.S. treatment programs deal with delinquents and addicts.[17] U.S. drug addicts are self-centered, narcissistic petty criminals who see other people as objects—not as persons with feelings of their own to be considered. In order to get these narcissists to pay more attention to other people, they are treated in intensely controlled and highly structured little social systems like Synanon, Phoenix House, Odyssey House, and Daytop Village. "The Community," as the social group in these settings is called, has a life of its own—intense and intrusive enough to catch the attention of even its most self-centered residents.

The Community provides group-centered activities, and tightly monitors the behavior of every one of its members. Addicts are told that—first and foremost— their behavior must conform; then, their thoughts and, finally, their feelings will follow suit. Guided by its authorities, the Community rewards and punishes its members according to a strict set of rules. The lesser part of punishment involves a loss of privileges and responsibilities; the greater part consists of shaming and isolation—for example, being forced to wear a sign proclaiming one's stupidity. These "learning experiences" are deliberately humiliating; they are designed to attack the transgressor's inflated sense of self, make him or her notice the scorn of the Community, and thus overcome the tendency to tune out others' reactions. The Community compels its members to care about social expectations; it forcibly glues them into a social structure.

Perhaps coincidentally, the guiding light of Soviet education and childrearing, Anton Makarenko, got his start by treating delinquents—"wild children" or- phaned by the Russian revolution and civil war. These children roamed the countryside in gangs, terrorizing and robbing.

Makarenko became the key figure in the establishment of special boarding schools— "colonies"—for delinquents, and while the regular establishment was off on a spree of total permissiveness, Makarenko began to achieve astounding success in the rehabilitation of these brutalized youngsters. His experimental methods leaned heavily on the creation of group-imposed discipline, with self-discipline as the ultimate goal.[18]

Makarenko believed that his experience and theories applied to all children— not just delinquents—and he is still the most popular Soviet writer on problems of bringing up and educating children. By Western standards, however, Soviet children are treated as if they were all born with antisocial personalities, requiring external controls because they cannot be trusted to develop internal ones. They are treated like narcissistic isolates who have to be glued into a social structure.

In Soviet education, the group is called "the collective," rather than "the Community"; but it functions in much the same way. First, the child is immersed in the group. In child-care centers for very young infants, the playpens hold two, three, or four children, rather than one as in the United States—not because of a lack of resources, but as part of a deliberate policy of early socialization. While in U.S. nursery schools, three- and four-year-olds are just getting used to working in pairs, the Soviet emphasis for toddlers is already on larger groups—especially group dancing and singing. All activities are group activities, and continuous social interaction leaves little time for developing a sense of separateness and independence.

The individual is made responsible to the group for his or her behavior, and group-imposed discipline is guided (or covertly directed) by an authority. This process starts with a great deal of moralizing in the games and songs in nursery school. Older Pioneers (Scouts) discipline younger ones, but very much under the eye of adult supervision. Collective responsibility is emphasized by collective punishments: Kindergarten children may be disciplined collectively by having to sit still in chairs for an hour. In higher grades, competition is always between groups or teams—not between individuals. This both suppresses individualism and encourages teammates to monitor each other's performance.

Individual children do get their own grades in school, but originality is detrimental to success: The highest grades go to those who conform best to the models, copy the drawings most accurately, recite the memorized poems most smoothly, and have the fewest blots of ink on their papers. *Success means embodying the group norm or group ideal—not rising above the group.*

For Russian children as for Russian adults, it is a sin to stick out from the group. One of the worst things a Russian can say about someone is that he is trying to be special, or calling attention to himself. American children also value peer-group membership, but their drive for conformity is weakened by the countervailing values of autonomy and independence. Furthermore, U.S. teenagers—although strongly conforming with each other—define their group by its differences from adult society. Also, at least to a degree, it's OK to be different from each other, and U.S. parents encourage their children not to be totally subservient to the group. Americans learn to take pride in their uniqueness— even if, in fact, they are not very unique. Soviet teenage society is generally less differentiated from adult society than is the case in the United States. And for Soviet children, group membership is not just valued, it is essential: The group's importance has been deliberately reinforced in so many ways. Thus, exclusion and ostracism from the group, the standard punishment used in Soviet schools and nurseries, is a Russian "learning experience" with echoes of parental discipline by rejection. Again, membership or exclusion is total. In or out—there is no in-between.

With membership so important, conformity so demanded, and independent identity so suppressed, what does it feel like within the collective? Membership in the peer group is total immersion in an intense social network, reminiscent of the child's immersion in the intense parent–child relationship. Friends are like identical multituplets. They can relax in their deeply felt bonds—their assumed group acceptance—because their differences are merely interesting, incidental nuances compared to their deep relatedness and essential sameness. Peers relate to each other as fundamentally identical comembers of the group, and as equal subordinates of higher, parental-style authorities. They have no experience of being separate, independent equals. They are always connected— always part of a large whole.

THE PSYCHOLOGY OF AUTHORITY

A child growing up so controlled and so cared for has two options, psychologically. He or she can become passive, (at least externally) compliant, and dependent; or the child can—instead—become controlling. The parents' style helps in determining how their child will handle this issue. For example, overbearing parental control can undermine a child's self-esteem—creating a sense of incompetence and fragility; and encouraging dependency, irresponsibility, and lack of initiative. A punitive parent may elicit and reinforce a child's hostility, which can be expressed by the child's becoming an aggressive, punitive authority. A more supportive parent will act as a leader, instead of treating the child as an infant; children with this experience will admire and desire the role of controller. They can become leaders themselves—especially within a paternalistic, highly structured organization. Ultimately, those who strongly identify with the role of controller—of whichever variety—will want to join the Communist party, since the party controls and "cares for" the masses.[19]

In fact, most people play out both sides of the authority relationship, they are both submissive and controlling, but with different partners. For example, party administrators intrusively control their subordinates, but submit to detailed supervision by their superiors. They also submit to "party discipline": Party scrutiny of their personal lives; obedience to job assignment; and "voluntary" political work outside their normal jobs. Their dependency needs are well cared for, too, with access to special stores, better health care, exclusive vacation spots, and better housing. These goodies are the dispensation of the state, and contingent on continued party membership and officeholding. Privileges are never the autonomous right of the individual. For example, the state retains ownership of the dachas used by the highest elite. The state has an ongoing nurturant relationship with its elite.

Party membership is thus not just an expression of parental, controlling behavior. The indulgent privileges accorded to party members, the need for support from above for both membership and advancement, and the required submission to party discipline—all are ways that party membership expresses the passive and dependent side of the original parent–child relationship.

Whatever his or her position in society, however, a Russian's authority relationships are enveloping (there is no escape), all encompassing (every aspect of behavior and every area of life is potentially subject to supervision), and centered on issues of dependency and control. There is no psychological independence; there has been no training for autonomy. Whichever side they play—submissive or dominant; dependent or patron—Russians recapitulate in these relationships the same engulfing child-and-parent game.

Along with dependency and control, guilt and resentment are possible themes of the Russian authority relationship. If the parent's intrusive control is mixed with enough love, it will produce a loyal, loving, socially hyperconscious child. However, if the parent's control is either not loving enough or too infantilizing, the child will resent it.

Forced to comply with parental wishes, the resentful child feels anger and self-contempt. The anger will be tinged with guilt to the degree that he or she still loves the parent; and in that case the child will also feel guilty (as well as angry and, perhaps, proud) when he or she disobeys. Feeling guilty encourages the child to comply more, which then produces more resentment—a cycle in which guilt leads to compliance and self-contempt, which leads to resentful cynicism, which leads to rule-breaking, which leads to guilt, and so on. This guilt, however, is dependent on the emotional ties of the relationship. Absent such ties—in impersonal situations—resentment and rule-breaking occur without guilt.

Constant external control means that discipline is never internalized; it never becomes self-contained self-control. For example, the group-imposed discipline of the children's collective is less a case of true peer discipline than one of submitting to the adult who is supervising in the background: It is not internalized. This means that, when the cat's away, the mice will play. Furtive rule-breaking—lip service to rules, and attempts to go around them—is rampant and guilt free.

Resentment of control is not expressed by frank opposition or rebellion, but—if not by furtive rule-breaking—by obstinate, passive noncompliance. As one Russian said that he had learned from the army: "Never disobey. Always say, 'Yes, sir,' and let *them* worry about whether you carry out the orders."[20] This fits the childhood experience (and the adult reality) of authority being overwhelmingly powerful. Remember that the choices are to go along—at least superficially—with the demands of authority (passive compliance), or to become an authority oneself. In nonauthority relationships—with friends—Russians can experience identical equality. With any others—if there is to be a relationship at all—passive compliance and active controlling are the only psychological roles available.

THE COMPARATIVE PSYCHOLOGY OF RUSSIANS AND AMERICANS

Russians are relaxed and secure in their friendships.[21] Having grown up immersed in intense, enveloping relationships—first, with parents and, then, with other children—they have a tremendous need for and satisfaction in personal relationships. Since there is only one degree of closeness—very close—Russians do not worry about testing or defining the nuances of a relationship: They have one, or they don't. Americans are raised to worry about their independence, so they fear their own desires for closeness; but Russians do not fear dependency. With such intense relationships, Russians feel less isolated than Americans. For Americans, approval comes in finely discriminated degrees; so, the mere appearance of friendship is not enough: Americans worry about whether and how much they are liked. Since Russian friendship is absolute—in or out—Russians can assume more in a friendship.

Russians also like being a part of large groups and, in social situations, feel comfortable about being themselves—"unbuttoning," they call it. They relax in the group's absolute acceptance of them. Unlike Americans, they do not worry about the fact that they conform: It's OK to be part of the crowd. (If anything, they worry about their desires for independence. "Am I being selfish?" they ask themselves.)

Because they feel so accepted, Russians are more emotionally expressive than Americans. Within close relationships, Russians express a delicate variation of emotionality by using numerous nicknames and diminutives. Lurking in the background is the unspeakable notion that too many differences could lead to a total break, and mutual exclusion; but, because of the strength of the relationship, that danger is very far away. Thus, Russians are more unrestrained with their friends than Americans are. Secure that their absolute relationships can stand up to the stress, they express anger at friends more easily than Americans do. In dealing with anger, loss, sadness, guilt, or other uncomfortable feelings, Russians look for sympathy and support from others.

Americans find such support-seeking to be uncomfortably dependent, and they have a slight feeling of being outsiders when in groups. Thus, they retain some of their independence, while worrying about how they will be evaluated. They cannot take acceptance for granted; so they monitor and control their degree of closeness, and learn complex ways of hiding or disguising their feelings. Americans are more likely to deal with their feelings themselves than look for outside support. They have learned to control themselves and take care of themselves.

Russians tend to see Westerners as cold because of the contrast between, on the one hand, Americans' self-control and regulated emotional distance and, on the other, Russians' emotional expressiveness and the intensity of Russian relationships. Russians value the social group so much more than we do that they see Westerners as lacking in spiritual values. Even after choosing to come to the West, a large proportion of the Russian émigré community feels that Westerners lack culture, altruism, and dedication to society. They see Westerners as narcissistic, self centered, and decadent.[22]

In business settings, Americans value bland, impersonal affability and self-control; Russians tend to take all their interactions personally. They are very sensitive to public humiliation or impersonal, cold treatment by superiors. This appears to them as a "violation of the dignity of the unique personality." This kind of treatment hurts on two counts: First, in such a conformist society, the uniqueness of their personalities is in some doubt; and second, cold treatment—like the coldness of the disciplining parent or the disciplining collective—implies a punitive rejection.

Thus, even for adults, group ostracism and public humiliation can be used as a disciplinary tool.

Use is still made in factories, universities and other institutions of "boards of shame" on which delinquent individuals are pilloried for failing to have their hair cut, cheating in examinations, seducing girls, neglecting to follow prescribed safety regulations—and of course, above all, for getting drunk. There are also show trials of a kind, still: the semi-public self-criticism sessions or kangaroo courts at which an erring individual may be called to order by his self-righteous workmates. . . . Such episodes are obviously rigged from start to finish by local Party officials, activists and busybodies.[23]

Being rigged by an authority to look like peer-group–imposed discipline, humiliating and isolating transgressors, and dramatically exaggerating the feelings involved—all these characteristics make these events both perfect examples of "learning experiences" and perfect expressions of Russian psychology.

Along with being more emotionally expressive in general, Russians can admit to their aggressive feelings more easily than Americans can. One reason for this is that Russians rely on outside controls to restrain misbehavior, whereas Americans' self-control is threatened by their fully experiencing aggressive feelings. Also, Russians have a very concrete conception of aggression: robbing, stealing, and depriving. An act is aggressive or it is not, there is no in-between or gray zone. Americans see aggression less clearly: There are so many subtle ways to be aggressive in their finely honed relationships. Finally, the American notions of friendliness, of giving the benefit of the doubt while keeping the doubt in mind, and of maintaining self-control—in sum, the American tendency to construct complex boundaries and relationships—make Americans feel more guilty about their aggressive feelings. Russians, on the other hand, do not feel much guilt about their aggressive feelings toward those outside their intense circles of friendship. However, once they have crossed some very well-defined moral frontier, they feel intensely—even histrionically—guilty. Subjectively, they are absolutely guilty—as guilty as it is possible to be—or they are not very guilty at all.[24]

Whatever their ability to recognize aggressive feelings, "neither the Russian nor the American groups reveal marked needs for dominance or aggression—two trends often emphasized in previous national-character studies—nor [are] the Russian people psychologically driven to be submissive, although we did find them to have a strong desire for supportive and nurturant superiors." Attitudes toward dominance and submission are founded on the parent–child relationship. Americans, for their part, want freedom and independence—not dominance. The Russian parental relationship, for its part, is not essentially aggressive. It is protective, nurturant, and controlling. Thus, Russians do not desire dominance, but parental-style control. And they don't want to be bossed around; they want to be taken care of.

The two faces of Russian parental authority—warmth and control—are separated in Russians' minds. "They see mothers as nurturant and supporting and fathers as arbitrary and demanding more markedly than do Americans." This splitting of the parents into a good one and a bad one allows Russians to express the resentment that is the flip side of their passive dependency, while reflecting the Russian tendency to draw heavy-handed distinctions. A mixed feeling—ambivalence—is too complicated: So each parent can't be both good and bad. Instead, the images are kept pure. One is good, and the other is bad.

In the absence of a friendly relationship, Russians are very mistrustful. When closeness is so close, one must be careful about who one allows in. With no gray zone in between, if you're not a friend—and a close friend at that—then you're a total stranger, and perhaps an enemy. "They ask, 'Is he wearing a mask?' 'Where does he really stand with respect to me?' But the dilemma is much more 'outside' in the relationship than within the self." With no gray zone, the issue is determining the true identity of the other—not checking one's own judgment. After all, there is no fine distinction to be drawn—just a yes or no judgment about something very fundamental.

"Americans, on the other hand, exhibit more acute self-awareness, self-examination, and doubt of their own inner motivations." Having to make fine discriminations in their relationships, Americans must give thought to the accuracy of their social judgments; they worry about being fair and balanced.

Russians are a little puritanical verbally, but have less confusion about their sexual identity than Americans—perhaps because Americans are, in general, both more confused about who they are in relationship to others, and more hesitant to draw such a heavy-handed, all-or-none distinction. In spite of the high frequency of women working in the Soviet Union, Russian sex roles are (even) more sterotyped and differentiated than Americans ones: Women's work at home remains exclusively women's. When Russians draw a boundary or make a distinction, it is usually not subtle.

Russians feel less guilty than Americans, because Russians have fewer internalized controls. If they break a rule, it is an external rule—not a matter of conscience. Thus, they also become less angry at others for misbehaving. This comparable to the way many Americans apparently feel about minor cheating on income taxes, or driving over the speed limit. For Russians, however, this attitude applies to a much wider range of behaviors.

In fact, because they experience control as an external "moral corset,"[25] Russians feel somewhat oppressed and constrained emotionally. They want to break out of their restraints. This shows up most clearly in Russian drinking habits, but also in their pleasure in *skandaly* (scenes). As Dostoyevskey wrote, "A Russian takes incredible delight in every kind of scandalous public upheaval" (quoted in Hingley). Visitors report on great arguments breaking out over trivial matters: In a peasant's market, for example, there was a case in which an old woman berated with great relish her accused scoundrel of a cheater until she was led away. "Everyone in hearing joins in, accusations and counter-accusations fly about until sooner or later authority steps in, if only in the person of a humble militiaman."[26] These histrionic outbursts bespeak the Russians' pleasure in throwing off the corset of restraint, and hamming up their feelings for the sheer pleasure of self-expression.

For Americans, such emotionality represents a humiliating loss of self-control. Far from joining in if someone else displays such feelings, Americans will often turn away in embarrassment.

As children, Russians are not encouraged to do much: Just being is enough. External achievement is irrelevant to their experience of emotional closeness. Their passivity is encouraged, and their desire for individual achievement is suppressed: It is not important, compared to fitting in and being loved. Thus, Russians do not measure people in terms of their accomplishments. Instead, they value people for personal qualities and attitudes, such as loyalty, respect, and sincerity.

Because they can't take social acceptance for granted, Americans worry about fitting in; yet they are also afraid of conforming too much. They resolve this tension between their desire for independence and their desire for approval by wanting others to appreciate them precisely for their individuality and their individual achievements. Socially insecure, Americans fall back on impressing people—and reassuring themselves—by reciting their activities and accomplishments, or displaying the symbols of money, achievement, and success. Americans have learned to get approval by saying, "Look, Mom! Look what I can do! Look at how independent and capable I am!"

Russians—on the other hand—feel more secure socially, but are concerned that they be worthy of their intimate, intense closeness. The issue for Russians is not external competency or achievements, but intrinsic values and unchanging essences.

"Americans are appreciably more worried about their failures in achievement, lapses in approved etiquette, inability to meet social obligations. Russians are shamed most deeply by dishonesty, betrayal, and disloyalty; they feel ashamed about taking care of number one (as Americans put it) at the expense of others. Americans have complicated explanations for their own transgressions—explanations founded on the relative nature of their loyalties. After all, their relationships are hedged by the caveats and reservations of various competing values. For Russians—whose relationships are absolute—betrayals are absolute.

Trained in being rather than doing, Russians are more passive, fearful, and pessimistic than Americans. Russians accept authority, but they worry about how authority will treat them—whether it will be nurturant or disciplining. They do not think of rebellion. Americans are more abivalent about whether to accept authority in the first place; they "exhibit more inner conflict as to the dilemma of 'rebelling or submitting,' " and even the nurturant side of authority threatens their independence. Faced with ambiguous situations, Americans look for problems to be solved. They are optimistic doers who define themselves by their activities. Russians worry about what the situation might do to them, they look for dangers and threats. They are passive pessimists who define themselves as essentially unchanging. Russians—except when exercising parental authority—are used to being acted upon, not acting; Americans—used to exercising some freedom even as children—want to be captains of their fates.

"The desire for 'mastery' is stronger in Americans than in non-elite Russians, but Russians of all kinds often manifest great bursts of activity." These bursts of activity come from Russians gathering their strength to overcome their passivity. But because of their passivity and pessimism, they are less persistent and more likely to give up than Americans. Their bursts of energy quickly subside. They thus tend to dischotomize even their levels of activity. They are absolutely active, or absolutely passive—with little sense of continuous, paced, productive activity.

Compared to average Russians, elite Russians are less expressive and more self-controlled than the average. Elite Russians are less embedded in the group, and more willing—if necessary—to be unpopular. They are more disciplined, more persistent, and more obedient. Being more controlled (in both senses), they are more controlling. These characteristics are not just the result of better education and training. Members of the elite do better in Soviet society precisely because of these personality characteristics.

Each nationality handles abstract, cognitive relationships in the same way it handles interpersonal ones. This is to say that the differences between Russian and American psychology are based on the two cultures' different ways of handling boundaries—connections and differences—in relationships. While Americans construct complex relationships with degrees and varieties of affiliation and trust, Russians have sharper, less complicated boundaries. Russians are close, or they are not.

Similarly, Russian mental categories—being so few and so heavily drawn—are palpable. Russians experience categories as real things—not as abstractions. In perceiving others, for example, Russians characteristically take a very large view initially (friend or no?), and then make a very detailed individualized, and unstereotyped analysis. Once they categorize someone, Russians then see that person very specifically, and more as a unique individual than Americans do. There are no intermediate, nuanced categories—just the broadest categories and the uniqueness of the individual.

Americans have many more intermediate categories, and a variety of independent systems of categories and classifications. (This mental structure is like the social structure of a myriad independent social groups and social identities in which Americans participate.) In perceiving others, Americans rarely get to the individual. They cannot assume as much as Russians do about the basic nature of their relationships; so they busily categorize and classify, looking more at the surface and seeing people as sterotypes or as performers of familiar roles.

For example, while an American might see a man as a shoe repairman—nothing more—a Russian will be more aware of the nature of his or her relationship with this repairman. First and foremost, have they established a friendly relationship or not? This is of the essence. If yes, then this shoe repair is more in the nature of a personal favor between friends than it is a business transaction. If not, then it is not clear that the work will get done at all. Then, as a matter of personal interest, is the repairman brusk or warm? Is he serious about his work? What are his habits in dealing with customers? Who is he? If this is not a friendly relationship, could it become one? Would I (the Russian) want it to? If the American gives any thought to the repairman at all, it might be to note that he is of Greek extraction, closes on religious holidays, is working class, and so on. All that is really important is that he repairs shoes. The Russian's interpersonal world is, in general, more intensely emotional; the American's, more cognitive and instrumental.

Because of the variety and complexity of their systems of classification, however, Americans see categories as tenuous abstractions—mere mental constructs and conveniences—not as absolute essences. To the American having shoes repaired, it is not the essential nature of the shoe repairman or of their human relationship involved that is important—if there is such a thing as an essential nature, at all. This is just an instrumental business relationship. Categories that the American might apply—"shoe repairman," "Greek," or "working class"—are merely convenient, unrelated helpers of thought, but not a coherent reality in themselves. Thus, Americans tend to focus on the concrete in their thinking, they start from the facts at hand in order to discover which categories usefully apply.

Since Russian mental categories have such strong definition, such firm boundaries, and such palpable reality, Russians naturally follow the method of scientific socialism—reasoning deductively from the general-categorical to the particular-concrete, from the context to the content, from the social to the personal, and from the group to the individual. Since American mental categories are so numerous, so tenuous, and so abstract, Americans reason inductively from the particular to the general, from the content to the context, from the personal to the social, and from the individual to the group.

For Westerners, drawing subtle categorical distinctions is comfortable and desirable. And so—familiar with thinking in terms of gradations—Westerners see compromise as a tool for moving relationships through phases of development. Russians find strong connections and closeness both comfortable and desirable, based on either a parent–child kind of tutelage or a shared sense of sameness. But ambiguity cannot be tolerated in so close an affiliation. In doubtful cases, therefore, it is easier for a Russian to make a clean break than to tolerate the ambiguity of compromise.

NOTES

1. S. Bialer, *Stalin's Successors* (New York: Cambridge University Press, 1980).
2. H. Smith, *The Russians* (New York: Ballantine Books, 1976).
3. The famous swaddling theory! On both upbringing and education, see: Smith, *Russians;* S. Jacoby, *Inside Soviet Schools* (New York: Hill and Wang, 1974); F. M. Hechinger, "Education: The Preschool Child" and "Education: Triumphs and Doubts," in H. E. Salisbury, ed., *The Soviet Union: The Fifty Years* (New York: Harcourt, Brace and World, 1967); U. Bronfenbrenner, *Two Worlds of Childhood,* (New York: Simon and Schuster, 1970); and D. Lane, *Soviet Economy and Society* (New York: New York University Press, 1985). Obviously, the composite description presented here cannot apply to every child and every family. It is instead a description of a cultural norm—a modal upbringing.
4. Hechinger, "Education."
5. This is probably for reasons of economics: the high frequency of women working, and—even more important—tight housing.
6. Smith, *Russians.*
7. Ibid.
8. Hechinger, "Education." Also see Smith, *Russians.*
9. A. Shevchenko, *Breaking with Moscow* (New York: Knopf, 1985).
10. Hechinger, "Education."
11. Note that this is true at all system levels. Children learn to see themselves as complexly connected even internally, for example, by being told that their behavior is not an essential part of them and so may be judged separately.
12. Smith, *Russians.*
13. Ibid.
14. Jacoby, *Soviet Schools.*
15. Mrs. Smith, quoted in Smith, *Russians.*
16. You can't be right *against* the party, or any authority—only *with* the party, or authority. This is because the party (like the customer) is always right—not necessarily factually right, but politically right. This connection was pointed out to me by Leon Lipson.
17. See S. Minuchin et al., *Families of the Slums* (New York: Basic Books, 1967); and L. Yablonsky, *Synanon: The Tunnel Back* (Baltimore: Penguin, 1965).
18. Hechinger, "Education." See also A. Makarenko, *The Road to Life* (Moscow: Foreign Language Publishing House, 1951).
19. The major route to success is through the party. Anyone with much responsibility in management, administration, the army, law, and so on, has joined. Those who have achieved some success without being party members are invited—virtually forced—to join, or else they jeopardize their careers. So, except in scientific research and the arts—less political endeavors—talented and ambitious people in all endeavors must become party members. Of males over 30 years of age, half of the college graduates and one-third of the high school graduates are party members. Nonmembers among total graduates include a disproportionate number of women, who are underrepresented in the party because their childrearing responsibilities interfere with their ability to do the extra work that membership entails: meetings, lectures, and political work with

the masses. See J. Hough and M. Fainsod, *How the Soviet Union Is Governed* (Cambridge, Mass.: Harvard University Press, 1979). Those who are "forced" to join the party presumably are less attached—psychologically—to the role of controller. These are not the members that we would expect to rise to positions of political authority, and therefore they are of less interest to this study.

20. Smith, *Russians*, emphasis in original.

21. This section is based in part on psychological testing that was performed by a group at Harvard's Russian Research Center on Russians who were stranded in, and defecting to, the West after World War II. That comprehensive study of a broad cross-section of Russian people has not been duplicated since. Because these cultural patterns run deep, however, it is still useful. The test results are recast here into the terms of this chapter. For the results of that study—and for quotes in this section, except where otherwise noted—see "Modal Personality and the Soviet System" in A. Inkeles, *Social Change in Soviet Russia* (New York: Simon and Schuster, 1968); and R. A. Bauer, A. Inkeles, and C. Kluckholn, *How the Soviet System Works* (Cambridge, Mass.: Harvard University Press, 1956). Interwoven with those results, this section contains psychodynamic interpretations of the material in the earlier sections, and a cognitive analysis based on differences in boundary regulation. Throughout this section, I speak of "Russians" and "Americans" as if these were homogeneous, standardized categories. This, of course, is not true. Even the psychological testing results that I quote are only summaries of trends—generalizations that (like statistics) apply over large groups, but do not apply to any particular individual.

22. Aleksandr Solzhenitsyn is a prominent exponent of this position.

23. R. Hingley, *The Russian Mind* (New York: Charles Scribner's Sons, 1977).

24. Their guilt can be compartmentalized, however, such as in the guilt–resentment cycle discussed earlier.

25. H. V. Dicks, "Observations on Contemporary Russian Behavior," *Human Relations* 5 (1952), quoted in Inkeles, *Social Change*.

26. Hingley, *Russian Mind*.

APPENDIX B
WHAT MAKES VANYA RUN?
The Psychodynamics of Soviet Career Builders

SUBMISSION AND CONTROL

The Soviet "man on the make" (and they are male; the limited role of women in the party has been mentioned in Chapter 2 and elsewhere) has a need for approval and advancement sufficient to overcome any psychological conflicts over submission to authority. To attain his goals, he needs enough self-control for full submission, without bargaining or questioning. He cannot have rebelled even in his youth. He couldn't be late to class too often, or come to lecture drunk. He makes—first unconsciously, and then consciously—a sacrifice of his autonomous sense of self in return for the nurturance, protection, and support of the authority/father figure.

The climber can use, compliance manipulatively, and thus—strangely—it becomes a form of control. The alternative form of compliance is a genuine seeking after authority's approval. Either way—either truly seeking approval or manipulatively seeking it—the loss of autonomy is willing or even eager. Paradoxically, this allows for the affirmation of control via the chosen destruction of the autonomous self. Or as the Soviet say, freedom equals the recognition of necessity.

Mere belief in the system—acquiescence—is not sufficient, because it may be too passive. The climber must have the energy of a leader. He needs a sociopolitical orientation. He must survive successive rounds of selection—showing both technical competency and political skills at each stage, but with the emphasis increasingly shifting to the political side. He must be in the vanguard of the ambitious, the calculating, and the socially oriented.[1]

Note: I have confined my ideas about psychodynamics to an appendix because they are so speculative.

DEPENDENCE AND NARCISSISM

The climber's attention is directed upward. The group whose values he values are his superiors. He wants to be like them; he wants them to like him.

To some degree, the Soviet climber resembles the U.S. executive. In a study (Henry 1949) of more than 100 U.S. executives that included extensive psychological tests, the typical executive was shown to be attached to and identified with sponsors. Meanwhile, the executive was detached and impersonal with subordinates, who were seen as mere "doers of work"—except for those who were seen as junior versions of himself.

In a study of 8,000 "business leaders" (Warner and Abegglan 1955), it emerged that men had to leave home "psychically" to relate with ease to other males in authority. This "leaving home" meant that they were freed from too close an emotional tie to their mothers; that is, they did not require too much direct nurturance.

For the mobile, self-made type of executive, the focus on mobility derives from the amibition of the mother, who is in general an energetic pusher. The mobile executive's father is, in general, bad—distant, not supporting, and unreliable. The son is left with a feeling of loss or deprivation. He has the idea that the father is withholding something from him. During adolescence, he has some positive experience with a male authority figure (a teacher or coach, for example), who gives encouragement and aid—thus reinforcing the training and life view implanted by the ambitious mother. In his youth, our mobile executive is the leader of the gang, the athletic team captain, and like that. "Bill was always president of everything he ever joined," says a childhood friend. Some early sucess shows him that goal-directed activity works. This success may be in athletics, music, offices, or honors, and is usually not scholarly success (Warner and Abegglan 1955).

Denied satisfying relationships with the father, these mobile men are well equipped psychologically to accept relationships with father-figures; because of their mistrust of, and hostility toward older males, they are also able to terminate such relationships, as they must in their business careers to obtain maximum advantage from them . . . Later in life they are able to continue relating themselves easily to figures of authority, never too close for disattachment when necessary—never too far away when continuity and closeness are necessary for advancement . . . The whole process of mobility requires a subtle balance between this drive for independence, withdrawal, and departure, and the opposing and necessary need to attach to others, to be respected and honored by them. (Warner and Abegglan 1955)

Some of this ability to detach is necessary for the Soviet climber, in whom it shows up especially in a desire to build his own network and reduce dependency. But "[mobile men] have difficulty accepting and imposing the kinds of reciprocal obligations that close friendship and intimate social contacts imply" (ibid.). This does not sound like the intensely social Russian climber.

In contrast to the self-made type, the American birth-elite executive is embedded in his community. He cannot be oblivious to his role in the broader non-business community without frustrating his mobility. He and his colleagues went to the same prep school; he grew up with his wife; and so on. The father's role in this case is very different from that of the mobile man's, and very important. The birth-elite executive has a need for both independence and subordination to his father. The father is admired, but from a distance. The two have a cool relationship, in which the father is basically helpful but somewhat impersonal.

Therefore, the birth-elite executive must be willing to subordinate himself to his father even as an adult, while still being able and energetic. He identifies himself with the family firm, and has a less personal and more long-range perspective than the self-made man. He is not going to quit and work for a competitor. His long-range perspective derives in part from family ownership and the possibility of inheritance. He has no need to permanently break off all contact with family and old friends. Solutions must be worked out in terms of continued relations with the past and the people in the past. "Far from leaving the past or denying it, he is concerned with building on it" (ibid.). The Soviet executive is like the birth-elite executive in being tied to his network.[2]

In general, the executive has broken the attachment to his parents. His father is seen as helpful, but not restraining: The tie to the father or substitute authority figure must be positive. Dependency on the mother must be eliminated; but if he is to work in a large organization, the executive must retain some dependency—psychologically speaking—on his father. He needs a framework of overall goals provided by authority (Henry 1949).

But for all that he can't have too much narcissism (be too self-centered), the organizational climber also can't be too dependent. The security of sponsorship frees the protégé to focus on work. "No, I was never anxious about a promotion. ... Maybe my association with the boss has something to do with that: as long as he was secure, I felt I was" (quoted in Warner and Abegglan 1955).

The path to leadership is successful subordinacy. People who advance in large bureaucracies generally understand this principle.... The psychology of subordinacy is the capacity to work closely with an authority figure and to involve oneself with work without the intrusions of infantile dependencies. (Zelaznik and Kets de Vries 1975, emphasis added)

An executive can "mature only by learning how to depend upon figures within the corporate triangle in much the same way that a child learns to depend upon members within the family triangle. We know that if the child learns to submit or rebel too much against these powerful figures, he is not capable of dealing with them in terms of his own interests or needs" (quoted in Packard 1962). Given Russian childrearing patterns and their patterns of authority, more dependency should be the norm in the Soviet Union than in the United States.

The minimum man is the true bureaucrat.

The minimum man's relationship to peer and parent figures is the key to his style of leadership. The parents lurk in the background as the main source of reward. The consensus leader keeps his attention fixed on the parental authorities, toward whom he remains passive, but he actively manipulates his siblings or peers, over whom he seeks control. Calculation and manipulation are his tools. If he gains power by calculation, he does not take an autocratic role; he manipulates relationships so that rewards pass through him on their way to others. (Zelaznik and Kets de Vries 1975)

This sounds like a better description of Brezhnev than Gorbachev.

The minimum man devotes his energy to questions of procedure rather than substance. Questions of substance make clear all dimensions of a power struggle, requiring a man to take a firm stand. Procedure, on the other hand, tends to be neutral and to include everybody, so long as people believe the procedure is fair to all and to every point of view. This, again, is peculiar to the culture of peer relations. (ibid.)

Again, this is reminiscent of Brezhnev's pseudoreforms.

The maximum man—on the other hand—is charismatic; he is a great innovator, but not always a good leader because he is dismissive of contrary opinions. His self-esteem is too high, so he has narcissistic independence (ibid.). This narcissism comes from having had his parents' unstinting love, which he has internalized.

He relentlessly pursues a single point of view without flexibility, but with deep commitment. The minimum man is a survivor, while the maximum man is an aggressor. The minimum man is pragmatic without strong ethics (ibid.). Perhaps we need to see the new Soviet leaders as more of an amalgam, as the pendulum swung from Stalin's maximum (or pseudomaximum—this is open to debate), to Brezhnev's minimum and back a bit.

FAMILY HISTORY

The most motivating family constellation for a Soviet climber—I hypothesize—is a controlled, somewhat distant father who functions as an ego ideal— a model to be emulated. The mother, on the other hand, is for the most part taken for granted. The father is demanding, and his caring is cool as well as contingent. His caring is real, however, albeit from a distance. Any anger or aggression toward the father is resolved by authority-pleasing at work, while being difficult with subordinates.

In fact, a variety of backgrounds are plausible. Instead of the father being a positive if distant model, for example, there might be reaction formation: the father as a negative model to be compensated for. But the father as ego ideal will provide the strongest and most positive, least conflictual background, and therefore will be most conducive to success. For a heroic but distant father, how about one killed in the war, à la Gorbachev?

I make the hypothesis described here on a number of bases. One is by analogy to what is known of U.S. executives in general, and what I learned in the course of treating some successful executives in my own psychiatric practice. Another is that, on a number of occasions, fathers were spontaneously discussed in the study interviews: I did not bring up the subject. With one subject who left a budding career, I hypothesized that his father had been too close and warm, as a way of explaining both his disaffection with the Soviet system and—more importantly—his autonomy. This was also the subject who, as a secondary school student, had wanted to pursue a nonpolitical route, but was pressured by a teacher and his parents into accepting a komsomol position of prestige. This may have caused resentment. Pure careerism was not enough to hold him; he enacted his rebellion against the system and left when he heard news of the death of his father.

Some withholding on the part of the parents is required in order to produce the requisite dependence, the externality of vision, the feeling that the solution to one's tension lies outside oneself and within the other. In general, Russians see "mothers as nurturant and supporting, fathers as arbitrary and demanding" (Inkeles 1968). This general case will produce sons who are passive compliant and/or passive aggressive toward superiors, and aggressive toward those with whom they can get away with such behavior. This is the average Soviet worker. If the father is too available, on the other hand, the son will become individualistic and narcissistic. But if the father is just a bit available and much more admirable, then a son might seek authority's approval, and endeavor to become an authority—a leader—himself.

NOTES

1. Frequent calls for demandingness and an exacting attitude from Soviet executives, combined with the "exhausting" nature of climbing, implies that at least some fast-trackers are *forcing* themselves to work hard. For these climbers, their internal split will lead to personal collapse eventually, unless they find some sinecure for an "easy life."

2. Applied to the Soviet case, such analysis would imply that Gorbachev will not make a truly radical break with the past—unlike China's Deng Xiaoping, whose own life was filled with radical breaks.

SELECTED BIBLIOGRAPHY

Andreev, B. G., ed. 1986. *Partiinaia Organizatsia. Trudovoi Kollectiv. Nauchno-technicheskii Progress.* Leningrad: Lenisdat.

Anonymous. 1979a. "Konsul'tatsiia: Passmotreniie Personal'nykh Del." In M. I. Khaldeev and G. I. Krivoshein, eds., *Pervichnaia Partiinaia Organizatsii Opyt Formy i Metody Raboty.* Moscow: Politizdat.

Anonymous. 1979b. "Konsul'tatsiia: Rol' Partorganizatsii v Podbore i Passtanovke Kadrov." In M. I. Khaldeev and G. I. Krivoshein, eds., *Pervichnasia Partiinaia Organizatsii Opyt Formy i Metody Raboty.* Moscow: Politizdat.

Antoniuk, V. S., and Mochenov, G. A. 1984a. "Improving the Social-Psychological Climate of the Collective as a Factor in Perfecting Management" (trans.). In F. M. Rusinov and V. S. Antoniuk, eds., *Psykhologicheskie Aspekty Upravlenia.* Moscow: Ekonomika.

———. 1984b. "Objective Conditions of Economic Development and the Socio-Economic Reserves of the Collective" (trans.). In F. M. Rusinov and V. S. Antoniuk, eds., *Psykhologicheskie Aspekty Upravleniia.* Moscow: Ekonomika.

———. 1984c. "Workers' Health as a Factor in Raising the Collective Labor Efficiency" (trans.) In F. M. Rusinov and V. S. Antoniuk, eds., *Psykhologicheskie Aspekty Upravleniia.* Moscow: Ekonomika.

Azrael, J. R. 1966. *Managerial Power and Soviet Politics.* Cambridge, Mass.: Harvard University Press.

Banfield, E. C. 1958. *The Moral Basis of a Backward Society.* Glencoe, Ill.: Free Press.

Bass, B. M. 1981. *Stodgill's Handbook of Leadership.* New York: Free Press.

Berliner, J. 1957. *Factory and Manager in the USSR*. Cambridge, Mass.: Harvard University Press.

Bialer, S. 1980. *Stalin's Successors*. New York: Cambridge University Press.

Blau, P. M. 1963. *The Dynamics of Bureaucracy*. Chicago: University of Chicago Press.

Blau, P. M. and Meyer, M. W. 1971. *Bureaucracy in Modern Society*. New York: Random House.

Bowman, G. W. 1964. "What Helps or Harms Promotability?" *Harvard Business Review* 42.

Brown, A. 1985. "Gorbachev: New Man in the Kremlin." *Problems of Communism* 34 (May–June).

Bunce, V., and Echols, J. M. III. 1980. "Soviet Politics in the Brezhnev Era: 'Pluralism' or 'Corporatism'?" In D. R. Kelley, ed., *Soviet Politics in the Brezhnev Era*. New York: Praeger.

Chandler, A. D. 1962. *Strategy and Structure*. Cambridge, Mass.: MIT Press.

Cocks, P. 1976. "The Policy Process and Bureaucratic Politics." In P. Cocks, R. Daniels, and N. W. Heer, *The Dynamics of Soviet Politics*. Cambridge, Mass.: Harvard University Press.

———. 1980. "Rethinking the Organizational Weapon: The Soviet System in a Systems Age." *World Politics* 22 (January).

Cocks, P., Daniels, R., and Heer, N. W. 1976. *The Dynamics of Soviet Politics*. Cambridge, Mass.: Harvard University Press.

Conquest, R. 1961. *Power and Policy in the USSR*. New York: St. Martin's Press.

———. 1983. Introduction to G. D. Ra'anan, *International Policy Formation in the USSR: Factional "Debates" during the Zhdanovshchina*. Hamden, Conn.: Archon.

Crozier, M. 1973. "The Cultural Determinants of Organizational Behavior." In A. Nejudhi, ed., *Modern Organizational Theory*. Kent, Ohio: Kent State University Press.

Dalton, G. W., Thompson, P. H., and Price, R. L. 1977. "The Four Stages of Professional Careers—A New Look at Performance by Professionals." *Organizational Dynamics* (Summer).

Dalton, M. 1959. *Men Who Manage*. New York: John Wiley and Sons.

Daniels, R. V. 1976. "Office Holding and Elite Status: The Central Committee of the CPSU." In P. Cocks, R. Daniels, and N. W. Heer, *The Dynamics of Soviet Politics*. Cambridge, Mass.: Harvard University Press.

Downing, G. D. 1967. "The Changing Structure of a Great Corporation." In R. M. Kanter and B. A. Stein, eds., 1979. *Life in Organizations*. New York: Basic Books.

Downs, A. 1967. *Inside Bureaucracy*. Boston: Little, Brown.

Drucker, P. F. 1954. *The Practice of Management*. New York: Harper and Row.

Ershov, A. A. 1986. "The Moral-Psychological Climate of the Collective: From the Experience of the Education Work of Party Organizations" (trans.). In B. G. Andreev, ed., *Partiinaia Organizatsia. Trudovoi Kollectiv. Nauchnotechnicheskii Progress*. Leningrad: Lenisdat.

Ezhov, V. A., Kozlov, Iu. B., and Filippov, G. G., eds. 1985. *Partiniaia Organizatsiia: Voprosy Metodologii i Metodiki Obobshcheniia Opyta Raboty*. Leningrad: Lenisdat.

Fatkin, L. V. 1984. "Demands Taxing the Leader's Psychological and Sociol-Psychological Qualities" (trans.). In F. M. Rusinov and V. S. Antoniuk, eds., *Psykhologicheskie Aspekty Upravleniia*. Moscow: Ekonomika.

Fleishman, E. A., and Peters, D. R. 1962. "Interpersonal Values, Leadership Attitudes, and Managerial 'Success'." *Personnel Psychology* 15.

Gaenslen, F. 1986. "Culture and Decision Making in China, Japan, Russia, and the United States." *World Politics* 39:1 (October).

Gerschenkron, A. 1962. *Economic Backwardness in Historical Perspective*. Cambridge, Mass.: Harvard University Press.

Golubkov, Ye. P., and Fatkin, L. V. 1984. "The Social Psychological Content of the Functional Responsibility of a Leader" (trans.). In F. M. Rusinov and V. S. Antoniuk, eds., *Psykhologicheskie Aspekty Upravleniia*. Moscow: Ekonomika.

Gouldner, A. W. 1952. "The Problem of Succession in Bureaucracy." In R. K. Merton et al., eds., *Reader in Bureaucracy*. New York: Free Press.

————. 1954. *Patterns of Industrial Bureaucracy*. New York: Free Press.

Granick, D. 1954. *Management of the Industrial Firm in the USSR*. New York: Columbia University Press.

————. 1961. *The Red Executive*. New York: Doubleday.

————. 1972. *Managerial Comparisons of Four Developed Countries: France, Britain, U.S., and Russia*. Cambridge, Mass.: MIT Press.

————. 1973. "Managerial Incentives in the USSR and in Western Firms: Implications for Behavior." *Journal of Comparative Administration* 5:2.

————. 1975. *Enterprise Guidance in Eastern Europe*. Princeton, N.J.: Princeton University Press.

Grusky, O. 1961. "Corporate Size, Bureaucratization and Managerial Succession." *American Journal of Sociology* 67 (November).

Gustafson, T., and Mann, D. 1986. "Gorbachev's First Year: Building Power and Authority." *Problems of Communism* 35 (May–June).

Hanfmann, E., and Getzels, J. W. 1955. "Interpersonal Attitudes of Former Soviet Citizens, as Studied by a Semi-projective Method." *Psychological Monographs* 69:4.

Hardt, J. P., and Frankel, T. 1971. "The Industrial Managers." In H. G. Skilling and F. Griffiths, eds., *Interest Groups in Soviet Politics*. Princeton, N.J.: Princeton University Press.

Hegarty, E. J. 1976. *How to Succeed in Company Politics*. New York: McGraw-Hill.

Henry, W. E. 1949. "The Business Executive: The Psychodynamics of a Social Role." *American Journal of Sociology*, 54.

Hoffmann, E. P. 1973. "Soviet Metapolicy: Information-processing in the Communist Party of the Soviet Union." *Journal of Comparative Administration* 5:2 (August).

Hoffmann, E. P., and Laird, R. F. 1982. *The Politics of Economic Modernization in the Soviet Union*. Ithaca, N.Y.: Cornell University Press.

Hofstede, G. 1980a. *Culture's Consequences: International Differences in Work-related Values*. Beverly Hills, Calif.: Sage Publications.

————. 1980b. "Motivation, Leadership, and Organization: Do American Theories Apply Abroad?" *Organizational Dynamics* (Summer).

Hough, J. F. 1969. *The Soviet Prefects: The Local Party Organs in Industrial Decision-making.* Cambridge, Mass.: Harvard University Press.

———. 1971. "The Party Apparatchiki." In H. G. Skilling and F. Griffiths, eds., *Interest Groups in Soviet Politics.* Princeton, N.J.: Princeton University Press.

———. 1973. "The Bureaucratic Model and the Nature of the Soviet System." *Journal of Comparative Administration* 5:2 (August).

———. 1976. "The Brezhnev Era: The Man and the System." *Problems of Communism* 25:14.

———. 1977. *The Soviet Union and Social Science Theory.* Cambridge, Mass.: Harvard University Press.

———. 1980. *Soviet Leadership in Transition.* Washington, D.C.: Brookings Institution.

Hough, J., and Fainsod, M. 1979. *How the Soviet Union Is Governed.* Cambridge, Mass.: Harvard University Press.

Ianni, F. A. J., and Ianni, E. R. 1972. *A Family Business: Kinship and Social Control in Organized Crime.* New York: Russell Sage Foundation.

Inkeles, A. 1968. *Social Change in Soviet Russia.* New York: Simon and Schuster.

Jennings, E. E. 1967. *The Mobile Manager: A Study of the New Generation of Top Executives.* Ann Arbor: University of Michigan Press.

Jowitt, K. 1974. "An Organizational Approach to the Study of Political Culture in Marxist-Leninist Systems." *American Political Science Review* (September).

———. 1975. "Inclusion and Mobilization in European Leninist Regimes." *World Politics.*

———. 1983. "Soviet Neotraditionalism: The Political Corruption of a Leninist Regime." *Soviet Studies* 35.

Kanter, R. M. 1977. *Men and Women of the Corporation.* New York: Basic Books.

———. 1979. "Power Failure in Management Circuits." *Harvard Business Review* (July–August).

———. 1983. *The Changemasters.* New York: Simon and Schuster.

Kanter, R. M., and Stein, B. A., eds., 1979. *Life in Organizations.* New York: Basic Books.

Kaplan, N. 1970. "Research Administration and the Administrator: USSR and U.S." In H. A. Landsberger, ed., *Comparative Perspectives on Formal Organizations.* Boston: Little, Brown.

Kelley, D. R., ed. 1980a. "The Communist Party." In D. R. Kelley, *Soviet Politics in the Brezhnev Era.* New York: Praeger.

———. 1980b. *Soviet Politics in the Brezhnev Era.* New York: Praeger.

Kennedy, M. M. 1980. *Office Politics: Seizing Power, Wielding Clout.* New York: Warner.

Khaldeev, M. I., and Krivoshein, G. I., eds. 1979. *Pervichnaia Partiinaia Organizatsii Opyt Formy i Metody Raboty.* Moscow: Politizdat.

Klugman, J. 1986. "The Psychology of Soviet Corruption, Indiscipline, and Resistance to Reform." *Political Psychology* 7:1.

Kontorovich, V. 1985. "Discipline and Growth in the Soviet Economy." *Problems of Communism* 34 (November–December).

Koriushkin, V. A. 1986. "Pervoprokhodtsy." In B. G. Andreev, ed., *Partiinaia*

Organizatsia. Trudovoi Kollectiv. Nauchno-technicheskii Progress. Leningrad: Lenisdat.

Kram, K. E. 1980. "Mentoring Processes at Work: Developmental Relationships in Managerial Careers," unpublished dissertation, Yale University, New Haven, Conn.

Kruk, D. M. 1973. *Upravleniie Obshchestvennym Proizvodstvom pri Sotsializme.* Moscow: Ekonomika.

Leites, N. 1952. "The Politburo through Western Eyes." *World Politics* 4:2.

Levinson, D. J., et al. 1978. *The Seasons of a Man's Life.* New York: Knopf.

McClelland, D. C. 1975. *Power: The Inner Experience.* New York: Irvington Publishing.

March, J. G., and Simon, H. A. 1958. *Organizations.* New York: John Wiley and Sons.

Martin, N. H., and Sims, J. H. 1956. "Thinking Ahead: Power Tactics." *Harvard Business Review* (November–December).

Martin, N. H., and Strauss, A. L. 1959. "Patterns of Mobility within Industrial Organizations." In W. L. Warner and N. H. Martin, eds., *Industrial Man, Businessmen and Business Organizations.* New York: Harper.

Meyer, A. 1964. "USSR Incorporated." In D. W. Treadgold, *The Development of the USSR.* Seattle: University of Washington Press.

———. 1965. *The Soviet Political System.* New York: Random House.

Miller, R. F. 1976. "The Scientific–Technical Revolution and the Soviet Administrative Debate." In P. Cocks, R. Daniels, and N. W. Heer, *The Dynamics of Soviet Politics.* Cambridge, Mass.: Harvard University Press.

Moore, B. 1954. *Terror and Progress USSR.* Cambridge, Mass.: Harvard University Press.

Norr, H. 1986. "Shchekino: Another Look." *Soviet Studies* 38:2 (April).

Packard, V. 1962. *The Pyramid Climbers.* New York: McGraw-Hill.

Papulov, P. A. 1985. *Kadry Upravleniia Proizvodstvom: Deitale'nost, Formirovaniie.* Moscow: Ekonomika.

Pfeffer, J. 1981. *Power in Organizations.* Boston: Pitman.

Popov, G. Kh. 1976. *Otsenka Rabotnikov Upravleniia.* Moscow: Moskovskii rabochii.

Powell, R. M. 1963. "Elements of Executive Promotion." *California Management Review* 6 (Winter).

Randle, C. W. 1959. "Promotable Executives." In W. L. Warner and N. H. Martin, eds., *Industrial Man, Businessmen and Business Organizations.* New York: Harper.

Reich, M. H. 1985. "Executive Views from Both Sides of Mentoring." *Personnel* 62 (March).

Rigby, T. H. 1964. "Traditional, Market, and Organizational Societies and the USSR." *World Politics* 16 (July).

———. 1977. "Stalinism and the Mono-organizational Society." In R. C. Tucker, ed., *Stalinism.* New York: W. W. Norton.

Roche, G. R. 1979. "Much Ado about Mentors." *Harvard Business Review* (January–February).

Rumer, B. 1986. "Realities of Gorbachev's Economic Program." *Problems of Communism* 35 (May–June).

Rusinov, F. M. 1984. "The Leader in the System of Social-Economic Relations" (trans.). In F. M. Rusinov and V. S. Antoniuk, eds., *Psykhologicheskie Aspekty Upravleniia*. Moscow: Ekonomika.

Rusinov, F. M. and Antoniuk, V. S., eds., 1984. *Psykhologicheskie Aspekty Upravleniia*. Moscow: Ekonomika.

Ryapolov, G. 1966. "I Was a Soviet Manager." *Harvard Business Review* (January–February).

Schwartz, D. V. 1974. "Decisionmaking, Administrative Decentralization, and Feedback Mechanisms: Comparisons of Soviet and Western Models." *Studies of Comparative Communism* (Spring–Summer).

Shakhovoi, V. A. 1985. *Kadrovyi Potentsial Sistemy Uplravleniia*. Moscow: Mysl'.

Skilling, H. G., and Griffiths, F., eds. 1971. *Interest Groups in Soviet Politics*. Princeton, N.J.: Princeton University Press.

Stein, B. A. 1976. "Getting There: Patterns in Managerial Success," unpublished report prepared for Center for Research on Women in Higher Education and the Professions, Wellesley College, Wellesley, Mass.

Stein, B. A., and Kanter, R. M. 1980. "Building the Parallel Organization: Creating Mechanisms for Permanent Quality of Work Life." *Journal of Applied Behavioral Science* 16:3.

Stewart, P. D. 1986. "Gorbachev and Obstacles toward Détente." *Political Science Quarterly* 101:1.

Stolyarenko, A. 1983. *The Psychology of Management of Labor Collectives*. Moscow: Progress.

Stone, R. C. 1952. "Mobility Factors as They Affect Workers' Attitudes and Conduct toward Incentive Systems." *American Sociological Review* 17.

Swinyard, A. W., and Bond, F. A. 1980. "Probing Opinions: Who Gets Promoted?" *Harvard Business Review* (September–October).

Tashakori, M. 1980. *Management Succession*. New York: Praeger.

Tichy, R. 1973. "An Analysis of Clique Formation and Structure in Organizations." *Administrative Science Quarterly* 8.

Tushman, S. 1977. "A Political Approach to Organizations: A Review and Rationale." *Academy of Management Review* 2.

Valsiner, J. 1984. "The Childhood of the Soviet Citizen: Socialization for Loyalty," Uren Memorial Lecture, Carleton University, Ottawa, Canada.

Vasil'ev, B. N., and Novikova, V. C. 1985. "Vneshtatnyi Sotsiologicheskii Sektor." In V. A. Ezhov, Iu. B. Kozlov, and G. G. Filippov, eds., *Partiniaia Organizatsiia: Voprosy Metodologii i Metodiki Obobshcheniia Optya Raboty*. Leningrad: Lenisdat.

Vendrov, Ye. Ye. 1969. *Psikhologicheskie Problemy Upravleniia*. Moscow: Ekonomika.

Warner, W. L., and Abegglan, J. C. 1955. *Big Business Leaders in America*. New York: Harper and Brothers.

Warner, W. L., and Martin, N. H., eds. 1959. *Industrial Man, Businessmen and Business Organizations*. New York: Harper.

Whyte, W. H. 1956. *The Organization Man*. New York: Simon and Schuster.

Williams, N. M., Sjoberg, G., and Sjoberg, A. F. 1980. "The Bureaucratic Personality: An Alternate View." *The Journal of Applied Behavioral Science* 16:3.

Winter, D. G. 1973. *The Power Motive*. New York: Free Press.

Wright, J. P. 1979. *On a Clear Day You Can See General Motors*. New York: Avon Books.
Zelaznik, A., and Kets de Vries, M. F. R. 1975. *Power and the Corporate Mind*. Boston: Houghton Mifflin.
Zinoviev, A. 1984. *The Reality of Communism*. New York: Schocken Books.

INDEX